THE HOME OFFICE
& THE CHARTISTS
1838-48

To Margaret,

Best Wishes,

From Neil

THE HOME OFFICE & THE CHARTISTS 1838-48

Protest and Repression in the West Riding of Yorkshire

1838-48

NEIL PYE

MERLIN PRESS

Published in 2013
by Merlin Press Ltd
6 Crane Street Chambers
Crane Street
Pontypool
NP4 6ND
Wales

www.merlinpress.co.uk

Chartist Studies Series No. 11

© Neil Pye, 2013

ISBN. 978-0-85036-634-1

Catalogue in publication data is available
from the British Library

Printed in the UK by Imprint Digital, Exeter

CONTENTS

Tables

Maps

ABBREVIATIONS

CID	Criminal Investigation Department
HO	Home Office
ILP	Independent Labour Party
PRO	Public Records Office
QC	Quarter Sessions Committee
TS	Treasury Solicitor
WO	War Office
WYL	West Yorkshire Archives Service, Leeds

ACKNOWLEDGEMENTS

In writing this book, first and foremost, I wish to acknowledge the help and support of the University of Huddersfield, particularly Professors Keith Laybourn, David Taylor and Paul Ward who gave me the opportunity to research this area as part of a doctorate degree. I am very indebted to them for sharing their expertise, along with their advice and encouragement over the years. I would personally like to reserve special praise for Professor Laybourn, who has been a major source of inspiration. Secondly, I would also like to thank Professor Owen Ashton, who has been fully supportive of this book – not only in terms of his academic expertise, but also for his shared passion for the study of Chartism, which has been invaluable. Further thanks must be given to Joan Allen, Malcolm Chase, Clive Emsley, Janette Martin, Rohan McWilliam, Ian Pitchford, Matthew Roberts, Mike Sanders, John Shepherd, Chris A. Williams and Philip Woodfine for all the support that they have given over the years. I am also very grateful for the assistance received from the librarians and archivists at the National Archives, Kew, University of Bangor Archives, University of Bradford, Edge Hill University, University of Huddersfield Archives, Huddersfield Local History Library, University of Leeds, University of Liverpool, London School of Economics, Mulgrave Estates, The People's History Museum, Manchester and Sheffield Archives and Central Library. I would also like to thank Anthony Zurbrugg and Adrian Howe at Merlin Press for making this publication possible. Last and by no means least, thanks to my parents Ronald and Jean Pye; close relatives such as Albert Pye, along with friends and colleagues such as Christopher Cheetham, Patricia Cullum, Christopher Ellis, William Marshall, Colin Montgomery, Brian Newton and David Platt, who have also been very supportive throughout this academic and writing journey.

Finally, the vast majority of information in this book has been drawn from primary evidence gathered from the previously mentioned archives and repositories. In providing a historiography of debate, reference has been made to vital secondary books and articles. Whilst these sources have been referred to in the context of the debate in the form of short quotations, in no way have they reached or exceeded the guidelines usually accepted by publishers. Furthermore, every effort has been made to avoid any infringement of copyright and apologies go out to any copyright holders whose permission has been overlooked.

Map 1: The West Riding of Yorkshire

I. INTRODUCTION:
THE HOME OFFICE AND CHARTIST
HISTORIOGRAPHY

The Home Office and its suppression of the Chartist movement in the West Riding during the period 1838 to 1848 has been largely overlooked as a topic of historical debate. Instead, the historiography of the Home Office contains studies that have largely concentrated on its basic powers of domestic policy, along with those of the Home Secretary who was in charge of its departmental affairs. With regard to modern theoretical approaches to history there has been very little written about the Home Office and its wider relationship with local government agencies. This is especially important in terms of the development of the British state and the machinery of public order, during the latter part of the first half of the nineteenth century. Secondly, very little is known about the role of the Home Office and how it impacted on the suppression of political protest throughout the era, and especially upon the Chartist movement. During the late-1830s, the Chartists appealed to large sections of the working classes and sought to unite a whole host of radical groups that existed throughout the period, under the banner of the People's Charter. This document contained the Six Points drawn from a wider range of established radical programmes for the democratic reform of the political system. The People's Charter was a response to anger amongst the politically disenfranchised over their lack of representation and ability to shape the affairs of the nation, with its policies drawn from a battery of traditional radical proposals.[1]

The supporters of the Chartist movement embraced both moral and physical force protest. The former inclined to non-violent means of protest through the use of the press and peaceful political and cultural events, whilst the latter relied largely upon direct action to effect swift political change. Direct action was designed to make the country ungovernable and force the government to accept Chartist demands for the Six Points. The bond that united all Chartists was their anger not only against the aristocracy but also towards the new middle classes who they felt had betrayed them over the 1832 Representation of the People's Act. This legislation, which gave the vote to many propertied middle-class voters, permitted the middle classes to forge a loose alliance with the aristocracy, whilst at the same time it enabled them to gain greater access to the state and its machinery which was subsequently used to suppress Chartist agitation.

Chartism attracted a large number of working-class supporters because it was a vehicle that allowed them to challenge what was seen as an injustice. They were upset and angry about not being able to direct, shape or influence the environment around them which underwent significant social and economic transformation as a result of industrialisation and the growth of towns. The process of change was well represented in locations such as the West Riding of Yorkshire. Throughout the first half of the nineteenth century, the West Riding was a major centre of radical activity against government. The demand for the vote, opposition to the new Poor Laws, the quest for better working conditions and the campaign for press freedoms were issues that gave rise to Chartism within the county.

In recent times, there has been very little research conducted that has explored the general link between the government and the state repression of the Chartist movement. Over the years, there have been numerous calls for such a study to be written from a wide range of historians such as Neville Kirk, Miles Taylor and John K. Walton.[2] The subject has been both largely ignored and overshadowed by the disagreements that emerged during the 1980s concerning the 'linguistic turn' and how the language of Chartist protest was interpreted.[3]

The aim of this book is not to explore the mechanics of the 'linguistic turn' or discredit the many assertions made by Gareth Stedman Jones, but instead to offer an alternative perspective in the hope that this will stimulate further studies of Chartism and its interaction with the state, especially within the area of public-order policy. A full discussion of the 'linguistic turn' would involve an intricate analysis of the effects of banking, mining and factory legislation introduced by Sir Robert Peel's administration during the period 1841-6.

Whilst Gareth Stedman Jones's study explored the language and meanings taken from Chartist literature, this book is concerned about what was said and written by the state, in particular the Home Office, and how it responded to a major challenge to its authority. By both examining and interpreting the language used by the Home Secretary and the personnel which made up the various branches of the Home Office, the intention is to not only construct a picture of how this government department functioned, but also to analyse how the Home Office and its public-order policy changed over a period of time in response to Chartism. Doing so will involve questioning an issue that is still relevant today: how centre-local relations changed, along with improvements that were made to the machinery of public order, especially in relation to matters such as provincial policing. The developments which occurred in those areas as a reaction to Chartist unrest enabled the governance of the nation to become more cohesive by the end point of this study in 1848; whereas previously it was disjointed due to the lack of infrastructure and sufficient communication links between the centre and localities.

In building a picture as to how these changes occurred, this research has drawn its inspiration and evidence from the vast catalogue of Home Office, War Office and Treasury Solicitor papers which are kept at the National Archives at Kew, as well as a number of local sources taken from various archives across the West Riding. Many of the Home Office papers used have not been examined properly for roughly thirty years. These sources provide remarkable insights not only into how the Home Office tried to suppress Chartist protests, but also state relations and the way in which the machinery of public order functioned. The various letters and notes written by the Home Secretary and staff at the Home Office reveal confusion, particularly during the early stages of Chartist unrest. The papers also highlight how each chameleon-like Home Secretary had a different strategy for dealing with disorder. Whilst the Whig approach was generally quite measured, as reflected by the responses of Lord John Russell and Sir George Grey (the exception was the Marquis of Normanby, who at times was heavy-handed), the Tory response to disorder carried out by Sir James Graham was decidedly robust.

By analysing how the Home Office policy towards the Chartists impacted on the West Riding, the responses to various stages of unrest highlighted the need for new mechanisms of social control in the form of policing. With the exception of Leeds, the absence of any organised police forces across the region was a major problem in tackling disorder and social unrest caused by the Chartists. Industrialisation and the growth of densely-populated urban centres highlighted the need for permanent and better organised civilian measures of law enforcement to protect the local population, as opposed to the use of ad hoc and temporary quasi-military solutions such as the yeomanry and militia, which by this time, had outlived their usefulness. The demand and gradual introduction of police forces to the West Riding brought the Home Office into direct conflict with local magistrates and the military. Both agencies tried to resist changes to the structure of the local public-order apparatus, fearing that this would lead to the erosion of their political powers. The sources used in this study highlight the problems and tensions which the Home Office in London faced in managing local law and order agencies. More importantly, the evidence reveals how the Home Office response to Chartist agitation speeded up the pace of reform, along with the implementation of many other improvements to the state and machinery of public order, which made it work more efficiently by the end of the period.

Although the main methodology employed is one of comparative historical analysis, in bringing this subject up-to-date, modern computer technology has been used widely. All of the sources used in this dissertation have been digitally photographed, scanned and enhanced using current software. As the vast majority of Home Office papers were handwritten, the use of computer technology has meant that the information taken from those sources can be fully examined, whereas previously, there have been areas of activity, especially in relation to policing, which have been overlooked because of the difficulty faced in deciphering the manuscripts. This evidence is crucial in adding something extra to existing studies and building a fuller picture as to why Home Office suppression was a major factor in the gradual decline of Chartism.

In order to further our knowledge through the use of new methodologies, this research explores why few studies have been written about the operation and effectiveness of the Home Office for the early nineteenth century. As part of the introduction it will therefore focus on a number of key issues, including the current state of the debate concerning Chartist studies and how our understanding of Chartism can be advanced. It concentrates on the strengths and weaknesses of previous studies of the state in its suppression of Chartism, and it also attempts to understand why new studies in this field have not emerged for over twenty years.

The historiography of the relationship between the Home Office and the Chartists is sparse. There have been a number of biographies written about various Home Secretaries who have served the department, with the exception of the Marquis of Normanby.[4] During the early 1970s, several unpublished dissertations appeared which concentrated on Sir George Grey's stewardship as Home Secretary, along with a political and administrative history of the department. In addition, there has been research conducted into the development of the Home Office after 1848, but following its publication in 1982, the historiography ends.[5]

The first book to explore the role of the Home Office was written by the former Permanent Under-Secretary, Sir Edward Troup, in 1926. This looked at both the origins and functions of the government department, based upon Troup's own personal experiences whilst serving the department in a number of capacities; it was meant to be used as a general guide for people with an interest in public affairs and not for specific academic purposes.[6] Within its narrative, Troup suggested that the power of the Home Office was largely concentrated in the hands of the Home Secretary. However, Troup does not explore in great depth the wider roles of some of the other key members of staff such as the Permanent and Parliamentary Under-Secretaries who served this highly important government department.[7] Further, as a piece of historical evidence it is very weak. The study contains no theoretical approach, nor does it tell the reader where the Home Office was situated in relation to the power and structure of the British state during the Chartist era. In addition, it is largely focused upon late nineteenth and early twentieth century developments.

In 1954, Troup's pioneering study was revised and updated by Sir Frank Newsam, also a former Permanent Under-Secretary at the department, who attempted to explore how the relationship between the Home Office and local agencies evolved.[8] The main point that Newsam raised in relation to the chaotic growth and development of the department since 1782 was that it had been both 'casual and haphazard'.[9] Like Troup's study, there is very little mention of how the Home Office developed its powers during the period of Chartist protest. The book also has very little relevance to this study as it covers developments during the early to mid-twentieth century, by which time many of the functions and duties of the government department had changed beyond recognition in comparison to the late 1830s and 1840s.

In the early 1970s, there was an attempt to rectify this imbalance when two major surveys appeared which examined the Home Office and its broader powers. The main driving force behind these works was a concept promoted by administrative historians Henry Parris and Oliver MacDonagh who suggested that during the nineteenth century there was a 'Revolution in Government'.[10] Parris and MacDonagh argued that Jeremy Bentham's ideas and theories brought about the expansion of bureaucracy, in the shape of experts, inspectors and statisticians. They maintain that the problems which emanated from industrialisation and the growth of towns meant that the doctrines of laissez-faire capitalism and collectivist state intervention existed alongside each other.[11] Both theorists questioned arguments put forward by A.V. Dicey, who had written extensively about Jeremy Bentham's role in the growth of government.[12]

A.V. Dicey argued that following the 1832 Reform Act Benthamite liberalism used scientific means to bring about 'a startling change in legislation' which began to reflect public opinion.[13] In recent times this assertion has been questioned by Peter Jupp who has argued that although the government began to take notice of public opinion, this was not representative of the entire population because it was limited to 'a powerful and metropolitan and provincial press', along with interest-specific pressure groups, such as, for example, the factory reform movement.[14] It can also be argued that because most of the working population was uneducated and disenfranchised, government legislation was not democratically framed, nor did it represent the wishes of the entire population. Whilst it is difficult to measure how much influence Jeremy Bentham's utilitarian ideas had on the Home Office, it is fair to argue that they did have some impact on policy areas such as policing and penal reform. This was reflected by need to create a more disciplined society, which was undergoing transformation due to the combined effects of industrialisation and urbanisation.[15] It was from those areas of discussion that, during the 1970s, two unpublished dissertations by D.F. Smith and A.P. Donajgrodzki appeared which touched upon the impact of Bentham's influence on the Home Office.[16]

Smith looked at Sir George Grey's tenure at the Home Office and attempted to question the notion that there had been a 'Revolution in Government'.[17] Though it only covered Chartist activity during the period 1846-8, its main strength was that it drew quite heavily from a vast range of parliamentary and government sources. This research also covered many aspects of Home Office activity.

Smith described Grey as being 'a typical Whig' who believed in the liberal principles of laissez-faire economics and devolved powers to the localities.[18] Many of his beliefs, in relation to the power of the state, stemmed from his role as a major landowner and member of the aristocracy.[19] Whilst serving in office, Grey attempted to introduce legislation and policies that favoured the very social class he represented. As an opponent of the commercial and industrial middle classes, Grey believed in 'progressive improvement' which emanated from the outcome of the 1832 Reform Act.[20] Accordingly, he supported political principles in which he believed whilst, at the same time, he reluctantly adopted practical measures that leaned towards centralisation. This was particularly evident in areas such as policing and prison reforms.[21] Grey's stance was reflected when dealing with Chartist unrest throughout 1848. On many occasions central government had to step in to assist the machinery at local level as pressures imposed on the magistracy and military became too great. Smith also argued that this state of affairs placed the Home Secretary and his administrative staff under too much strain. This later prompted parliamentary questions over how the Home Office conducted its business.[22]

This important study was followed by another vast, but unpublished, thesis written by A.P. Donajgrodzki which looked at the development of the Home Office during the period 1822 to 1848.[23] The growth of the government department and how it coped with both 'traditional' duties (such as Royal Prerogatives and Petitions) and 'new' demands such as control of the Metropolitan Police, prisons and factory reform were its central concerns.[24] Donajgrodzki argued that in the 1820s the Home Office underwent a period of transformation in which it developed legislative powers and began to interact more extensively with external agencies. This led to an expansion of its business that was both 'unplanned and unqueried' which turned the department into 'an administrative waste-paper basket'.[25]

Donajgrodzki's research examined the roles and functions of both key and minor personnel who worked at the Home Office, from the Home Secretary at the very top to the librarian at the very bottom of the pyramid-structured department.[26] It also explored areas such the administrative structure, the social composition of its staff and their tasks, along with the key attributes of the Secretary of State and major office-holders.[27] The outcome of this investigation led Donajgrodzki to conclude that whilst the powers of the Home Secretary had evolved and expanded since the 1820s, the administrative and bureaucratic progress of the Home Office had remained static.[28] This broad analysis of the development of the department during the period led Donajgrodzki to assert 'that it was possible to have a revolution in the scope of government, without a revolution in bureaucracy'.[29]

Whereas Donajgrodzki used the 1848 Parliamentary Select Committee on Miscellaneous Expenditure and their investigation of the inner-workings of the Home Office as an end point for his study, in 1982 Jill Pellew used this as a starting point for the third and last major book to appear about the government department. She charted the development of the Home Office from 1848 to 1914, during which time she asserted that its operation became more professionalised.[30] This could be seen following the 1853 Northcote-Trevelyan Report which brought about the creation of a civil service.[31] However, whilst Pellew's study contained hardly any mention of the effect that Chartist unrest had on the Home Office, significantly, it did offer a broad account as to how the department became more efficient during the Victorian era, through the emergence of a Secretariat and the greater use of inspectors. This was despite the pace of reform being relatively slow.[32] It is at this stage that the relevant historiography abruptly ends.

There have been a number of studies of the state and the Home Office but none that have dealt directly with the issue of the suppression of Chartism. The historiography of current Chartist studies can be divided into three main phases. The first, which lasted from 1959 to 1987, saw a plethora of books and articles written that reflected localised and class-based studies. This era culminated with the dispute over the 'linguistic turn' which challenged class-based approaches to Chartism. Following this major disagreement, the second phase from 1987 to 2000 saw very few books and articles written about Chartism. Indeed, during this period there was a shift away from class towards studies which were largely cultural, biographical and gender specific. The transition fed directly into the most recent phase of activity, in which there has been a significant range of books, articles and dissertations written that reflects both the language and culture of politics. These have both been written within and beyond the United Kingdom, in places such as Australia, as highlighted by historians such as Paul Pickering. The latter trend has recently been highlighted by Janette Martin's unpublished thesis which explores the mechanics of political oratory and itinerant lecturing during the Chartist era, along with the creation of a new narrative, which was written by Malcolm Chase in 2007.[33]

The resurgence of interest in Chartism has largely come about through the internet as specialist websites such as *Chartist Ancestors* have enabled members of the public to use the world wide web as an interface for family history studies. Further to this, the wider availability of source materials through the National Archives that can now be viewed digitally via the internet has attracted the attention of historians, as has the advent of the annual Chartist Conferences which have recently been held at both Sheffield and Leeds universities and much further afield at the Sorbonne, Paris. However, despite this renewed interest in Chartism, there are still a number of areas within the modern historiography that continue to remain contentious. The most notable issue which surely needs to be addressed is the relationship between Chartism and the state and how it led to improvements in the development of the machinery of public order.

Further investigation is needed to add to our knowledge of Chartism, as well as to help explain why the movement fell into decline. In doing so, this study offers a chance to expand upon areas that have already been touched upon, especially in relation to the closure of urban and public space, and what was perceived as being extreme forms of political activism in the shape of mass gatherings and arming and drilling. Throughout the period, territorial disputes led to frequent clashes between the authorities and the Chartists. Furthermore, the Home Office clampdown on Chartism demonstrated that the state was looking to steer the public away from extreme forms of activism towards more disciplined and moderate methods of political participation as suggested by James Vernon.[34]

In evaluating the first phase of activity from 1959 to 1987, before this period many studies of the Chartist movement were written from a biographical and narrative perspective. The work of pioneering historians such as Robert Gammage and especially Mark Hovell, who was one of the very first historians to explore the link between the Government and its suppression of Chartist protest, exaggerated the impact of poverty and hardship, along with the internal disputes that dogged the development of the radical movement.[35] However, it was during the late-1950s that there was a major sea change in the way that Chartism came to be viewed. Asa Briggs and F.C. Mather looked at the growth of the movement within the localities.[36] This brought about a new narrative in which traditional ideas were fused into a town by town approach that threw up a number of random explanations as to how and why Chartist activity emerged in given places.

In analysing what this methodology uncovered the main advocate of this approach, Asa Briggs, described Chartism as a 'snowball movement' in which localised disputes came together under the banner of the 'Six Points' to form a 'nationwide agitation' against the Government and the state.[37] Briggs, along with many other writers with similar convictions, argued that the support base of the Chartist movement was made up of an alliance forged between followers of the Factory Reform movement and opponents of the New Poor Law. This collaboration was bolstered by craftsmen and textile workers who turned to the radical movement when their domestic and handcraft trades were affected by industrialisation and the growth of machine-based production methods.[38]

The localised approach to Chartism placed a heavy reliance upon economic causation. Many previous studies used W.W. Rostow's research into trade-cycles as a barometer to measure peaks and troughs of radical activity.[39] From this statistical evidence, it was suggested by Briggs that periods of unemployment and economic depression coincided with peaks in Chartist agitation.[40] This narrow interpretation overlooked wider issues such as the impact of colonial and foreign events that prompted measures to be taken by the government to suppress the movement during 1847-8.[41]

Another problem associated with the localised approach is that it gave the impression that Chartism was a backward-looking form of protest which wanted to stem both the tide of economic and urban progress.[42] It was suggested that the early development of the organisation was shaped by Tory Radicals such as Richard Oastler. His influence was previously assessed by G.D.H. Cole in the book *Chartist Portraits*, published in 1940, for which

Briggs wrote the introduction.[43] Whilst there is some truth in the assertion, it must be qualified by the fact that Oastler was a product of aristocratic and landed interests. Further to this, as a major figure in the development of the Factory Reform movement and anti-Poor Law protest, Oastler had been very much at odds with major Chartist leaders such as Feargus O'Connor over earlier issues like the 1832 Reform Act and Catholic Emancipation. The difference between Oastler and O'Connor was that whereas the Tory Radical believed in the gradual reform of the political system, the Chartist leader wanted the immediate imposition of universal suffrage for the unrepresented, along with an overhaul of the system that was in place.[44] In addition, Richard Oastler supported the anti-Poor Law and Factory Reform protests because he felt that for the Tory Party to safeguard its future, it had to engage with the working classes for the purposes of renewal and to broaden its support base.[45]

The notion that class conflict and social division led to the rise of the Chartists as a major working-class political force was promoted by Edward Thompson, who wrote the hugely influential book *The Making of the English Working Class*, which appeared in 1963.[46] This was one of the first major studies to place emphasis on culture and the 'history from below' approach in the years leading up to 1830. Whilst the book was not specifically written about the Chartist movement, Thompson argued that the focal point of its protestations was the injustice of the 1832 Reform Act. This in turn, led to the development of a greater working-class consciousness that surfaced towards the end of the decade.[47] Thompson's book heralded the beginning of a more politicised methodology.

Edward Thompson's assessment of the growth of a radicalised working class that gave rise to Chartism, later provided a basis for Dorothy Thompson to conduct her own research into the subject. She was highly critical of the localised approach. She felt that many studies were too simplistic and only touched the surface, in terms of the development of the movement. In one of her earlier books on the subject, Thompson argued that Chartism was a response to the 'economic and social change of an urban working-class' which was why its protestations were primarily located within the manufacturing districts.[48] She also said that the movement was 'pervaded by a sense of class' which acted as 'both a positive sense of identification and a negative hostility to superior classes'.[49] She argued that those class tensions were 'stronger' than at any point during the nineteenth century.[50]

In examining the factors that gave rise to Chartist agitation, Dorothy Thompson felt that the changing nature of the state provided a central theme. She argued that 'a question on which the working-class radicals found common cause with many middle-class reformers and even some Tories was the hostility to the Whig-Radical policies of centralisation'.[51] For instance, the 1834 Poor Law Amendment Act and the 1839 Rural Constabulary Act were highlighted as two examples of legislation that posed a danger to traditional forms of governance. This led Thompson to assert that the creation of a 'continental-type state administration' was 'widely feared'.[52] She also suggested that that those fears caused 'a great deal of division' as well as 'hesitancy' amongst 'some magistrates in the face of insurrectionary' threats.[53] Additionally, there was also 'intense hostility towards the Metropolitan Police when they were introduced into provinces centres'.[54] Whilst Dorothy Thompson made some very interesting observations, a major criticism of her line of thought is that it did not go far enough in explaining how state repression impacted on Chartist protest.[55]

The quest for the reform of state institutions and the way in which government conducted its business had been in motion since the late-eighteenth century. Publications such as Adam Smith's *Wealth of Nations*, Thomas Paine's *Rights of Man* and Jeremy Bentham's *An Introduction to the Principles of Morals and Legislation* had stimulated much debate which carried on into the following century.[56] During that period, whilst central government created the rules and held responsibility for the management of internal dissent, it adopted an 'arms-length' approach to domestic affairs, in which social tasks were carried out by self-help and voluntary agencies, along with the support of factory owners.[57]

It was against this backdrop that, whilst Dorothy Thompson indicated that government suppression was fairly clear-cut, a much more thorough analysis of the source materials would suggest that this was a highly complex process in which Chartist agitation threw up a number of questions, especially in relation to the lack of cohesion that existed between central and local government. Because government was not joined up properly - due to the lack of an infrastructure and modern internal communications - the Home Office and regions such as the West Riding existed as two separate entities. What Chartism did was speed up the need for changes which brought the centre closer to the localities. In doing so, regions such as the West Riding became far easier for the Home Office to police and control from the centre. However, despite Dorothy Thompson's rather simplistic view of state repression, she was correct in her assertion that the debate about Chartism needed to establish a closer focus between what was happening nationally and locally.

In 1973 when J.T. Ward made an attempt to bridge this gap, he asserted that the Chartists were the first major working-class political party in the world.[58] He also reinforced an observation made by Asa Briggs, fourteen years earlier, that the Chartist movement acted as an 'umbrella' organisation for a wide range of social, economic and political causes.[59] Ward's study fused together aspects of the local approach with Dorothy Thompson's national methodology in order to create a new narrative. Ward delved into the deeper history of the movement and suggested that the entire concept behind the Charter and the 'Six Points', stretched back to the seventeenth century when constitutional struggles between radical and conservative ideologies were in their infancy.[60] Ward's take on the subject was later underlined by David Jones who, in 1975, argued that the ideas of the Chartists were steeped in old traditions but as a political organisation it was 'relatively new'.[61] Whereas Ward argued that the radicalism dated back to the seventeenth century, Jones claimed that the ideas behind Chartist protest were evident in late-eighteenth century publications such as Paine's *Rights of Man*, which was written in 1791. They were also present in the battles that took place in around parliament over the issue of 'Old Corruption' which was opposed by John Wilkes.[62]

The criticisms put forward about conventional studies of Chartism were given further impetus when James Epstein, who at the time was a protégé of Dorothy Thompson, questioned the local approach. He said too many studies had been conducted in this area and that there was no structure to the research.[63] This assertion is questionable on the basis there are still numerous local gaps that need to be filled, especially in relation to areas such as Scottish, Welsh and Irish Chartism.[64] More work is needed in analysing how incidents such as the Bull Ring and Newport disturbances in 1839 affected Chartist activity outside their immediate areas. In addition historians, such as Roger Swift, have argued that greater research is needed into government suppression, especially in relation to the role of policing.[65] Clearly, here is a case to argue that more case-studies are needed in relation to the impact of provincial policing on Chartist protest in which there is a wealth of Home Office sources that have not been fully explored.

Following James Epstein's observations concerning the state of the debate, the criticism of established Chartist theories was taken a stage further by Gareth Stedman Jones. In 1983, he wrote the essay 'Rethinking Chartism' which launched an assault on class-based methodology. Stedman Jones argued that the Chartists and their grievances could only be understood by language and how they used it. The author created the so-called 'linguistic turn', and although it was not entirely dismissive of class as an explanation behind the emergence of the radical movement, he felt that there was a need for a new approach in order to galvanise studies in this field.[66] Stedman

Jones felt that the political organisation contained far more substance than had been suggested in earlier case-studies, particularly those that revolved around class-based and the localised approaches.

The 'linguistic turn' attracted much criticism from liberal and Marxist theorists who found many flaws in its key arguments. In 1987, Neville Kirk staunchly defended the class-based approach. He argued that his counterpart had created an overtly political interpretation of the Chartists that greatly under-estimated the influence of social and economic factors behind the rise and fall of the movement.[67] Kirk reiterated the view put forward by Dorothy Thompson that the Chartist movement was motivated by class conflict and tension.[68] In contrast, Stedman Jones attempted to explain how the commercial and industrial middle classes used the powers which they had gained during the 1830s to transform and remodel society. Alternatively, Kirk was highly critical of the lack of attention Stedman Jones had given to the impact of 'concrete' state policies. He believed that the 'linguistic turn' relied far too heavily upon 'empirical supports' as opposed to primary evidence which can found in Home Office sources taken from the period.[69] Neville Kirk also suggested that state policies towards the Chartists were 'complex' and 'uneven' and not as clear as Stedman Jones implied.[70]

The dispute over the 'linguistic turn' continued on into the second phase of the Chartist historiography. What followed was a transitional period as the emphasis shifted away from localised and class-based approaches towards studies that were largely cultural, biographical and gender specific. This was driven by Patrick Joyce whose revisionist book *Visions of the People* suggested 'alternatives to class in popular perceptions'.[71] Joyce argued that class was just one of many identities used in articulating the language of radical politics.[72] He examined areas such art, literature and song and suggested that these various forms of 'populism' crossed over within political culture. In a departure from Edward Thompson's earlier narrative, Joyce argued that there was 'a righteous and dispossessed people rather than a working class' which was more liberal in outlook than socialist.[73] Whilst Joyce's book was not written specifically about Chartism, this study opened up major avenues for the growth of cultural studies in this field.

Patrick Joyce's study was followed with two books by James Vernon who felt that there were certain deficiencies within the historiography which had to be addressed.[74] In doing so, Vernon wanted to create 'a new cultural history of politics'.[75] He suggested that the narrative had moved away from the 'linguistic turn' towards the language of politics.[76] His key argument was that during the period 1832 to 1867, 'English Politics became progressively less democratic'.[77] He attributed this development to what he saw as the regulation of mass forms of political participation which stemmed from the 1832 Reform Act. Vernon argued that the closure of the political system was a top-down process largely because of 'a growing degree of uncertainty' at central government level over whether local government could deal with the social changes brought about by urbanisation and industrialisation.[78] He suggested that over a period of time, the political system became more regulated and disciplined as populist and violent methods of activism associated with the mass platform were reshaped and simplified.[79] Vernon saw the use of print culture and the growth of the party system as being central to the shaping of cultural identities and allegiances in the closure of the political sphere.[80]

Vernon's arguments came in for some criticism. Whilst he openly admitted that he could not exactly pinpoint when the disciplining and regulation of politics began, the historian Jon Lawrence questioned the methodology of his main study. Lawrence felt that the motives behind reforms designed to regulate the political system were not fully examined. Further to this, he felt that Vernon had exaggerated the control of physical space in which, Lawrence suggested, a closer examination of state policy and high politics was needed.[81] There is validity in the assertion made by Lawrence that not enough research has been conducted in examining the relationship between Chartism and the control of public space. Lisa Keller and Antony Taylor have looked at how parks and public meeting places in London were regulated by the authorities to prevent Chartist protest.[82] Beyond the metropolitan and urban heartlands, Katrina Navickas has explored the culture and symbolism attached to the use of fields and moorlands as an arena for Chartist gatherings, with specific emphasis placed on the West Riding and South Lancashire.[83] All three studies are important but work is clearly needed over the way in which Chartism was controlled spatially within an urban environment.

Despite the emergence of these new narratives, during the mid-1990s the problems of whether Chartism could be understood in terms of class or culture continued to be a major source of contention amongst historians. Questions were raised about the damage that this disagreement had done to the historiography. In an article written in 1996, Miles Taylor tried to draw a line through this dispute. He compared and contrasted the areas at the centre of the Gareth Stedman Jones and Dorothy Thompson debate. Taylor suggested that despite disagreements over their 'fundamental approaches' to the subject, they actually agreed on many things. This was particularly evident in the way in which they viewed Chartism as a national movement that dated back to the struggle over the 1832 Reform Act.[84] However, where both of them did disagree was over issues such as the role of the state. As a consequence, Stedman Jones was singled out for criticism and blamed for causing an impasse in the historiography. Taylor suggested that instead of creating a platform for new research, the 'linguistic turn' had resulted in 'over a decade of disagreement' amongst historians.[85]

Miles Taylor's pessimistic view of the state of research into Chartism was criticised by Andrew Messner. Whereas Taylor pessimistically blamed the 'linguistic turn' for stalling the Chartist historiography, Messner believed that there was still a need for existing approaches. He felt that prior to the collision between class-based and linguistic approaches to Chartism, studies of the radical movement had existed within an 'intellectual vacuum'.[86] Messner suggested that fresh work was needed in areas such as the Land Plan, the latter part of Feargus O'Connor's life and the 'wider cultural aspects' of the movement.[87] Messner also wanted the historiography to be extended towards the colonial realm. His article examined how the Chartist model of protest was exported to places such as Australia, where many activists caught up in unrest on the mainland were later transported.[88] A more productive approach would examine how Ireland was used by the British government as a testing ground for public-order policy. During the nineteenth century and before Chartist unrest had taken place, there had already been many examples of state intervention in Ireland, which included areas such as policing, education and public works.[89] Chartism in the colonial realm has already been responded to by Pickering, but in order to further our knowledge of the interrelationship between Chartism and the state, more clarification is needed about the level of intervention that occurred and how much influence this had on domestic government policy both before and during the suppression of Chartism.

As the Chartist historiography drifted into the third phase of activity from 2000 to the present, the huge emphasis placed on cultural studies has continued unabated. The narratives created by Patrick Joyce and James Vernon fed directly into the work of historians such as Mike Sanders, who has investigated areas such as the use of Chartist poetry and hymns as a vehicle for radical protest. Similarly, studies conducted by Ian Haywood and work by Joan Allen and Owen Ashton have looked extensively at the print culture that enveloped the movement.[90] These studies were substantially expanded upon by Malcolm Chase in his *Chartism: A New History* in 2007.[91] This hugely important study has done much to fuse together issues such as class and gender, along with the link between the local and national organisation of the Chartist movement. However, it only touches upon aspects of the role of the government and the state in its suppression of Chartist unrest in which there are many issues that need to be addressed so that the historiography can progress.

It should be apparent that very little research has been conducted about the role of government and its interrelationship with the Chartist movement. The first study to broach the subject of the government and its suppression of the Chartist movement was written by F.C. Mather in 1959. It was titled *Public Order in the Age of the Chartists*.[92] The book followed on from his unpublished dissertation written in 1948 which examined how the public order apparatus meshed together.[93] It also expanded upon an article published in 1953 that explored how improvements to internal communications improved the efficiency of the machinery of public order.[94] Mather asserted that during the 1830s and 1840s the government response to Chartist unrest spawned many innovations which removed the threat of riot from English society. The assertion that riot had been totally eliminated from English society was highly contentious. Since the 1960s, many incidents have taken place which would suggest otherwise.

Mather's study was a vast narrative which covered a number of areas and gave a broad description of the machinery of public order and how it functioned at both central and local levels. It examined the nature of the 'old' and 'new' police. It also compared and contrasted the roles of the military and intelligence services.[95] According to Mather the machinery of public order during the Chartist era underwent improvement but exhibited a number of flaws which hindered its effectiveness. One of those areas was in the field of policing. The author suggested that radical unrest could have been easily suppressed had the magistracy embraced reforms much more quickly. This was particularly the case in places such as the West Riding.

The major strength of Mather's seminal work is the amount of factual data that it contained. It possessed an overwhelming amount of detail and is littered with references to various Home Office, War Office and government sources. Where the investigation is weak is through its lack of theoretical analysis. The book was written at a time when social history was in its infancy. As a consequence, it does not fully explain why the state acted in the way that it did. Nor does it give any sociological reasons why the Chartists resorted to the protest they undertook.

Following on from this, it was not until the mid to late-1980s that fresh research conducted in this field began to adopt a more theoretical framework. In 1987, John Saville wrote about the events of 1848. This publication appeared very shortly after Neville Kirk had penned the article 'In Defence of Class', in which he attacked Gareth Stedman Jones's 'linguistic turn'. Kirk called upon historians to produce a study of the state and its suppression of the Chartist movement.[96] Like Mather's previous investigation, John Saville's manuscript was very much a product of the time. It was written against the backdrop of the Thatcher Conservative government's politicisation of the police as a coercive instrument of the state in the control of inner-city riots and industrial unrest. Another major influence behind Saville's research was Irish Republican and Ulster Unionist terrorism which was at its height. John Saville tried to address the arguments put forward by Neville Kirk for a study based on the coercive aspects of the state.

The book began by highlighting the problems with the historiography at that particular moment in time. Saville agreed with James Epstein's perception that many previous studies of Chartism had focused too heavily on the localised approach. Further to this, in response to Gareth Stedman Jones's attempt to politicise the debate, Saville wanted a broader study of the movement in relation to the development of the early-Victorian state. Saville rightly said that this area had been overlooked; it continues to remain so to this day. He also suggested that there was a need for an analysis of the link between Chartism and other political movements that existed around that time. The historian felt that this had previously been explained in terms that were too simplistic.[97]

Saville looked at how the British government did its utmost to avert insurrection by curtailing the spread of French revolutionary ideas on the mainland and stemming the threat of rebellion in Ireland during the aftermath of the Potato Famine. Saville's research concentrated on those urban centres worst affected by the mass migration of Irish inhabitants: Liverpool, Bradford and Manchester. The three towns and cities also became major centres of Chartist unrest during the period 1847-8. At the time, the movement had aligned itself with the Irish Confederates. In doing so, it played on social and political tensions in order to cause mass unrest which the government tried to suppress.

The main weakness of this in-depth study is that it covers only one year of Chartist activity. In doing so, it fails to offer a fuller picture of how the Home Office and its mechanisms of control developed during the ten years of Chartist agitation. However, despite this deficiency, John Saville's month-by-month account suggested that the state machinery had become more effective in dealing with Chartist unrest throughout 1848 than at any stage during the main years of the movement's existence. He argued that the radical movement was suppressed by the government due to its control and use of physical force with great effect but also because it won a propaganda battle. This did much to gain the hearts and minds of the population under its control.

A year later, Saville's study of the events of 1848 was followed by Stanley H. Palmer's monumental book on policing, which examined the relationship between Britain and its use of Ireland as a colonial testing-ground for police reforms during the period 1780 to 1850.[98] Palmer argued that the police were highly ineffectual in dealing with Chartist riots and disturbances. He suggested that the military was largely responsible for the suppression of the radical organisation. Palmer was extremely dismissive of the threat to public order posed by the Chartists. He argued that despite their revolutionary intentions, the movement was based upon 'bluff and verbal intimidation' as it lacked the power to trouble the authorities in any shape or form.[99] Whilst his study is vast it contains very little mention of the events that occurred in the Chartist heartland of the West Riding. Further to this, Palmer's suggestion that during the period 1838-9 Birmingham was the main centre of the Chartist movement is a somewhat contentious view.[100]

Since the research of Saville and Palmer was carried out almost 25 years ago, there has been very little attempt made to expand upon these studies. Neville Kirk's attack on the 'linguistic turn' and Gareth Stedman Jones's decision to overlook state suppression as a reason behind the decline of the Chartist movement was followed by John Walton's perceptive assessment of the state of the debate during the mid-1990s. He argued:

> What needs more attention is the nature, strength and adaptability of the forces against which the Chartists were pitted: the power of the state not only to coerce, repress, make propaganda and deny the space in which to act but also to set the agenda, to calibrate responses and to present itself as responding modestly and responsibly to those grievances which it chose to recognise as legitimate.[101]

Miles Taylor has also identified a number of avenues for future research, underlining an examination of the role of the state. He maintains that there was the need for 'a definitive account of the relationship between the Chartist movement and the state throughout the 1830s and 1840s'.[102] He argued that 'if ultimately the rise and fall of Chartism is to be understood in political terms, then this deficiency needs remedying'.[103] A second area of exploration that Taylor alluded to revolved around 'the changing political strategies of the Chartists' and how the movement responded to state coercion. A third major theme is the need to re-examine the main reasons why the radical organisation failed and whether or not this could be linked to a more responsive and conciliatory state,[104] the case being that during the period the state was chameleon-like, changing its spots to suit various situations and crises. It was to this end that Taylor also suggested that analysis needs to revolve around the 'geography of Chartism'.[105] He argues that political studies of the movement have 'seen off the local emphasis' which had not only made it 'difficult to appreciate the national dimensions' of the radical organisation, but also presented the danger of ignoring the relationship between 'locality and centre'.[106] Many of the questions that Miles Taylor raised have yet to be answered properly.

Throughout the period there was a pattern to the behaviour of the Chartist responses to coercion. Before the Newport disturbances in November 1839, there was an air of confidence about the Chartists and their intention to overhaul the state and achieve the democratic reforms they craved. After the Newport massacre, which claimed the lives of twenty-two people, this confidence was shattered and a harsh realism set in amongst its leadership as to what could be achieved. As a consequence, whenever any conflict with the state and its machinery occurred, the Chartists usually dispersed, largely because they lacked the firepower and the will to be able to mount any sustained challenge to its authority. This can be seen in the key incidents that happened after Newport, which included the attempted uprisings of January 1840, the 1842 Plug Plot disturbances and the incidents that occurred throughout 1848, which were mainly centred on London and Bradford, and will be examined in more detail throughout later chapters.

Given the strengths and weaknesses of the Chartist historiography this book explores in much greater depth some of the areas of research suggested by both Miles Taylor and John Walton, along with many of the gaps in the studies of Stanley H. Palmer and John Saville. However, in order to create an approach that fuses together the history from above with that from below, a far more focused perspective will be taken that examines how Home Office suppression impacted on a major heartland of Chartist activity: the West Riding of Yorkshire. Studies of the radical movement in this region have been largely ignored, especially in relation to areas such as state development and the growth of policing, where there are major gaps in the historiography. At the same time, it will be mindful of comparable developments in other Chartist strongholds such as Birmingham, industrial South Wales and mid-Wales.[107]

The historian J.T. Ward once made the obvious point that the West Riding 'had a long tradition of radicalism and agitation'.[108] However, despite this observation, over the past thirty years or so, there has been comparatively little research into the Chartist movement within the region.[109] The studies that have previously been written tend to mirror the town-by-town approach advocated by Briggs, which was commonplace throughout the 1960s and 1970s. On the surface, they offer a sketchy overview as to how Chartism impacted on a given place. In terms of class and identity, there have been no studies as to how radical unrest associated with the movement had an effect on the region as a whole. Past investigations have touched on the growth of the *Northern Star* newspaper, established in 1837 in Leeds, along with riots that took place during the three main waves of agitation. However, there has been no overarching study of the movement, particularly regarding centre/local relations, state repression and the development of the public order apparatus. A broader analysis of the historiography can give us clues about the gaps that need to be filled in order to construct an understanding of the relationship between the Home Office and the Chartist movement in the region.

The West Riding is one of three historic subdivisions of Yorkshire. Its geographical territory spans over 1,500,000 million acres, from Sedbergh in the north-west to Sheffield in the south, stretching ninety-five miles from north to south and forty-eight miles from east to west (See Map 1). Two-thirds of its landscape was rural, yet during the nineteenth century, the region underwent significant social, economic and political change. The development of radicalism was directly linked to the growth of towns and industrialisation. The regional economy specialised in cotton, wool, silk and flax spinning. This gave rise to the growth of important industrial towns such as Leeds, Bradford, Huddersfield and Halifax that were connected to the radical south-east Lancashire region.[110] An indication of the remarkable pace of progress and growth can be measured by the impact that industrial development had on places such as Leeds, which at the time was a major commercial centre for woollen and worsted trades. The town was directly linked to Manchester and Liverpool by canals. Between 1700 and 1840, its population multiplied by twenty times.[111] In the context of the growth of the West Riding as a whole, as Table 1 below shows, the number of inhabitants in the town doubled between 1801 and 1841, from 572,168 to 1,165,580.[112]

Table 1: Population of Major Cities and Towns in the West Riding, 1801-51[113]

City/Town	Population					
	1801	*1811*	*1821*	*1831*	*1841*	*1851*
Bradford	13,264	16,012	26,307	43,527	66,715	103,778
Halifax	12,010	12,766	17,056	21,552	27,520	33,582
Huddersfield	7,268	9,671	13,284	19,035	25,068	30,880
Leeds	53,162	62,534	83,796	123,393	152,074	172,270
Sheffield	45,755	53,231	65,275	91,692	111,091	135,300
Wakefield	10,581	11,393	14,164	15,932	18,842	22,057

By looking at how industrial and demographic changes influenced the development of Chartism in the region, early research was influenced by the local model introduced by Asa Briggs during the late 1950s. In 1959, J.F.C. Harrison's influential 'Chartism in Leeds' appeared in *Chartist Studies*. The author believed that the radical organisation in the town had emerged 'from the early autumn of 1837'.[114] During the decade, the municipal area was 'second only to Manchester as a centre of radical and working-class movements in the North'.[115] Harrison went on to state that:

> Nowhere was the variety and complexity of the pattern of working-class endeavour more clearly demonstrated. Trade Union activity, Short-Time Committees for factory reform, the struggle for the unstamped press, Owenism, co-operative stores, and the extension of the suffrage – all claimed the support of Leeds working men. These movements were not so much rivals competing for support, nor even complementary parts of a greater national movement, as different expressions of a general discontent and reaching out to a more just and equitable organisation of society. The movements tended to fade into one another.[116]

Harrison argued that the Chartist movement in Leeds was based upon radical leaders such as Joshua Hobson, John Francis Bray and David Green, who were actively involved in causes such as the Factory Reform movement and Owenism. He attempted to discover why the Chartist movement in Leeds failed to attract the same level of interest that it did in Bradford. Harrison argued that the organisation that existed in the town was like 'a small group of able, intelligent enthusiasts' that was 'almost a general staff without an army'.[117] The intellectual nature of the Chartist movement in Leeds led Harrison to conclude that it failed to attract mass support because it was in direct competition with many middle-class radical organisations. The only avenue where it did gain success was in the field of local politics. Harrison's research went on to explore the impact of 'Municipal Chartism' and how the movement interacted with Improvement Committees in the field of civic development.

All in all, Harrison offers a generalised account of how the movement took root in Leeds; he did not make full use of the sources that were available. A more thorough investigation based on government suppression would examine how the Borough Police and the military kept a lid on tensions within the town. In effect, the control of public space forced the Leeds Chartists to pursue a more moral force strategy as opposed to the direct action which occurred in other parts of the region.

The next major investigator of West Riding Chartism, David G. Wright, looked at the rise and fall of the movement in Bradford. This research, concluded in 1966, formed the basis of an unpublished doctoral thesis and was largely written from the perspective of working-class consciousness. The dissertation reflected the sea change that had taken place in the study of Chartism through the influence of Edward Thompson. Wright located events in Bradford as being a 'class war' between the authorities and the disenfranchised. He looked at how workers, who had been made redundant as a result of economic depression, became the main agitators behind Chartist disturbances and unrest. The case-study also alluded to tensions within Bradford that were caused by the increasing presence of an Irish community which was at the centre of a rebellion in 1848.[118] This was an area that had also been explored by F.C. Mather who had emphasised the role of Feargus O'Connor in the development of the movement. Mather argued that 'from the very beginning of his Chartist career', O'Connor 'planned an alliance of the common peoples of Great Britain and Ireland'.[119] He also suggested that the radical leader harboured ambitions of 'uniting Irish peasants', along with 'Irish immigrants living in the towns of England and Scotland, with British working men, in a single agitation for social and political reform'.[120]

In keeping with an observation of Asa Briggs, his supervisor, made six years previously, Wright argued that radicalism within the West Riding was dominated by Nonconformist attitudes. In contrast to the argument put forward by E.P. Thompson in *The Making of the English Working Class* he suggested that Wesleyan Methodism was an anachronistic force behind the agitation that took place in Bradford during the first half of the nineteenth century.[121] The Chartist movement, like many Yorkshire radical organisations that went before it, saw the union of the Church and state as an obstacle to its objectives. The two institutions were seen as an 'unholy union' in which religious differences were bound up with political inequality. Chartist leaders believed that religious diversity 'could not exist in a state' where 'civil liberty was complete'. Evidently, an aim of the radical movement was to destroy the 'Cannon Creed' by Universal Suffrage, in order to provide a base for 'the Altar, the Throne and the Cottage'.[122] This was a concept promoted by Richard Oastler at the height of Poor Law and Factory Reform agitation which was adopted by the leadership of the Chartist movement - despite misgivings about Oastler's role amongst some of the more socialist radicals.

On 7 April 1838, the *Northern Star* blamed the union between the Church and state for causing poverty and distress amongst the working classes. It saw the relationship between the two institutions as being highly representative of a corrupt political system:

The Church and State are too firmly, and have been too long, politically united, to adopt the spiritual admonitions of the Hierarchy, otherwise than as political lessons. We find religion supported by force; liberty trampled upon; comforts abridged; rights abstracted; and wrong following wrong, in rapid succession; and yet we are told that our salvation will much depend upon our mild endurance of those multiplied evils. But that such sophistry and blasphemy can be preached accepted and acted upon, is not wonderful, when we see the Altar based upon the Throne, and Religion made subservient to political purposes.[123]

Wright's local analysis of the religious and political tensions that existed at a time of social and economic changes provided a balanced appraisal of the causes of riot and disturbance in Bradford throughout the major period of Chartist agitation. Although his study contained much detail, Wright stressed the need for a more expansive study. It came in 1990, when Theodore Koditschek examined the question of class formation in Bradford.[124] At that time he questioned existing methodologies, such as that of E.P. Thompson, maintaining that the process of class formation was far more complex than was previously thought. Koditschek argued that during the nineteenth century, in Bradford, the processes of industrialisation and urbanisation were intertwined.[125] He showed that the emergence of a proletarian workforce in the town ran parallel to the growth of a capitalist 'entrepreneurial bourgeoisie', which was not only concerned with making profits but also creating the conditions for social progress.[126] When Chartist agitation occurred, it was at this point that a major collision occurred between liberal, conservative and radical Chartist factions, which turned Bradford into a 'massively crisis-ridden and unconditionally divided city'.[127] Polarisation gave rise to a number of shifts in the town's political power structure, in which he suggested that Chartism has to be viewed as 'a transitional movement', which only offered a vision for the 'politically disenfranchised and dispossessed worker'.[128] He made this statement on the basis that what came after the Chartist struggle with the state authorities during 1848, was the emergence of a 'more orderly urban community', in which politics became dictated by 'class and resolution'.[129] Despite the depth of his study, one of the weaknesses in Koditschek's analysis of Chartist agitation is the very little usage of Home Office source materials. It suggests that there are gaps within the historiography that still need to be filled in explaining what happened in Bradford, especially during 1848, which the subsequent research appears to have overlooked.

In 1969, Wright's work was also followed up by Alfred Peacock's pamphlet about Bradford Chartism, which looked at the origins of the movement in the town as well as the reasons behind the failed rebellion of January 1840. Unlike Wright's study, Peacock examined how socio-economic and political factors shaped the growth of the Chartists in Bradford. However, unlike Wright's study which explored Chartism from its very conception to its demise during the 1850s, Peacock's work was only concerned with two years of Chartist activity. In his investigation, Peacock cited the advent of the power loom and developments in machine weaving as the causes of unrest. The technological advances spelt low wages and unemployment in the woollen and worsted trades. He maintained that 'the handloom weavers were swept away in the decade between 1836 and 1846 … and they were the depressed masses who provided the bulk of support for the Chartist movement'.[130] Those discontented workers formed a strong trade union movement that was bound together with Richard Oastler's campaign for Factory Reform. They later provided the backbone of a mass protest movement against the authorities which was motivated by causes such as the campaign against 'taxes on knowledge' and opposition to the 1834 Poor Law Amendment Act. According to the author, this gave Chartism a momentum and longevity that lasted throughout the 1840s and early-1850s.[131]

Peacock's study went on to examine the roles of Peter Bussey and Robert Peddie, two main Chartist agitators. The latter figure was referred to as being 'the most important figure in the story of West Riding Chartism'.[132] In his analysis of the causes of the attempted uprising in January 1840, Peacock made the observation that historians had 'accepted that there were plans afoot for some kind of rising in Bradford at various times in the history of the Chartist movement, yet nothing happened at the times of great distress'.[133] He also said that there were 'too many questions unanswered', in explaining why in the end the rising took place. For instance, 'what was Peddie doing in Bradford at that time?' and 'how was he, a total stranger in the town, able to get into a movement that from the end of the Convention, had been conducted so secretly, that the magistrates could obtain no evidence of what was going on?'[134] This led Peacock to conclude that the rebellion was 'a last desperate attempt to promote a national rising'.[135]

Peacock's pamphlet was followed in 1972 by H.M. Docton's detailed and intensive study of Chartism in Dewsbury. The research drew upon many local sources as well as Home Office papers which gave a well-rounded account of the movement and its impact in the town.[136] Docton argued that the anti-Poor Law movement merged into early Chartism for which a similar process also occurred in Huddersfield.

Following on from Docton's thesis, two unpublished dissertations appeared during the mid-1970s which examined Chartist protest in Barnsley and Sheffield respectively. The first study written by Frederick Kaijage in 1975, looked at the social and economic history of Barnsley and how the town shaped radical and Chartist protest during the first half of the nineteenth century.[137] This dissertation contained a huge chapter about the rise and fall of Chartism in which Kaijage argued that there were four elements at play: 'class'; the 'decline of the linen industry'; a 'long radical tradition' and 'the presence of Irish immigrants'.[138] Kaijage argued that the Chartists were 'at war with oppression and vested interests', which included 'magistrates', 'manufacturers', the 'lower middle class' and 'conservative operatives'.[139] He also suggested that the Chartists wanted to become citizens in the political system 'in order to protect themselves'.[140] This was especially reflected by events after 1842 in that as the movement fell into decline, its leaders in Barnsley wanted 'class harmony' instead of 'class war', which later gave rise to respectable politics.[141]

Frederick Kaijage's study was later followed in 1976 by John Baxter's dissertation, which examined the class struggle, in particular within Sheffield and its surrounding areas.[142] Baxter's study, which is overtly Marxist in outlook, devotes an entire chapter to Chartism. He argued that its protestations went through three phases - 'preliminary', 'popular' and 'revolutionary' – which, after its peak activity, became 'tired politics' and descended into respectability.[143] In terms of its source base, Baxter's study was largely reliant upon the extensive use of Sheffield newspapers and the *Northern Star*, plus the occasional reference to Home Office and Treasury

Solicitor papers.

Since these dissertations, the study of Chartism in the West Riding has been virtually non-existent. Apart from a key essay written by Kate Tiller on Halifax Chartism for the period 1847-56, there have only been one or two minor books and articles on, for example, Benjamin Rushton's influence on the movement in the town and on Samuel Holberry's role during the 1839-40 Sheffield disturbances.[144]

The long-neglected purpose of this study is to consider how the Home Office suppression of the Chartist movement in the West Riding as a whole impacted on the development of the state and the machinery of public order. It will do so by comparing and contrasting the strength and nature of the state apparatus that was in place at the beginning and end of the period in order to build a picture of how centre-local relations operated. This study will therefore examine how various home secretaries responded to and handled the Chartist movement. It will argue that the actions of and responses by the Home Office gave rise to a power struggle with local agencies which it won and in doing so gradually gained hegemony over the state and its machinery. Further, it will open up a wider debate as to whether Home Office suppression gradually led to what James Vernon has described as the 'closure and disciplining' of mass political protest associated with Chartism.[145]

2. THE HOME OFFICE
AND THE NETWORK OF REPRESSION

In recent years there has been much discussion over the strength and nature of the British state during first half of the nineteenth century. Early studies were characterised by a view that it was weak due its tiny bureaucracy and lack of control over the population. Many comparisons were drawn between Britain and her European counterparts France and Prussia, whose states were structured along absolutist lines with heavily staffed administrative apparatus.[146] However, in 1989, John Brewer challenged the notion that the British state was weak when he devised a 'fiscal-military' model. He argued that the main strength of the state lay in its centralised and efficient system of tax collection and customs duties. The revenue generated from these two areas funded the development of the Royal Navy. This was used as a vehicle for warfare and commercial growth on a global scale through the acquisition of colonies. The policy of expansionism later provided the economic foundation for industrial development throughout the late-eighteenth and nineteenth centuries.[147]

During the 1990s, the debate surrounding the development of the British state was extended into areas such as public-order governance. Studies by David Eastwood and Richard Vogler focused on the relationship between central government and local agencies such as the Lord Lieutenant and Magistracy. Eastwood suggested that the strength of the British state rested with the localities.[148] He argued that the main source of its power was the magistracy on the basis that it was the chief nexus between central and local government. Eastwood also argued that despite the amateurish nature of this agency, the main strength of local magistrates was that they took their duties very seriously.[149] In 2004, the debate over where the source of state power lay was investigated further by David Philips. Having looked at the arguments of both Brewer and Eastwood, he believed that their studies should be consolidated and extended into areas such as policing.[150] However, a topic that has been completely overlooked is the role of the Home Office, which is central to this discussion.

In order to establish where the power of the Home Office was situated in relation to this debate, modern approaches to state development have concentrated on the concepts of 'political geography' and 'spatial dynamics'.[151] By using the description of 'territory' as 'a portion of geographic space which is claimed or occupied by a person or group of persons or by an institution', and 'territoriality', meaning the process where 'individuals or groups lay claim to the territory/land', there is scope to argue that the source of state power rested with the localities.[152] This argument rests on the basis that Home Office control over regions such as the West Riding was relatively weak due to poor communications and the constraints of geography.

The theorist Michael Mann has argued that state power can be measured through an analysis of the strength of 'despotic elites'. These are the personnel in charge of the machinery that generates physical force.[153] A second form of measurement is through its 'infrastructural' capacity, which is the ability of the apparatus to penetrate places where political and civil unrest is being conducted.[154] We need to consider the strength of the British state and whether the source of its power was situated at the centre or in the localities. The answer to this question is not particularly straightforward.

If we look at a state as being an entity that is made up of institutions where power radiates outwards from the centre over a given territory and has the capacity to claim and legitimately use physical force violence to maintain public order, at first sight, this model would suggest that its power rests at the centre.[155] This assertion is on the premise that the Home Office exerted total control over the public-order apparatus. However, on closer inspection, in using the description of 'territory' as 'a portion of geographic space which is claimed or occupied by a person or group of persons or by an institution', and 'territoriality', meaning the process where 'individuals or groups lay claim to the territory/land', there is scope to argue that the source of state power rested with the localities.[156] This argument rests on the basis that Home Office control over places such as the West Riding was relatively weak due to poor communications and geographical limitations.

In order to establish the early difficulties which the Home Office faced in denying the Chartists space to conduct their protests, as well as where the power of the British state lay, the chapter will compare and contrast the central and local mechanisms of control that were in place. The first part of this debate will examine the powers of the 'despotic elites' who staffed the Home Office and consider how they lacked the necessary 'infrastructural' capacity to wield any form of direct influence over the West Riding. The second part will analyse the strength and nature of the apparatus within the region itself. This will demonstrate how geographical considerations enabled local agencies to act almost independently from central control.

At the very beginning of the period, the British state was effectively a two-tiered structure in which central and local authority co existed alongside each other. This meant that any response to disorder organised on a mass scale was uneven. At the top of this configuration was the Home Office which theoretically, through its key office-holders and personnel, controlled the entire apparatus. However, in practice, the paucity of internal communications meant that the provincial machinery largely existed independently of central control. As a result of this division, many practices went unchecked and the system was rife with abuses.

There has been some dispute over how much control the Home Office and the Home Secretary possessed when dealing with civil unrest. Troup and Newsam have argued that the office-holder exerted absolute supremacy over the state machinery. On the other hand, Smith and Donajgrodzki have suggested that the functions of the Secretary of State were delegated amongst various individuals and branches which came together in emergency situations.[157] The latter argument appears to carry more weight because in theory the Home Secretary had a huge number of powers at his disposal. These ranged from sharing tasks such as the maintenance of law and order, especially in relation to the judicial system; the deployment of various military forces to deal with disturbances; control of the Metropolitan Police, along with the use of surveillance mechanisms such as the Post Office and spies to monitor political groups and individuals intent on causing insurgency with a view to challenging the authority of the state. However, despite having those powers, on a practical level, the Secretary of State and his staff were hampered by political and ideological changes, which significantly increased the workload of the Home Office.

The first major alteration that affected the operation of the Home Office was carried out by Sir Robert Peel during the early 1820s, when it was given the power to legislate.[158] This allowed the Home Office to shape directly domestic policies in response to the vast number of abuses and problems that emerged as a result of industrial and urban development. Peel opened the doors of the Home Office to outside agencies such as experts, statisticians and theoreticians whose influence played a major part in the way in which government policy was formulated.[159] The effect of this development was a major explosion in the portfolio of its business. During the late 1820s and throughout the 1830s, its remit was gradually expanded into areas such as policing, prisons and factory reform.[160]

Before 1822, the role of the Home Office and its staff was largely administrative. Many of its practices dated back to a time when the department had existed under a number of various guises. The history of this major office of state stretches back four hundred years to the Tudor period.[161] When Sir Robert Peel's reforms were introduced, the Home Office became increasingly politicised and more accountable to parliament.[162] In order to pass legislation, the Home Office forged closer relations with the House of Lords.[163] Traditional duties such as its prerogative powers and those relating to the maintenance of public order were merged with newer responsibilities such as the creation of the Metropolitan Police Force in 1829.[164]

The growth of those tasks went hand in hand with profound ideological changes, which was the second major alteration that affected the operation of the Home Office. Theorists such as Jeremy Bentham and, later, Edwin Chadwick believed that in order to remedy the abuses of laissez-faire capitalism and industrialisation, legislation should be introduced and designed for the 'greatest happiness of the greatest number'.[165] The Benthamite argument came about in response to an increase in crime and the need for greater regulation of social and living conditions in burgeoning towns.[166] The two political idealists believed that there was a huge need for state interference in social affairs, especially in relation to the conditions of the working classes. They both understood that the ruling upper and middle classes had to forge better relations with the disenfranchised working classes in order to renew the political system and prevent it from succumbing to the threat of revolt.[167]

During the Home Office conflict with the Chartists, whilst the insurgency challenge was prevented throughout the period 1838 to 1848, the state remained small and minimalist in outlook. The main realm of government activity revolved around foreign policy; colonial and national defence; the raising of revenue to fund naval and defence costs; trade and industry; and law and order.[168] Whilst the state was tentatively broadening its scope in areas such as public health and industrial conditions, the main source of investment in those fields came from private enterprise, industry and voluntary organisations.[169] However, it is clear that the need to improve internal security was becoming a major priority in order to maintain national stability as a response to changing social conditions.

These changes impacted on the working practices of the Home Office, especially those of the Home Secretary, who was consumed by the growth of parliamentary and cabinet responsibilities. The duties of the Home Secretary were divided between judicial, military and police functions.

Whilst the Home Office had many powers at its disposal for dealing with potential Chartist unrest and insurgency, its authority, and that of the Home Secretary, was hindered by its antiquated practices. Given the poor internal communications, local agencies enjoyed considerable independence from central control.

In judicial matters, the Home Secretary advised magistrates how the law should be interpreted and used as a means of preserving public order.[170] A good example of how this relationship worked was demonstrated when effigies of people who had supported the new Poor Laws of 1834 were burnt on the streets of Huddersfield. The Home Secretary responded by ordering magistrates to punish anyone caught carrying out this illegal activity by charging them with a breach of the peace.[171]

This role took on even greater relevance when magistrates were unsure how to enforce the law under certain circumstances. For example, in November 1837 when two people were committed to gaol after being charged with rioting at Bradford, the acting Justices of the Peace did not know whether to grant bail. In such cases, a magistrate usually decided what type of punishment should be administered according to the circumstances of the criminal act that had been committed. However, because of the extreme nature of this particular case, the magistrates had very little alternative but to seek guidance from the Home Secretary, who later told them to set bail at £150-£200 per person. A surety of such a large amount of money was demanded by the state because it ensured that prisoners could be produced and brought to trial.[172]

Similar action was often taken by the Home Secretary when it came to the prosecution of individuals involved in treasonable activities against the government which were commonplace during the era of Chartist turbulence. In such cases, state trials were organised and funded by the Lords of the Treasury who paid the court expenses.[173] Decisions about what course of action should be taken in such extreme circumstances were made by the Home Secretary following consultation with Law Officers of the Crown, the Solicitor to the Treasury and the Attorney-General who was responsible for making the laws.[174] The type of punishment that was administered to state offenders carried a deterrent status. However, there were limitations to the lengths that the Home Office could go to in bringing to justice parties caught up in treasonable activity.

First of all, there was the issue of public safety to consider. This would explain why insurgents such as the ringleader of the 1840 Sheffield disturbances, Samuel Holberry, and the Chartist leader Feargus O'Connor in 1839, escaped execution for their involvement in insurrection and the use of seditious language to incite political violence.[175] The government could not come down too heavily on such individuals because an intention of the Chartists was to make the parts of the nation ungovernable. Any draconian form of action would directly play into their hands. Quite often, imprisonment in gaol or transportation was applied as a suitable form of punishment. This was the fate of John Frost in 1840 for his involvement in the Newport Rising.[176]

A second limitation imposed on the Home Secretary was the non-interference with decisions made by magistrates. Trials that were held at Borough and Petty Sessions could not be influenced and as a consequence, judges could not be pressurised into making decisions that favoured the government. Once a decision had been made by a magistrate or judge concerning a case or individual, it could not be overturned.[177] In practice, the only way in which the judicial process could be interfered with was through the Prerogative of Mercy. This was a traditional power enforced by the Home Secretary on behalf of the monarch and often used when offenders were wrongly convicted.[178] However, the Home Office found a way to intervene by using a loophole in the system that involved the offer of financial rewards to witnesses in return for their evidence and attendance at court. Such incentives were offered following outbreaks of severe rioting.[179] For instance, when anti-Poor Law disturbances broke out in Dewsbury in 1838, a sum of £50 was offered for any information about the offending parties and was paid pending a trial.[180] The enforcement of this measure required military assistance, which had its limitations, especially when dealing with riot and disorder.

In order to uphold the law, the Home Secretary handled requests from Lord Lieutenants and magistrates for armed assistance whenever there was a perceived or actual outbreak of violence. In most cases the Regular Army was deployed as an instrument of repression.[181] This was an institution made up of various regiments in which the soldiers were primarily used as 'domestic policemen' to maintain public order and pursue criminals.[182] In 1835, the Home Secretary had 23,559 troops from infantry, cavalry and artillery regiments at his disposal.[183] The United Kingdom was divided into military districts, each of which, according to F.C. Mather, was led by a commander 'whose rank varied with the size and importance of the troops at his command'.[184] The West Riding came under the boundary of the Northern District, which stretched from the Scottish border through the north-eastern coalfield, the textile belts of Lancashire and Yorkshire into Leicestershire and Nottinghamshire.[185]

The Home Secretary was responsible for the placement of troops.[186] The post-holder was in frequent communication with commanders of the various district armies which were based across the country.[187] They issued reports in relation to the state of towns and denoted whether cavalry and infantry soldiers were needed by magistrates to repress any attempts by individuals and political movements to disturb the public peace.[188] The deployment of soldiers was carried out at the discretion and judgment of the Home Secretary, who also acted on any information received from the Lord Lieutenants concerning the state of their counties and any proceedings that had taken place within them.[189]

As an instrument of repression, the deployment of the regular army was slow and hindered by bureaucracy.[190] The process of deployment began when members of the general public made a complaint to the local Justice of the Peace who on acting upon this forwarded details of the incident to the Home Secretary. At Home Office level, the request was passed onto the Permanent Under-Secretary who wrote a letter with a covering note to the Horse Guards requesting military assistance in a given place. The Horse Guards were led by the Commander-in-Chief of the British Army, who specifically dealt with requests for military aid. He was assisted by the Adjutant-General who was responsible for the infrastructure and administration of the army, along with the Quartermaster-General, the most senior general in command. Beneath those key officials was the civilian staff who conducted the daily affairs of this highly-important office of state.[191] When notice of the situation had reached this level, the Commander-in-Chief instructed the District Officer who commanded the military district nearest to the affected area to march troops to the scene.[192] On many occasions, communications between various agencies broke down causing considerable confusion.

The use of regular soldiers to suppress Chartist unrest within the West Riding was a highly unpopular, but much needed, 'preventative measure'.[193] In the management of 'numerous small disturbances' the forces were often inadequate and highly unsuitable, whether they were assisted by a civil force or not.[194] There was a similar pattern when military force was used to deal with the 'repression of large commotions'.[195] The regular soldiers were often armed with muskets. This meant that they could cause injury or indeed death by 'firing or stabbing' and, in effect, could only repress incidents by forceful measures.[196] The Home Office and local magistrates were reluctant to deploy troops on the basis that their responses to flashpoints were often 'indiscriminate'.[197] This was later proven by the reaction of soldiers towards armed insurgents at Newport in 1839 and also during skirmishes with the Chartists in the West Riding throughout the 1842 Plug Plot disturbances.

The absence of any 'efficiently organised' policing to deal with riots and disturbances meant that the Home Office and local magistrates had little alternative but to call upon soldiers to maintain the authority of the state.[198]

As well as the over-aggressive nature of the armed forces, an additional problem that the Home Secretary had to deal with was indiscipline within its ranks. Troops were often placed in the centre of highly populated towns. Skirmishes with local inhabitants, along with petty criminal incidents were commonplace. This resulted in soldiers receiving draconian punishments whilst at the same time the military, as an institution, received a bad press. A couple of typical incidents were reported by the *Northern Star* on 17 February 1838. This resulted in soldiers stationed at Leeds Barracks being flogged for their crimes. The first incident involved Private Roylance, described as being 'a poor fellow who was punished for taking a saddle' in what amounted to a misunderstanding over a horse.[199] The unfortunate soldier 'had to subsist on 6d. a day for eight days' and had '1s. 6d. to pay for the cats he was flogged with'.[200] The second case of flogging reported was a separate incident that involved Private C. Burton who was drunk during the 'evening stables'.[201] He was caught by his sergeant and reported to the troop sergeant-major who ordered him to be sent to 'the Guard Room'.[202] One onlooker reported that:

> On hearing this, Burton ran out of the stable by the back gate, and the Sergeant after him, when he made a jump to get over the gate, but the Sergeant pulled him back, and I believe, struck him with a stick he had in his hand: though I did not see the beginning, I saw the Sergeant strike him over the head, and then Mr Hargreaves called to the Sergeant to strike him; but the riding master ran and assisted the Sergeant, and struck Burton like a dog. He was sent to the guard room, and tried by court martial, and sentenced to receive 150 lashes, which he received.[203]

A week later, further incidents were reported by the *Northern Star*. Six men of the 15th Hussars had been flogged in 'little more than five months' and the newspaper questioned the severity of the punishments meted out to the soldiers by stating:

> As to those offences for which, by the articles of war, soldiers can be punished, by sentence of the court martial, we have frequently acted as counsel for men charged with having stolen goods, watches, regimental clothes, and other apparel connected with military appointments; but we never before heard of a man being flogged for an offence, which might be tried at common law.[204]

The problem of indiscipline within the Regular Army was also rife in the third area of public-order management which the Home Secretary oversaw in the shape of policing.

The police, as a mechanism which the Home Secretary turned to when dealing with Chartist riots and disturbances, must not be viewed simply as an agency of suppression. Indeed, political opinion was, and has been, divided over their origin and purpose. Whereas the traditional Tory view of policing suggests that policing came about as a centralised measure to protect capital and property, the Whig interpretation viewed the creation of police forces as a necessary measure to rectify the ineffective nature of the parochial policing which existed at the end of the eighteenth and beginning of the nineteenth century.[205] During the mid-1970s, those assumptions were challenged by Robert Storch who argued that the police came into existence largely because the ruling classes wanted to maintain their hegemony and socially control the industrial working classes.[206] All these interpretations may have played a part in the gradual creation of police forces in the West Riding and elsewhere, especially when related to the activities of the Home Office.

As a centralised measure of repression, the Home Secretary controlled the Metropolitan Police. The force was established in 1829 by Sir Robert Peel and consisted of roughly 3,300 officers that were deployed in and around London.[207] The Secretary of State was responsible for the approval of all appointments, promotions and pay conditions.[208] He was also in charge of the selection of Police Commissioners and Assistant Police Commissioners whose role it was to train and instruct the police in their duties.[209] In the maintenance of public order, both parties came together and decided amongst themselves 'whether meetings should be declared illegal; public notices should be issued, crowds should be dispersed or whether ringleaders should be seized'.[210] When local magistrates were short of military or policing provisions, Metropolitan Police officers were often used to assist in the organisation of constabulary forces and monitor disturbances on behalf of the Home Secretary. When sworn-in under the command of a magistrate, their expenses were usually paid out of the county rate via the provisions of the thirteenth section of the 1831 Special Constables Act and later through extended legislation that was introduced in 1838.[211]

A good example of how this agency was deployed occurred during anti-Poor Law demonstrations in Bradford during 1837. The assistant Poor Law Commissioner, Alfred Power, was assaulted and heckled by a crowd who struck him with 'a tin can', along with 'umbrellas, stones and mud'.[212] After the incident, Power complained to the Home Office that none of the local constables offered him protection from an angry mob. The Home Secretary responded to this complaint and sent Metropolitan Police officers to the town to give Power some adequate security, despite not being sworn-in by magistrates.[213] This episode was just one of many flashpoints that the Home Office had to deal with. During the period 1830 to 1838, it was estimated that 2,246 Metropolitan Police officers were sent to various places across England and Wales to assist the civil power in the preservation of public order.[214]

The deployment of the Metropolitan Police, who were also called the 'blue locusts' or 'Peelers', was a highly unpopular measure.[215] The force operated along military lines and had a chain of command that was almost identical to the regular army. With ex-army figures in charge of the constables, whenever they were called upon to police crowds, they frequently used excessive force that often incited rather than suppressed disturbances.[216] One such an incident took place in London on 13 May 1833 at Cold Bath Fields, when a Metropolitan Police officer was killed by a dagger, and two others stabbed following the attempted suppression of a political gathering.[217] Before magistrates had read the Riot Act, the police had acted illegally and used indiscriminate force, by beating men, women and children with their truncheons.[218] Street corners and access routes in and around the location were blocked. This meant that the only way protesters could flee from the scene was by running over the fields where they were chased and assaulted.[219] The authorities intervened because they were convinced that it was illegal. In turn, they acted without waiting until the crowd had been incited by inflammatory speeches.[220] Many onlookers who later gave evidence at an investigation said that the crowds offered very little resistance to the police. There were also allegations that some constables were 'intoxicated by liquor'.[221]

Despite being exonerated, the incident at Cold Bath Fields called into question the conduct of the Metropolitan Police. A Parliamentary Select Committee felt that excessive force had been used by constables. Many witnesses who presented statements and gave evidence to the committee were alarmed at the rough treatment meted out by the police to protesters at the scene.[222] Incidents such as these led to reluctance on the part of the Home Secretary to deploy officers beyond the boundaries of London and, instead, to try to find a solution to the problem of provincial policing. This was later evident by particular reforms initiated by the Home Secretaries Lord John Russell and Sir James Graham throughout the Chartist era.

The affairs of the Metropolitan Police also concerned other senior figures at the Home Office, such as the Permanent Under-Secretary, who was effectively the second in command to the Home Secretary. Throughout the 1830s and 1840s, as the Home Secretary became increasingly overloaded with cabinet and parliamentary responsibilities, many public order duties were delegated to the Permanent Under-Secretary. His role was to gather information about the state machinery and devise ways in which its effectiveness could be improved.[223] The office-holder dealt directly with magistrates, military generals, senior police commissioners, judicial figures and spies. The information gathered from those sources was used to paint a picture of the state of the nation.[224] However, what the Permanent Under-Secretary actually saw was a limited view of national affairs. The paucity of internal communications meant that he could not actually see what was occurring on the ground, especially in distant regions such as the West Riding. Much of the information that he received from the agencies under his control was manipulated and not entirely accurate. However, such was the importance of this role that every letter that came into the Home Office passed through his hands for scrutiny.[225]

The main responsibilities of the Permanent Under-Secretary mirrored those of the Home Secretary. In judicial affairs, the person appointed to this role was normally a former barrister with all-round legal skills. Those attributes were used in an advisory capacity to the Secretary of State, particularly when public order legislation was produced.[226] In turn, the Permanent Under-Secretary had a close relationship with the Attorney-General, who was responsible for making laws. In tandem with the Solicitor to the Treasury and Law Officers of the Crown, all of these parties came together and examined the legal boundaries that the Home Office could operate within.[227] A good example of how decisions were taken in this field came during the aftermath of the 1842 Plug Plot disturbances, when senior members of the government department interpreted laws to decide the fate of those arrested for their involvement in rioting.[228]

As well as judicial responsibilities, the Permanent Under-Secretary wielded much influence in military affairs. This key figure managed the finances of the armed forces and issued warrants which enabled soldiers to receive adequate firearms and stock piles of ordnance, in order to carry out their duties effectively.[229] The Under-Secretary also advised the Home Secretary when it came to the deployment of regular troops in putting down provincial disturbances. This influence did not always please local magistrates whose requests for military assistance were not always granted. They held the belief that the Home Office should act upon each and every demand they made for soldiers, which caused tensions between the centre and localities.

Beneath the regular army, the Permanent Under-Secretary also had at his disposal a number of auxiliary forces that could be used to deal with riots and disturbances such as the yeomanry, militia and enrolled pensioners. These forces were deployed on a temporary basis and used to satisfy local magisterial requests for assistance. The yeomanry was a horse-based cavalry force and operated in the West Riding under the title of the Yorkshire Hussars. It was made up of volunteer regiments and staffed by tenant farmers who were employed by the Lord of the Manor.[230] The force consisted of 420 soldiers and underwent an inspection by a Field Officer of the Regular Army each August following the annual harvest.[231] Although the Permanent Under-Secretary oversaw its national operation, at a provincial level, the yeomanry was controlled by the Lord Lieutenant who was responsible for its maintenance. When called upon to deal with an incident, there were limitations to the use of such regiments as they could only be deployed on a permanent basis for a maximum of eight days. This included time set aside for marching and training purposes.[232]

Throughout the 1830s and 1840s, both Whig and Tory governments were very wary about using the yeomanry as a measure for controlling disturbances. Politicians such as Lord John Russell, believed that its presence created more 'ill-will and dissension' within communities than the regular army.[233] First of all, the deployment of the forces was expensive as they had to be paid for marching days as well as permanent duties.[234] Secondly, when dealing with crowds the yeomanry was often over-aggressive. There were numerous instances where they charged at innocent bystanders with their horses. They also used their weaponry to indiscriminately lash out at people. This was particularly highlighted by memories of the Peterloo Massacre on 16 August 1819, when 15 people were killed and around 400-700 injured. The incident happened when troops charged and assaulted a crowd of 60-80,000 people that had gathered at St Peter's Field to attend a political meeting.[235] The momentous events certainly damaged the reputation of the yeomanry and were a major factor behind its later decline as both the Whigs and Tories looked towards civil rather than quasi-military responses when dealing with crowds and disturbances.

The failings of the yeomanry went hand-in-hand with those of the militia, which also came under the control of the Permanent Under-Secretary. As 'a bulwark against a foreign invasion', this force was made up of volunteer foot soldiers who were used to defend land and property from attack by insurgents.[236] At a provincial level, the militia was controlled by the Lord Lieutenant. Magistrates could call upon the forces to assist in crowd control situations. In terms of composition and practices they were almost identical to the yeomanry. The regiments could only be used on a permanent basis for a limited number of days within a year.[237] Like its counterpart, the troops that made up the militia forces were also prone to mete out similar aggression when confronted by angry mobs.

From the late 1820s onwards, the Home Office made an attempt to scale down the yeomanry and militia forces.[238] This was particularly evident just before the beginning of Chartist unrest, when the Whig government wanted to reduce public expenditure.[239] The decline in their use meant that the maintenance of order in places such as the West Riding was extended to agencies such as the Enrolled or Embodied Pensioners. These were regiments of those who had previously served with the regular armed forces.[240] The men had been discharged from their normal duties on medical grounds or because their regiments were either disbanded or reduced. On leaving the regular army, they received a pension. The amount varied in relation to the nature of their wounds, disabilities or the length of service that they had given. This allowance was paid to them through the commissioners of the Chelsea Hospital, with the consent of the Secretary of War.[241]

Army pensioners were often called upon to act as special constables to deal with the suppression of riots and disturbances. They were mainly used in emergency situations when magistrates could not get enough civilian staff to perform this role. Although, in theory, the Home Secretary had the power to deploy the forces for a maximum of twelve days service, in practice it was the Permanent Under-Secretary who issued the warrants which authorised their deployment.[242] Further to this, the appointment of soldiers to various regiments across the country was handled by the Lord Chamberlain and Vice-Chamberlain.[243]

The use of army pensioners to deal with civil unrest was problematic as the Permanent Under-Secretary had to consult the Lord Lieutenant and the Commander of the Military District over how they should be deployed. This led to many disagreements about their role. When used to control crowds and put down disturbances, army pensioners resented being told what to do by magistrates, especially when it came to putting in place tactical arrangements; it caused anger and bitterness amongst both parties.

The limitations of auxiliary forces as a means of preserving the peace meant that the Permanent Under-Secretary had to find other ways of monitoring radical groups and individuals who were intent on carrying out treasonable actions against the state. A way of achieving this was by spying on people and their activities. The Under-Secretary oversaw a spy network that was funded by the Treasury and used to monitor individuals and radical groups who intended to subvert the state and its institutions.[244]

For instance, between 2 September 1839 and 4 August 1841, Samuel March Phillipps was paid £590. 5s. 5d. to oversee the operation of this system.[245] Money was paid to spies who went into the provinces and obtained information by mingling with crowds at political gatherings. More covertly, they sometimes passed themselves off as agitators in order to infiltrate political groups. Surveillance activity was commonplace in the suppression of Chartism, especially in the West Riding during the 1830s and 1840s. The information gathered from spies, though frequently inaccurate, allowed the Permanent Under-Secretary to build a picture of the state of feeling within places. This was later used to put in place preventative measures for dealing with unrest.[246]

During the 1830s, the Home Office and the Permanent Under-Secretary devised more suitable means of monitoring the affairs of individuals and groups who had political grievances against the government and the state. One of those methods was the use of newly-created Factory Inspectors who were appointed by the department following the passing of the 1833 Factory Act. Their main role was to ensure that laws concerning the use of child labour in the mills, along with early health and safety conditions were being adhered to by factory owners.[247] Mostly based in the industrial North, the inspectors frequently came into contact with local magistrates who often alerted them about attacks on property and political unrest. Their use as a surveillance mechanism raised questions about their natural responsibilities. The *Northern Star* alleged that the inspectors were appointed to spy on the working classes, particularly those caught up in anti-Poor Law unrest within the West Riding. Whilst the allegations were vehemently denied in Parliament by Tory politicians such as Sir Robert Peel, one of his counterparts, the Whig Parliamentary Under-Secretary of State, Fox Maule, later admitted that the inspectors were being used for this purpose.[248] The allegation was given further impetus in July 1838 when the Treasury granted the Home Secretary, Lord John Russell, permission to allow letters to be sent between factory inspectors and the Home Office, free of charge. This made the flow of information between the centre and provinces more cost effective.[249]

In addition to the use of factory inspectors, for many years previously the Home Office relied on the Post Office, created in 1657, as a means of spying on the population.[250] The government department had the power to intercept and open letters as well as packages that contained treasonable content.[251] Both the Home Secretary and the Permanent Under-Secretary were in direct contact with the Postmaster-General who oversaw the entire operation of the Post Office. This included postmasters based in many towns and cities across the country who serviced the system. In the suppression of the Chartist movement during the 1830s and 1840s, the Home Office often received reports from William Moore who was the postmaster of Huddersfield, via Colonel Maberly, the Postmaster-General, concerning the state of the town. The letters were forwarded to the Permanent Under-Secretary who acted upon the information that he received.[252]

The intelligence supplied by postmasters to the Home Office about radical groups and individuals was more reliable than the evidence supplied by magistrates. The reports of the state of feeling, which they gave to the Home Office, carried a hidden agenda in the form of demands for military assistance. A major advantage of postmasters over magistrates was their ability to mix with local inhabitants and overhear snippets of information and rumours. Furthermore, with knowing which individuals were behind radical discontent, they knew exactly what letters to put aside, so that they could be tampered with and scrutinised by central intelligence services for sources of information about plots against the state.[253]

However, there were limits to the use of the Post Office as a means of surveillance. Before the advent of railways, the mail was carried in horse-drawn coaches along turnpike roads. This was not only a slow method of conveying messages from one place to another – it also carried dangers. The Postmaster-General often received reports about collisions involving mail coaches and dog carts that often resulted in the post being lost.[254] This created much ire, particularly within military circles as senior figures were largely dependent on the steady flow of information to maintain public order. During the Chartist era, the Commander of the Northern District Army, Sir Charles Napier, often complained that he had not received letters that had been addressed to him. This would suggest that communications at the very highest level of government were not entirely reliable.[255] In 1840, some attempt was made to remedy this situation when the Post Office acted on the advice of Sir Rowland Hill and put in place a Penny Postage Scheme.[256] The system later gave rise to innovations such as pre-printed envelopes with postal towns, adhesive postage stamps and the weighting of letters. Along with the development of railways during the 1840s, a more efficient service of conveying messages from one place to another was created. New regulations also meant that military and civil institutions such as Clerks of the Petty Sessions were exempt from paying any postal charges that enabled information to be distributed freely.[257]

In the maintenance of public order, an efficient administrative structure was needed to process messages so that decisions taken by senior figures at the Home Office could be filtered down to local agencies. Beneath the Home Secretary and Permanent Under-Secretary were a number of individuals and branches charged with performing such tasks. They also carried out lesser repressive roles that were delegated to them due to the overworked nature of the Home Office.

The person in charge of its administrative staff was the Senior Clerk, who was answerable to the Permanent Under-Secretary. This office-holder also managed the affairs of the yeomanry and militia forces. He was directly in contact with Lord Lieutenants and magistrates, and responsible for the appointment of troops to those forces.[258] In order to carry out that task, the Senior Clerk referred to a vast amount of statistical evidence which documented the strength of each regiment that was in operation. The role involved monitoring the number of troops that each company had and reinforcing them when necessary. Militia Acts that dated back to 1802 acted as a reference point for the Senior Clerk. Those legislative tracts contained details and statistics of the number of troops that each regiment had that were based upon returns sent into the Home Office by the Lord Lieutenants.[259] Further to this, throughout March and August of each year, the Senior Clerk spent two to three hours a day examining letters in relation to the annual inspection of auxiliary forces, which were sent in from the same source. The management of both administrative staff at the Home Office and the affairs of the yeomanry and militia forces meant that the person who oversaw this aspect of departmental activity was overloaded with too many duties.[260]

There was a similar pattern of activity at the Domestic Branch which carried out much of the administration in relation to public order matters such as Breaches of the Peace. This office handled hundreds and thousands of letters that were sent into the Home Office by provincial Lord Lieutenants and magistrates who looked for assistance from senior figures over a vast range of matters.[261] The branch was staffed by five clerks who throughout the Chartist era were overwhelmed by the huge workload with which they were confronted on a daily basis. The clerks handled incoming mail that was directly passed on to the Permanent Under-Secretary for scrutiny. Having read the contents of each letter, the Under-Secretary of State issued a response that contained instructions from which hand-written circulars were produced and sent to the Lord Lieutenants and magistrates. Those circulars often contained recommendations made by the Home Secretary and Permanent Under-Secretary in relation to policing and prison affairs, along with magisterial directives for dealing with disturbances.[262]

Throughout the Chartist era, the number of circulars issued by the Domestic Branch grew in number. The production of the documents on such a broad scale was a tiresome and monotonous exercise for its staff. On a given day, the clerks handwrote hundreds if not thousands of letters which were later franked and posted at short notice. One of the clerks who served this branch commented that in 'quiet and peaceable times, the correspondence is not oppressive but when the Country is disturbed, then the correspondence increases to a very considerable degree'.[263] The harsh and brutal working conditions altered very little throughout the 1830s and 1840s. As a result of Chartist unrest they worsened considerably.

Much of the information sent to the Home Office was often turned into statistical evidence and used to formulate parliamentary legislation. The two individuals and branches that carried out the tasks were the Keeper of the Criminal Register and the Criminal Branch. The keeper oversaw a register of criminals who had been arrested, as well as tried and convicted. This register was created in 1805 and initially confined to Middlesex but was later extended to other counties across England and Wales, including the West Riding.[264] The register was compiled from returns which contained details of court proceedings that were sent in to the Home Office by Clerks of the Peace.[265] Up until the late 1820s, the operation of the branch had been fairly straightforward but from the late 1830s onwards its role became very complicated, especially when it took onboard a number of additional responsibilities. One of those included the administration of the Metropolitan Police and its affairs. As the force was used on numerous occasions during the decade to deal with provincial disturbances, this branch of Home Office activity was placed under considerable strain. This increased throughout the turbulent 1840s when it became responsible for the administration of the Constabulary Acts.[266]

With regard to the type of work that was carried out for the Metropolitan Police, the Keeper of the Criminal Register was responsible for the approval of appointments, promotions, pay, expenses and complaints, although the Home Secretary was the main authority behind the force.[267] On a weekly basis, roughly forty to fifty letters were sent into the branch. These were later passed onto the Home Secretary, Permanent Under-Secretary and Metropolitan Police Commissioners. The administrative duties in relation to the Metropolitan Police took up more than half the time of the Keeper of the Criminal Register. This severely impacted on his main role in the collation of statistical evidence.[268]

There were similar difficulties in the work carried out by the Criminal

Branch, which kept records of individual offenders. The details of many convicted Chartists passed through this particular branch which specifically dealt with all correspondence in relation to criminal cases, along with records and evidence sent into the Home Office by Judges, Clerks of the Peace and Recorders.[269] Such information was passed on to the Home Secretary and Permanent Under-Secretary for closer scrutiny. The staff within the Criminal Branch also administered documentation concerning the operation of the prison system. This involved handling paperwork regarding the removal and transportation of convicts to the penal colonies.[270] Throughout the 1830s and 1840s, the growth of the population and criminal activity that went with it significantly increased the workload of the branch. One of its clerks later observed that it had fallen into 'an extensive and inconvenient arrear' which could not be addressed.[271]

The difficulties faced by the Home Office in coping with its vast workload were compounded by the lack of authority it exerted over the local mechanisms of control. At the beginning of the period, the machinery that was used to preserve public order was relatively weak and fragmented. In a letter written to the Duke of Wellington on 7 August 1837, Lord John Russell described civil power as being 'inefficient and useless'.[272] Using the West Riding as a working example of how the local machinery operated across the country as a whole, the system of control was largely feudal in origins and structure. Further, many of the agencies that the Home Office dealt with were mainly self-serving and out of step with profound social, economic and political changes that had taken place during the first half of the nineteenth century. However, despite this criticism, a major source of strength that the local apparatus had was its distance and detachment from central government interference. Poor internal communications, along with the over-worked nature of the Home Office, meant that agencies such as the magistracy existed fairly independently from its control. As a consequence, there were a number of flaws and abuses that went largely undetected. An agency that typified this state of affairs was the office of the Lord Lieutenant, which was supposed to oversee the operation of the machinery of public order and the affairs of the county as a whole.

The office of the Lord Lieutenant dated back to the sixteenth century. The individuals appointed to this role were chosen by the head of state, on the recommendation of the Home Secretary.[273] The person selected for this post invariably came from an aristocratic and landed background. The narrow composition of this office and its exclusivity meant that it had very little appeal amongst middle-class commercial and industrial interests, who alternatively pursued seats in Borough governance.[274]

During the first half of the nineteenth century, the role of the Lord Lieutenant became problematic for a number of reasons. First, the office appeared to be outmoded in relation to social changes that had taken place. The role of the Lord Lieutenant dated back to a society that was both rural and less populated. Under those circumstances, it was easier for the individual appointed to this position to control the population and territory under his command. However, the advent of industrial and urban transformation changed this state of affairs. The rapid growth of towns brought about by the movement of the population from the land to meet the demand for labour required a more dynamic form of governance. It came about when legislation such as the 1835 Municipal Corporations Act was introduced.[275] The measure allowed the new middle classes to engage in local governance and, as a consequence, inter-class conflict emerged.

A second major factor that brought about the steady decline in the office of the Lord Lieutenant was the spread of Jeremy Bentham's ideas and the need for greater accountability at all levels of governance. As a result of this, questions were raised in Whig/Liberal quarters about some of the established practices of the head of the county. For instance, there was the serious problem of corruption. Many Lord Lieutenants did not reside in the counties that they were supposed to represent. Instead, they took huge advantage of privileges and the trappings of office that were conferred upon them.[276] The gulf that existed between central and local governance meant that many of those abuses went unchecked as the Home Office did not have the power and communication to police such behaviour. Moreover, the office of the Lord Lieutenant was called into question as many of the persons appointed to the role could not perform the duties asked of them because they were too ill and physically incapable of doing them. This problem impacted heavily in the area of public order governance and the ability of the Lord Lieutenant to adequately oversee county affairs.

As a consequence, whilst the office of the Lord Lieutenant had in theory, many repressive powers at his disposal, in practice they had gradually been eroded. The office-holder oversaw the affairs of yeomanry and militia forces which were used to put down riots and disturbances. However, the scaling down of those regiments from the late 1820s limited the post-holder's authority over this means of repression.[277] A similar pattern of activity occurred in judicial affairs. Traditionally, the Lord Lieutenant made recommendations to the Lord Chancellor regarding the appointment of county magistrates.[278] However, throughout the 1830s and 1840s the responsibility attracted much opposition and criticism from Whig-Liberals who felt that the selection process was not impartial, particularly as the Lord Lieutenant usually represented Tory interests. The political divide filtered down into the business of the Quarter Sessions. The problematic role of the Lord Lieutenant as a supervisory figure and lack of control that the office exerted over magistrates was later highlighted by divisions that emerged over the adoption of rural policing during the early 1840s.

Disputes between the Lord Lieutenant and magistrates were also visible in the suppression of riots and disturbances. The role of the Lord Lieutenant was to assist and guide civil power in the preservation of peace.[279] However, there were often occasions when the head of the county was nowhere to be seen. As a result, magistrates were frequently left to fend for themselves in handling unrest.[280] Indeed, in June 1837, when Anti-Poor Law disturbances broke out in Huddersfield, one of the magistrates bemoaned the lack of support from the Lord Lieutenant:

> We only regret that we did not from time to time communicate with our Lord Lieutenant from whom we should have received as we always had judicious advice, excellent counsel and firm support.[281]

Following the poor handling of this incident, the Lord Lieutenant was castigated by Lord John Russell over his failure to ensure that adequate support was given.[282] Usually, when the Lord Lieutenant was absent from his duties, the Vice-Lieutenant was called upon to act as a substitute. However, in a number of cases, this action was often not followed through. As a consequence, the responsibility for dealing with riot and tumult was passed on to the local magistrates, who were mainly aided by the military.[283]

Within the West Riding, the role of the magistracy involved upholding the law and suppressing any attempts by individuals and political groups to cause unrest.[284] Their main duty involved guarding the public peace.[285] From a political perspective, the magistracy was strong as it had a number of powers at its disposal but as an agency of repression it was relatively weak. Many of its representatives were not resident at the places that they served, as was particularly apparent across the West Riding during the build-up to the first wave of Chartist turbulence.[286]

At the beginning of the period, there were three types of magistrates who served the region at county, borough and parish levels. The highest rank that fulfilled judicial duties within the region was the county magistrates. They were appointed by the Lord Chancellor on the recommendation of the Home Secretary and Lord Lieutenant.[287] The Justices of the Peace, as they were also known, presided at quarter sessions which met four times a year.

In addition to their judicial powers, the magistrates oversaw the operation of the machinery of public order and they also set the county rate. This tax depended on the value of property. Within the West Riding, the inhabitants who lived in the agricultural districts paid significantly more than those that inhabited the manufacturing areas.[288] The revenue generated from this taxation paid for the military, policing and prison provisions that were used to secure the region from unrest. However, a major weakness with this institution was its division along borough and parish lines in which Whig and Tory political persuasions impacted on decision-making.[289]

There was also the borough magistracy which served the large towns. It was made up of aldermen and officials who were elected to unpaid council posts under the terms of the 1835 Municipal Corporations Act.[290] Thirdly, there were justices of the peace who served the parishes that were made up of villages and hamlets. They were often appointed by Charter and consisted largely of aristocratic and landed interests who supported the Tory Party. The main source of their power was the vestry - a church room where key decisions were made, such as the appointment of parish constables. The magistracy at this level was responsible for the administration of a number of tasks in relation to the poor laws and the maintenance of local highways. More importantly, they also presided over petty sessions, which were courts that administered justice on a minor scale.[291]

In the preservation of public order, magistrates across the board had direct police powers. They were ordered by the Home Secretary to obtain evidence by 'discreet and efficient means' about individuals and political groups.[292] This involved the deployment of spies and confidential reporters who attended political meetings and gathered information about speeches that were deemed to be seditious and could incite violence. As a further means of preserving public order, Justices of the Peace often issued notices that were put on display within a given place when radical assemblies were organised. The posters or hand bills warned people about the consequences that they faced if any form of illegal protest was conducted.[293] Before a notice was issued, a draft copy had to be sent for scrutiny to the Home Secretary who often made any amendments.[294] Many of the hand bills printed warned the public that the Riot Act would be read by magistrates in the event of a disturbance.

The reading of the Riot Act as a method of suppression was a practice that dated back to 1713. The main purpose of this measure was to make rioters feel guilty about the crimes they had committed following civil unrest.[295] When a disturbance was in motion, magistrates, assisted by troops or special constables, read the Riot Act from a sheet of paper or a placard. Once this had been recited aloud, the people involved in the commotion were given an hour to vacate the area. If they had not dispersed within that time limit, the magistrates had the authority to send in troops and police to clear the scene.[296] Those who refused to move were charged with committing a felony which could result in the punishment of transportation to a penal colony.

In the maintenance of public order, the reading of the Riot Act was determined by three factors. First, there was the 'state of excitement' that the crowd was in.[297] If it was too volatile, the magistrates often shied away from the enforcement of the measure due to the fear of inflaming the situation. A second factor involved the strength of the civil force in place and whether the magistrates were adequately supported by a military presence or special constables at the scene. A third determinant involved the danger of magistrates using the military without any need to do so. Usually, it was at the discretion of magistrates to decide on the basis of these factors whether it was safe to enforce the measure.[298]

There were many flashpoints when magistrates refused to enforce the measure because it was too dangerous to do so. A particular incident occurred on 5 June 1837 at Huddersfield, when a meeting of the Board of Guardians was convened at the local workhouse to elect a clerk in order to enforce the provisions of the 1834 Poor Law Amendment Act.[299] A number of magistrates refused to attend the meeting because they were too scared. In February 1837, an earlier attempt to elect a clerk was greeted with severe violence and intimidation.[300] When the Board of Guardians met at the workhouse, a large crowd gathered in front of the Druids Arms. They listened to Richard Oastler deliver a speech in which he used 'violent and inflammatory language'.[301] The 'Factory King' and his crowd of supporters proceeded to the workhouse where they forced open the gates of the premises. When people filled the yard and broke into the building, the Board of Guardians decided to halt the meeting and temporarily reconvene at the Albion Hotel. As they made their way to the venue, the guardians and magistrates were threatened and assaulted by the crowd. When they tried to protect them, the police and special constables sustained 'many personal injuries' in clashes with violent protesters.[302] The crowd followed the Board of Guardians to the Albion Hotel where the meeting was reconvened. Anti-Poor Law protesters continued to throw stones at the constables and the windows of the room where the assembly was being held to interrupt the proceedings.[303] The Chief Constable of the Huddersfield Police ordered two magistrates at the scene to read the Riot Act.[304] One of them, William Battye, refused to do so and was later reprimanded by Lord John Russell for his actions. This was despite the fact that there were hardly any means at his disposal to disperse the crowd.[305] It later emerged that out of 400 special constables sworn in by magistrates to preserve the peace, 399 ran away during a serious fight![306] As a result, mob rule triumphed and the Board of Guardians decided not to elect a clerk due to the 'dread of violence'.[307]

In addition to the problems of fear and intimidation experienced by magistrates, a further difficulty with the public reading of the Riot Act was its lack of impartiality in dealing with civil unrest. Within many industrial towns across the West Riding, the local magistrates were often factory or mill owners. When the peace was threatened they often turned to the local military commander for assistance. The majority of the insurgents with whom the magistracy and military dealt were working class. By continually using force to put down their protestations, such action not only widened social divisions but also resulted in poor labour relations between the factory owners and operatives. This pattern of behaviour was also rife in rural areas, especially in disputes between landowners and farm labourers. Those conflicts were often one-sided affairs in which such offenders were not only punished for causing riots and disturbances but they also lost their livelihoods by being removed from the land.[308]

In dealing with violent protest, the magistrates could not act in isolation. In many instances they had to rely upon the military for assistance in order to preserve the peace.[309] The relationship was problematic as conflicts frequently arose. The Home Office often found itself mediating between the two parties, particularly over areas such as troop accommodation. For instance, when dealing with anti-Poor Law unrest in Bradford the magistrates were told by the Home Office to provide suitable accommodation for the cavalry. Much to the annoyance of Sir Richard Jackson, who at the time was the commander of the Northern District Army, instead of being kept together the troops were dispersed in billets throughout the town. This course of action endangered the soldiers and left them vulnerable to violent assault. As a temporary measure, the Bradford magistrates hired rented accommodation in November 1837. They were later reimbursed by the Treasury for the costs incurred.[310]

A further source of tension between the magistrates and the army was the fact that when cavalry and infantry troops were deployed by the Home Secretary as a measure for dealing with a potential outbreak of violence, the officer in charge of the military detachment had to report to a magistrate on their arrival at a given place.[311] The two agencies usually communicated with each other and decided amongst themselves how many troops were required for a given situation.[312] The main problem with this relationship emerged when a riot or disturbance occurred. In such cases, when soldiers were placed under magisterial supervision, they could only act under the guidance of magistrates.[313] This arrangement caused huge resentment amongst military generals who objected to being told how to marshal their own troops and enforce discipline, especially if any of their soldiers stepped out of line. The relationship between the magistracy and military in dealing with civil unrest was strained even further when sporadic violence broke out. In an emergency situation, the response was often confused. However, if strong preparations for dealing with potential outbreaks of violence had been made beforehand, the relationship between the magistrates and the military worked effectively. In turn, many incidents tended to pass off relatively peacefully.[314]

Once trouble had ceased, further disputes erupted concerning the removal of troops from a given place after they had served their purpose. For this to be carried into effect, the Commander of the District Army had to enter into dialogue with the local magistrates. The military needed the consent of civil power so that the soldiers could be moved in the interests of public safety.[315] Without any adequate form of policing at their disposal, the magistrates relied largely upon the troops to keep the peace. As a consequence, there were many occasions when they refused to allow the removal of troops. In such cases, the Home Office stepped in and mediated between both agencies over the best course of action.[316]

The flawed relationship that existed between the magistracy and military prompted calls for the introduction of an organised police force as a more effective measure of suppression.[317] The *Northern Star* perceptively commented:

Magistrates are most efficient in times when there is no danger; but we have generally seen that when there is danger they dread exposing themselves, their property of their families to popular vengeance. Sir Robert Peel said some years ago that we had outgrown many of our institutions; and we have no doubt the conviction will soon become general that THE POLICE OF THE COUNTRY MUST UNDERGO A THOROUGH REFORM. It will never do to leave it to this or that Magistrate to trust to his neighbour, and make good the proverb that what is everybody's business is nobody's business. There must in every district be some functionary specially responsible for its peace, and against whom, it would be a matter of grave impeachment if disorder were to gain a head. This winter will try severely the value of our institutions.[318]

Throughout the ten years of major Chartist unrest, the attitude of both its newspaper and activists towards policing at local, regional and metropolitan levels varied considerably over time. At the beginning, the police were seen as an agent of the state and an attack on civil liberties, particularly over their use by the state as a mechanism of surveillance to crush internal dissent. They were compared to the French Gendarme system of policing which was seen in a highly negative light.[319] Furthermore, the quality of the early police recruits was very uneven.[320] Whilst there was some agreement amongst Chartists that police were needed to patrol large towns due to the ineffectual nature of magistrates, the debate later shifted towards questioning the cost to ratepayers of implementing police forces, as well as constitutional debates about the forces becoming fully centralised.[321] The feeling amongst Chartists was that both the public and ratepayers, not the government, should control the police.[322] Following on from those debates, towards the end of the Chartist period, questions were raised about the brutality of the police, especially before, during and after the presentation of the third Chartist petition in London during 1848.[323]

In examining the state of policing within the West Riding at the beginning of the period, the provisions were relatively weak, fragmented and uneven in quality. What existed was a patchwork of forces which had no uniformity and were largely divided along parish and borough lines. First, in the parish system there were major difficulties concerning the appointment of constables. The process dated back to the Saxon age when settlements were thinly populated and mainly consisted of tiny villages and scattered hamlets.[324] There were two ways in which parish constables were appointed. The first method was through the Lord of the Manor or Steward of the Court who decided whether an individual presented before a Courts Leet jury was suitable to serve their parish. A second mode of appointment was through the vestry where an applicant was interviewed by a local Justice of the Peace who judged whether the individual was a fit and proper person. If successful, the constable was sworn-in.[325]

The entire selection process was flawed. First, when the Lords of the Manor appointed a constable there were no objections or background checks conducted of the people appointed to the post. They often judged the fitness of an applicant without actually having met the person. Secondly, at vestry level, the appointment of a constable was carried into effect on the presumption that the parishioners had been consulted. Subsequently, they were given constables that they did not want. Corruption was rife as decisions were often made behind closed doors.[326] Allegations of nepotism were commonplace. On many occasions, tradesmen were appointed as constables without any measurement of their fitness for the office.[327]

In the discharge of their duties, the parish constables appointed were often unpaid. The role carried no incentive for them to perform their tasks with any real efficiency or motivation. When dealing with criminal activity, the constables were relatively impotent and afraid of confrontation. This made them especially unpopular amongst parishioners. Lawlessness was rife in villages and hamlets and, as a result of their ineffectiveness, criminals often got away with felonies.[328] There was a similar lack of police presence when it came to dealing with riots and disturbances. The parish constables often sent deputies and substitutes in their places because they were too afraid to tackle angry mobs.[329] An example of such behaviour occurred during anti-Poor Law riots in Huddersfield. The head constable, George Mallinson, was described by magistrates as being a 'very timid man' after he had shied away from handling crowds of angry protesters.[330]

Table 2: The state of policing in the West Riding, 1837-41[331]

Town	Constables	Night Watchmen	Population (1841)
Bradford	4	-	66,700
Halifax	4	-	27,520
Huddersfield	6	-	25,068
Leeds	28	70	152,074
Sheffield	71	-	111,091
Wakefield	3	11	18,842

As Table 2 clearly shows, the only place within the West Riding that had a proper police force was Sheffield. During the late 1830s, the town had a parish status and did not become a borough until 1842, yet its police force was well-managed and regulated.[332] The force was controlled by a superintendent who acted under the authority of the local magistrates. They allowed the office-holder to carry out his duties with minimal supervision. Sheffield had a population of roughly 110,000 inhabitants and seventy-one police officers served the town and its neighbourhoods.[333] However, despite such a presence, the system in place was flawed. First, there were problems concerning the boundaries of the force and its jurisdiction which stretched a mile either side of the parish church. As a result of this, the police force could not be used in areas beyond those confines. This meant that criminals often took advantage of the situation. Once crimes had been committed they fled to the parishes to escape detection.[334] Secondly, although the force had sufficient numbers to maintain public order, many of the policemen were in fact, night watchmen. This meant that there was very little presence on the streets during daylight hours and many criminal offences went unchecked.[335]

The failings of the parish system prompted the Home Office to create a system of Borough Policing through the 1835 Municipal Corporation Act.[336] It was a response to the growth of densely populated towns which needed a better form of social control. In places where this measure was adopted, a Watch Committee was appointed and a police force was created through the provisions of the 1833 Lighting and Watching Act. One of the first places in the West Riding to enforce this measure was Leeds which adopted Borough status in 1837. In 1831, the town had a sizeable population of 150,000 inhabitants and suffered from high rates of crime. Before the creation of its force, the police provisions were described by one local official as being 'manifestly deficient'.[337] The new force that was put into operation consisted of a chief constable, twenty-eight day policemen, and seventy night watchmen, which included nine inspectors.[338] This provision later proved sufficient in keeping Chartist unrest in check.

The borough system of policing had a similar organisational structure to that of the 1834 Poor Law Amendment Act. In theory, central government control was combined with local management. However, in practice the Home Office exerted very little authority.[339] Control over the forces was firmly placed in the hands of the Watch Committee, which was appointed by local magistrates. Quite often, conflicts between the two agencies emerged over issues such as the duties of constables and tactical arrangements. The problem of governance at senior level filtered down to the lower ranks of the forces which hindered their effectiveness. This led Mather to assert that many of the forces lacked numerical strength to preserve public order.[340] For instance, when dealing with outbreaks of violence, the constables were often unarmed and untrained to police such incidents. A further problem was indiscipline within the ranks which was widespread and often went unnoticed by the Watch Committee. It was compounded by the fact that many chief constables and inspectors appointed to supervise the duties of officers lacked the relevant skills to get the best out of the forces at their disposal. Calls were made for better training methods to be put in place.[341] Such was the situation that magistrates continued to rely heavily upon special constables, who were often sworn-in on an *ad hoc* basis. In the long term, they proved to be equally deficient when it came to dealing with riot and turbulence in the West Riding, especially throughout the Chartist era.

At the very beginning of Chartist unrest the strength of the British state, along with the source of its power, was evenly distributed between the centre and localities. In relation to the composition of the state, there was not what would now be termed as a modern structure in place. Instead, there were two forms of governance which co-existed alongside each other at central and local levels and vied for domination. The system was mirrored at a county level from the 1830s onwards in which the boroughs represented by the Whigs competed with the parishes led by Tory interests for political control.

At a centralised level, the Home Office had many powers at its disposal but could not directly apply them. This was largely because of poor internal communications and weaknesses within its own structure and composition. The main source of its power was the Home Secretary, who managed the affairs of the department and theoretically exerted total control over law and order mechanisms. However, from the 1820s onwards, this situation altered drastically. Whilst reforms introduced by Sir Robert Peel and the influence of Benthamite ideas gave the Home Secretary more powers, they also weakened his authority. The changes widened the cabinet and parliamentary duties of the Secretary of State which subsequently took precedence over public order functions.

During the 1830s, the role of the Home Secretary gradually evolved into that of a departmental chairperson or figurehead, which was more in keeping with its later twentieth century purpose. A key beneficiary of those changing circumstances was the Permanent Under-Secretary, who was the head of internal security. The second most powerful person within the department, he controlled the staff at the Home Office and scrutinised every piece of incoming mail that was sent into the department from central and local agencies. Whilst the Home Secretary was theoretically the main decision-maker and possessed overall control of the department and machinery of public order, it was the Permanent Under-Secretary who, in practice, carried out its major tasks.

However, beneath the Home Secretary and Permanent Under-Secretary was a chaotic and disorganised administrative apparatus. This was a major weakness of the Home Office and its capacity to effectively manage domestic and public order responsibilities. From the 1820s onwards, as British society changed, the workload of the department grew at such a rate that it was unable to cope when placed under any pressure, especially in cases such as the handling of provincial unrest. The Home Office was also hindered by a small bureaucracy. This meant that when information was sent in from local agencies such as the Lord Lieutenant and magistracy, it could not be processed quickly and efficiently. The lack of clerks, typists and copy writers that were needed to perform tasks which the Home Secretary and Permanent Under-Secretary demanded, meant that Home

Office responses to public order emergencies were reactive rather than proactive. This was largely because its staff could not cope with the number of documents that it had to produce manually. In addition, there was no pattern or organisation over the way in which the Home Office conducted its duties. For instance, within the area of policing, instead of being grouped under one branch or a sub-department, responsibilities were spread across four separate individuals and branches. This meant that many functions overlapped and tasks were often duplicated. The state of affairs also applied to the departmental handling of both judicial and military matters in which confusion reigned.

Such weaknesses at the centre had a huge impact on governance in the localities as agencies such as the Lord Lieutenant and magistracy took full advantage of the situation. In the period before the spread of the railways and the introduction of the electric telegraph there was a time-lag in communications between the centre and the localities, and vice versa, which meant that public order agencies in the localities governed with virtual independence from the centre. As a consequence, systemic abuses were rife and went unchecked, which was commonplace in practices such as the selection of constables. As elsewhere in the country, across the West Riding the machinery was weak, disjointed and in a state of flux as it struggled to cope with changing social and economic circumstances. The division of the magistracy and policing along borough and parish lines did little to encourage cooperation between Whig and Tory interests which had a negative impact on county affairs. These disputes fed into wider disagreements between the military and magistrates in a range of issues that the Home Secretary presided over, which came to a head during the early 1840s.

3. LORD JOHN RUSSELL: CONTAINMENT AND MODERATION, 1838-39

The first Whig response to Chartist agitation, presided over by Lord John Russell was a policy of containment. Ideologically, the approach to radical unrest revolved around the belief that 'a properly balanced government should have checks on its power, so that neither the monarchy, aristocracy, nor the people would be allowed to become too strong'.[342] This policy involved the refusal by the Melbourne Administration to meddle or introduce drastic reforms that would upset the political circumstances created by the 1832 Reform Act.[343] The same maxim applied to its policy towards the Chartist movement in the West Riding. The main objective of the Home Office involved keeping the militant organisation in check and preventing it from becoming a major political and revolutionary force. Evidence suggests that whilst Russell's containment approach worked, the hard-line policy adopted by Normanby failed.

In dealing with the Chartists the Home Office had to overcome major obstacles. The structure of the state and poor internal communications meant that the Home Office did not have the capacity to directly intervene in the affairs of the West Riding. As a consequence, a huge amount of trust was placed in the local machinery of public order, which was relatively weak and disorganised. In order to maximise its limitations, both Home Secretary's had to cultivate good working relations between the Home Office and the ruling elites in the localities. The nature of the state meant that interaction between the centre and localities existed on the basis of brinksmanship, whereby each department or agency knew the boundaries and limits that one could push, in terms of how much they could extract from each other. This method of governance can clearly be seen through demands for military assistance or the imposition of policing in provincial towns.

The first Home Secretary charged with tackling the threat of Chartist agitation was Lord John Russell, who served in this role from 1835 to 1839 as a key figure in Lord Melbourne's Whig administration. He later became

Prime Minister, managing two terms in office and, later, party leader, leading the Whigs in the House of Commons for eighteen years. Russell also represented Britain at many international conferences and was one of the most prominent statesmen of the nineteenth century, although he was not always highly regarded at the time.[344]

The first phase of the Whig approach to Chartist agitation was built around a policy of containment. Lord John Russell was a politician skilled in the art of the possible who fully understood the strengths and weaknesses of the Home Office. He refrained from an all-out assault on the Chartist movement and, instead, used the machinery of public order to act upon what he perceived as the more sinister aspects of the radical organisation that posed a danger to both people and property. In terms of central and local relations, Russell spent a great a deal of his time as an arbiter in the management of tensions between the justices of the peace, Lord Lieutenant and the military but was proactive in understanding that there was a need for better police provisions.

Russell's handling of Chartist agitation has been the subject of much debate. One of his biographers, John Prest, writing in 1972, suggests that the Whig politician viewed Chartism and its petition for the 'Six Points' as 'a demand for civil rights from the kitchen' in which its emergence was a product of 'a vague spirit of disaffection'.[345] Prest asserts that the Home Secretary 'never seriously asked himself how far the movement had its origin in the disappointment with the Reform Act of 1832', or his 'Finality Jack' speech.[346] He also suggests that Russell under-estimated the Chartists and their early demands for political reform.

Nevertheless, rather than being weak, Russell showed great strength. This was typified by his response to the 'People's Charter' which outlined the 'Six Points' for political reform. The connection between Russell and the Chartists was the dispute over the 1832 Reform Act, of which he was the main architect. This was a major source of tension amongst the working classes across the country who felt that they were politically isolated. When the Charter was published, the Whig politician reiterated the stance that he had previously taken on the issue of electoral reform a year earlier, when he made his infamous 'Finality Jack' speech.[347] He said that it would be 'a most unwise and unsound process' to 'form a new suffrage'.[348] Russell also argued that any amendments made to the system of representation would destroy the stability of institutions.[349] The Secretary of State made this speech at a time when many towns across the West Riding were severely affected by anti-Poor Law unrest.[350] Edward Vallance has recently argued that the 'Finality Jack' speech was seen by the Chartists and other disenfranchised radicals as being 'the end' and 'not the beginning of England's political reformation'.[351] Russell's decision to stand firm in the face of such pressure has to be seen as a sign of strength rather than weakness.

In rejecting John Prest's assertion that Russell was weak in his handling of Chartist unrest, it can be argued that the Home Secretary also showed great authority, as demonstrated by his reaction to the mass political gatherings that were held on a frequent basis across the West Riding. Local agencies such as the magistracy and the military were particularly concerned about these meetings, largely because of the size of the crowds that attended them, which on occasions amounted to many thousands. In addition, they were also seen at the time as being a fashionable form of symbolic protest, as suggested by the historian Charles Tilly who argues that:

> The individual performance we now call a demonstration entered Britain's repertoires of contention in essentially the same way as the sort of campaign we now call a social movement, indeed as social movements' indispensable device. A demonstration entails gathering deliberately in a visible, symbolically important place, displaying signs of shared commitment to some claim on the authorities, and then dispersing.[352]

Mass demonstrations and civil disobedience by the Chartists posed serious questions about the resources at the disposal of magistrates as some of them could not be policed properly. Many gatherings were often held illegally without the consent of the Lord Lieutenant and local magistrates. There was always a danger that provocation by the authorities could spark greater unrest.

The Home Office did not know whether to allow illegally held meetings to proceed or suppress them by force. Such action meant confronting the crowds and their ringleaders in a straight altercation. This type of response carried the danger of a repeat performance of the Cold Bath Fields incident. A good example of the difficulties that the Home Office faced occurred on 15 October 1838, when a major Chartist meeting was held at Peep Green, otherwise known as Hartshead Moor, near Brighouse. Over the years, this gathering has been the subject of much discussion, particularly over the size of the crowd that attended. At the time, one estimate was that roughly 250,000 people had gathered at the location.[353] However, the *Manchester Guardian* suggested that the number did not exceed ten thousand people, of whom three thousand were 'scattered up and down the moor'.[354] This meeting was attended by the main leadership of the Chartist movement in the form of Feargus O'Connor, the Reverend Joseph Rayner (J.R.) Stephens and a 'clique of Ultra Radicals from Halifax, Huddersfield and Barnsley'.[355] Radical speakers, such as Peter Bussey, used the gathering as a platform to incite the crowds into using violence in order to obtain the 'Six Points'. He believed that the United States acted as a model for revolutionary protest in so far as:

> What was it that gained the independence of America? It was common sense and American Rifles (loud cheers); and if ever the people of England intended to obtain their independence, if they ever calculated upon upsetting the tyranny which now pressed upon their industry, they would have to provide themselves with rifles too.[356]

When the authorities learned of Bussey's intentions, along with those of similar Chartist orators over the use of violence to effect political change, pressure was put on the Home Office to take a tougher stance against the movement. For instance, the Law Officer of the Crown, John Campbell, believed that the 'doctrines' which the radical organisation 'disseminated' were 'destructive to the rights of property and to social order'.[357] He was also fearful about the violent tone of language used by the Chartists and the formidable nature of crowds that attended mass political gatherings. The law officer was unsure how public order could be maintained under such conditions. Campbell believed that 'new laws of a coercive nature' were needed to stop the Chartists in their tracks.[358] As a further measure of repression, the law officer wanted a military force to 'crush those' who intended to 'disturb the public tranquillity'.[359]

The Home Office, under Russell's supervision, refused to bow to the demands of magistrates and law officers who wanted a full-scale crackdown on the activities of the Chartists. Russell believed that such a move was counter-productive. He was of the persuasion that civilian rather than militaristic means was a better way forward in containing the Chartists. He also believed that soldiers should be held back to aid civil forces, especially in emergency situations.[360] This shrewd approach was far more sensible, especially when dealing with the threat of potential agitation and possible flashpoints. However, the reality was that in the West Riding the civil authority was so poor that the Home Office had no other option but to rely upon the military for support. Further, the lack of direct influence that the Home Office could exert over the localities meant that many magistrates often defied Russell's instructions and continued unabated with their hard-line approach. This was highlighted by a number of reports in the *Northern Star* which criticised their role.

On 8 August 1838, the *Northern Star* accused magistrates of causing disorder in Dewsbury. They were seen as 'the men who did the dirty work of Lord John Russell, and two particular Justices of the Peace were singled out for special treatment.[361] It was alleged that Justice Ingram and a police magistrate called Greenwood wanted to enforce an 'English Coercion Bill', which would have given magistrates extra police powers to protect individuals and property from injury.[362] The very notion attracted stinging criticism from the Chartists, who accused the magistrates of 'causing outrage to every feeling of decency'.[363] They were also charged with committing 'insult upon a people' in which they demanded 'nothing more than a hearing through their representatives'.[364] The article highlighted a huge distrust within magisterial circles towards the working classes and the intentions of the Chartists and *vice versa*.[365]

A month later, tensions between Justices of the Peace and the Chartists were exacerbated when it was reported by the *Northern Star* that the Leeds magistrates planned to suspend the *Habeas Corpus* Act. This was a law in which a person could seek redress after being illegally detained by the authorities. The idea of its shelving was seen by the Chartists as a declaration of class war by Justices of the Peace against working people. The reason for the suspension of the act lay in a disturbance that had previously taken place at Leeds. The editor of the *Leeds Mercury*, Edward Baines who was also a member of the Wakefield bench of magistrates, was singled out for specific criticism by the newspaper and accused of showing contempt for the Magna Carta:

> A party of rioters are presented, each and every one of whom is entitled to be liberated upon bail, or summarily dealt with by the Justices. The Justices, however, in order to prove their fearlessness and respect for the law, at once, evince the most cowardly alarm and disregard for all law and custom and common decency. Lest they should appear to be intimidated, they stretch their powers and prove their alarm. They will not accept bail, lest the idea should be entertained that they were forced to comply. What an exhibition!!! [366]

As highlighted by this evidence, when magistrates were threatened they often displayed a tendency to overreact to situations. The Home Office found it difficult to control them, which forced Russell to take a tough line.

In December 1838, the Home Office tried to control Chartist agitation in the West Riding by issuing a proclamation which banned 'unlawful meetings'.[367] Justices of the Peace were ordered to use their 'utmost endeavour' to prevent illegal gatherings and they were told to punish any offenders associated with them.[368] Russell informed the magistrates across the West Riding that if an illegal meeting was held, they were to obtain written statements from witnesses and ensure that they attended future trials when proceedings were brought against any offending parties. The Home Secretary told them to take notes of the 'particulars of the meeting' along with the details of anyone 'principally concerned' with the gathering.[369] Russell wanted to know the number of people that were present at a given event; the nature of the language used by the speakers; the character of the emblems on the banners displayed, and whether firearms were discharged.[370]

One of the problems with this measure revolved around whether it could be enforced. There were complaints amongst magistrates that they had no funds at their disposal to gather information, and the pertinent question was what constituted an illegal meeting?[371] Russell responded to this query by stating that if a meeting was conducted in a 'tumultuous manner', it was deemed to be illegal. The Home Secretary also directed that if no breach of the peace or violence had occurred, the magistrates were not to disperse the meeting but issue proceedings afterwards. For instance, if a speaker used violent and inflammatory language, they were told to apprehend the speakers and gather as much evidence as possible retrospectively in order to secure a conviction. Russell felt that by acting after the event, the magistrates would avoid unnecessary confrontations and be less exposed to the risk of violence.[372]

Throughout the first quarter of 1839, as the mass movement gained momentum, this measure had little effect within the West Riding. Many illegal political meetings were held and the use of violent language by speakers to incite direct action against the state continued unabated. An example of this activity occurred during the first two months of that year when the oratory of the Chartist Peter Bussey attracted the attention of the authorities. On 28 January 1839, he gave a lecture at the Odd Fellows Hall in Bradford. It was estimated that 700 people heard Bussey attack the Whig administration and its handling of political issues such as the Corn Laws. He said that the agitation surrounding the question was nothing but a 'Whig trick' to divert the working classes from protesting for the vote. He believed that without any means of representation they were powerless to prevent 'other equally bad laws' from being introduced.[373] Bussey argued that the repeal of the Corn Laws would move a monopoly from the aristocracy to the moneyocracy, the agriculturalist to the manufacturer, and the changes would not benefit the working classes.[374] The views aired by him appeared to be more in keeping with Tory Radicals such as Richard Oastler, who also thought that society should be returned to a state of affairs that existed before the changes wrought by the Industrial Revolution.[375] Bussey then used his speech to incite open confrontation and told 'every reformer' in the crowd to 'arm themselves'. He famously said:

> Let those who cannot purchase a rifle get a musket, those who cannot get a musket, let them buy a brace of pistols, and those who cannot buy pistols must get a pike – aye a pike, with a shaft eight feet in length, and a spear, fourteen inches long at the end of it.[376]

Bussey's rallying cry troubled the authorities. In February 1839, Russell received information from the Commander of the Northern District Army, Sir Richard Jackson about the arming of Chartists, and wanted more information about its extent.[377] The Home Office also received depositions from J.C. Layock, the Clerk to the Magistrates acting at Huddersfield, concerning 'a dangerous weapon' that was seen in the hands of the Chartists, in the shape of a pike.[378] Some of the weapons had been supplied by 'the House of Catteneo and Fletcher', which was a hardware firm based in Leeds.[379]

The pike was an iconic weapon that became synonymous with Chartist protest and their attempts to assert their constitutional right to bear arms. The demand to use weaponry was later ratified as a policy at the Chartist National Convention, held on 9 April 1839.[380] David Jones has asserted that 'most Chartists regarded arming as a natural form of protection against Peterloo'.[381] He believes that the 'right to arm' was a deliberate response by radicals and a broad section of the working classes to the Whigs' invasion of people's rights and local customs through various measures such as the 1834 Poor Law Amendment Act.[382] Paul Ward has argued that the use of patriotic language was a key feature over the way in which radicals put across their demands.[383] It was against the backdrop of those tensions that David Jones also suggest that 'privately, the authorities often sympathised with the plight of the working class but in public the Chartists got it in the neck'.[384]

The threat of violence in the shape of arming and drilling and the use of the pike as a weapon against public order agencies gave rise to allegations that the Home Office wanted to put in place police measures to curtail such activities. In February 1839, it was rumoured that Russell wanted to extend the Metropolitan Police beyond its natural boundaries as part of a shake-up of provincial policing. This move attracted criticism from some quarters as it was seen as being a measure of further encroachment by central government over the affairs of the West Riding:

> See to what lengths our centralising ministers will go, for the gratification of their captious fancies! The Metropolitan Police is also to be extended to "other places". What those "places" are, we are not told. But this bill is obviously a part of the rural police scheme, and is in conformity with that great plan of concentration, which, if permitted to proceed, will become so fatal to the liberties of the country, Lord John Russell seems determined – are the people watchful? [385]

A month later, these rumours were given further impetus in another speech made by Peter Bussey who attacked the proposed measures and said that they 'stood in the way of political freedom'.[386] He believed that the bill which Lord John Russell wanted to introduce 'struck at the very roots of the liberties of Englishmen'.[387] The fiery activist, who had recently been elected as a delegate to the National Convention, claimed that the Home Office wanted to place 'the police under the control of an army of 27,000 men'.[388] He suggested that Russell had already written to the magistrates of Yorkshire and Lancashire as permission was sought to establish a force that would be 'drilled and trained like regular soldiers'.[389] Bussey alleged that weapons for the proposed force were being made in Birmingham. They consisted of a dagger-like instrument known as a 'dirk' that was 'sharp at both edges' and could be 'carried inside policeman's coats'.[390] Bussey also claimed that the new London to Birmingham railway line was being used as a testing ground for 'four hundred armed police'.[391] It was also contended that the government wanted to insert clauses in the corporate and railway bills to sanction their deployment at a provincial level.[392]

Peter Bussey's observations about policing were near the mark. Lord John Russell had earlier written to Major-General Sir Richard Jackson as he sought advice over which towns within the Northern District were ready to adopt locally-organised police forces.[393] However, on the question of direct action which Peter Bussey staunchly favoured, there were visible splits within the Chartist movement.

In March 1839, the Chartist leaders met at the Convention in the Crown and Anchor Tavern in the Strand, London, to discuss their national strategy for achieving the Charter. This meeting was chaired by John Frost and attended by Feargus O'Connor, William Sankey, Dr John Taylor, William Smith O'Brien and Julian Harney. When discussions got under way, Feargus O'Connor, who fully understood the repressive capacity of the state from his own experiences, said that 'a million petitions would not dislodge a single troop of dragoons'.[394] He asked those who were present at the meeting to reflect upon this statement. William Smith O'Brien responded to O'Connor's assertion in which he said that despite there being 'twelve hundred thousand signatures', the House of Commons would reject the petition for the Charter unless there were 'a similar number of pikes behind them'.[395] In essence, O'Brien believed that the Chartists could only obtain their goals through the use of force which involved a head-on collision with the authorities. Some of the moderate elements within the movement were realistic enough to accept that such action would end in bloodshed. Despite these divisions, the Home Office responded to the perceived threat of violence by calling upon the military for assistance.

In April 1839, Russell appointed Sir Charles James Napier as Commander of the Northern District Army. This was clearly a politically-motivated decision designed not only to put fear into the Chartists but also put at ease the minds of law officers and magistrates who had become increasingly concerned at the perceived threat of violence to people and property. There were a number of reasons why Russell turned to Napier for assistance, though not all of them were popular. First of all, the Home Secretary felt that tensions amongst the working classes could be soothed by the appointment of a person who was sympathetic to their cause. Napier's empathy towards the Chartists was a product of his upbringing in Ireland. He likened their aims to those of the Irish peasantry. During the 1790s, he saw at first-hand how army and yeomanry forces had waged terror against them.[396] His sympathy towards Chartist goals meant a reluctance to use force against its supporters, except in extreme circumstances. Secondly, Russell appointed Napier because he possessed a strong and forceful character needed to handle magistrates who were, in the main, self-serving. Napier distrusted politicians and his dislike cut across party divides. The general felt that he was above high politics. He had been an outspoken critic of both Whig and Tory policies, particularly those in relation to the new Poor Laws which he felt were unjust. As well as showing a dislike towards politicians, Sir Charles Napier also harboured a similar distrust of magistrates.[397]

From the very outset, Napier's tenure as Commander of the Northern District Army was problematic. Russell and the Home Office found themselves having to arbitrate constantly over feuds that erupted between the military and Justices of the Peace. Napier was critical about magisterial interference in the policing of crowds and disturbances. Magistrates had a tendency to demand military assistance over relatively trivial matters. The Commander of the Northern District Army believed that their 'small interests' and 'personal fears' of working-class agitation was counter-productive in dealing with radical unrest.[398]

The first dispute between the two agencies occurred over the way in which troops were dispersed across the Northern District. Napier believed that this tactical arrangement left the soldiers wide open to attack from the Chartists. He later spoke candidly about the potential ramifications of this:

> The soldiers must be kept together: the consequence of a military mishap would be a national misfortune; of a civil defeat only a trifling private loss. By dispersing the troops the greater evil becomes very possible, even probable. By concentrating the troops the smaller evil may happen; but the danger will give such a stimulus to private courage as will call forth more manly and effectual exertions from the middle classes, who are now supine and trust wholly to soldiers. This apathy I wish to rouse them from. I want to withdraw the detachments from Todmorden and Halifax and give them to Leeds and Sheffield, but Lord John Russell opposes me, being talked over by the magistrates.[399]

To secure the entire Northern District from Chartist turbulence, Napier wanted three regiments brought over from Ireland. Russell responded to the demand by only allowing one to be moved.[400] This emergency formed the backdrop to a second major disagreement that took place between Napier and the Justices of the Peace in the West Riding over the issue of troop accommodation. The general believed that magistrates looked for the cheapest possible means when it came to having a military presence in the region. In doing so, those circumstances placed the lives of the troops in danger:

> The magistrates are always trying to get soldiers, and never caring for their safety: they shall not have detachments unless they provide for their security, which they try to avoid as costly without regard for the soldiers' lives. I have written them a strong letter, and sent a copy to the secretary of state, whom they had enlisted on their side. He has the good sense to see I am right, and takes my side of the question.[401]

Russell later gave Napier the authority to hire temporary barracks to secure the safety of his troops.[402] The building of permanent stations to accommodate soldiers became a major source of conflict between the Home Secretary, Napier and the Lord Lieutenant, the Earl of Harewood. The Lord Lieutenant, along with many magistrates across the region, felt that new barracks were needed at Barnsley and Brighouse.[403] The Home Secretary had already chosen three sites where new permanent stations were to be built at Bolton, Blackburn and Rochdale, and refused to deviate from this position.[404] In the coming months, there were many instances in which the inhabitants of places such as Bradford offered to provide 'proper accommodation for troops' at their own expense if the Home Office allowed them to be quartered there.[405] But for the meantime, the issue of permanent troop stations within the West Riding was deferred by Russell who continued to act in an arbitrary manner as the Chartists tried to create further dissension within military ranks.

The *Northern Star* questioned the loyalty of troops in the event of an open conflict which might lead them to defect from their regiments to join the Chartists as they sought to overturn the government and the state:

> The bread wrung from the sweat of the father, so stinks in the nostrils of his brave and valiant son that he disdains to eat it when served up with a parent's blood. Well done, brave soldiers! Tell the tyrants that you will not commit murder – that you fight for the QUEEN, and not for the Poor Law; for the glory of a nation, and not for the monopoly of a faction. That being of the people, you are *for* the people; that the people being the only legitimate source of power, you hold muskets to defend their rights, and not to invade their privileges. Let every man think and reflect upon the horrors of civil war, when father is arrayed against son, and brother against brother. We have never gone out of our way to say a word of the soldiers of this country; but now we affirm that they are Chartists to a man, because the Charter restores God's gift, which is peace and plenty; and man's inheritance, which is liberty.[406]

The problem of dissension within military ranks and the difficulties caused by the appointment of Napier as Commander of the Northern District Army forced Russell to explore other means of securing the West Riding from the threat of Chartist unrest. However, as he discovered, none of those measures were suitable. The situation was made all the more pressing by the continued wave of arming and drilling, along with the expectation of large political meetings which posed a danger to the public peace.[407]

Initially, the Home Secretary considered the deployment of the yeomanry in towns such as Bradford, where 'four to five hundred agitators' possessed 'muskets, pikes and pistols'.[408] The Deputy Lieutenant of the County, Lord Wharncliffe, wrote to the Home Office and spoke of his intention to assemble the South-West York Regiment of the yeomanry cavalry under his command for 'eight days' permanent duty at Doncaster.[409] However, questions were raised at central government level over this development. Two issues emerged which revolved around the cost and limited time-scale of their deployment. The West Riding magistrate Matthew Thompson later received a letter from Russell, who after 'consulting the judgment of military men' felt that it would be 'injurious to allow troops to be distributed at Bradford, Halifax and Huddersfield'.[410] The decision not to deploy the cavalry was based on the grounds that its presence would do more harm than good.[411]

Informed that the use of the yeomanry was not a viable option, the Home Secretary considered the use of militia forces, a move that carried similar dangers to the deployment of the yeomanry. Questions were raised over whether the working classes could be trusted with firearms and 'taught military discipline' at a time when they were 'extremely agitated'.[412] There was the additional fear that extremist elements of the Chartist movement could infiltrate its ranks and then turn on the authorities.[413] The *Northern Star* reinforced this assertion when it claimed that 'thousands' of people with 'arms in their hands and Chartist doctrines in their heads' would ensure that 'every billeting house' contained 'a club of Conventionists'.[414] The radical newspaper suggested that an armed force could be raised 'from classes' who the army had been 'too afraid to trust with a pike or a pistol'.[415] The article also highlighted that a 'mighty change' had taken place amongst the working classes in which they decided to arm themselves in order to defend their local customs from foreign ideas and central government intrusion:

> They are no longer the ignorant serfs who could be stimulated by cries of 'Church and State', 'God Save The King', and 'Down with Bonaparte'. They demand physical and intellectual improvement, and a participation in the most esteemed rights of citizenship. They swell with a sense of indignity and wrong. That their present movement has proved a failure, whatever may be the cause, is no balm to their wounded feelings. It will only strengthen the resolve to coerce their adversaries when the means are with them. They will bide their time.[416]

Russell's decision to consider using the militia as an agency of repression came at a time when politicians became concerned about the level of arming and drilling that was taking place in towns across the manufacturing districts. On 15 May 1839, Sir Watkin Williams-Wynn, MP for Denbighshire, raised the issue in the House of Commons and said that 'deadly weapons' were being provided by 'a large number of people in the country'.[417] Wynn pointed out that 'special constables' were reluctant to carry out their duties because they were 'armed only with the weapon provided by law for a constable'.[418] The politician went on to argue that if the arming was allowed to go 'unchecked', the situation would lead to 'a lamentable degree of bloodshed'.[419] Wynn believed that in order to prevent such a scenario, measures were needed to strengthen 'the hands of the magistrates'.[420]

Russell responded to those concerns in which he said that the 'Government had not been unmindful of what was going on', and believed that it was better to rely on laws that were in existence.[421] He argued:

Because the objects of the persons influencing the minds of the people, and inciting them to arm, were so clearly mischievous – so many of their acts so clearly exposed them to the penalties of the law, that it was impossible that they could meet with any general sympathy.[422]

Russell told the House that 'when extraordinary measures were taken in Parliament', they created 'sympathy', along with excitement and 'jealousy' towards the constitution.[423] Questions were also raised in the Commons about the Home Office and its handling of torchlight gatherings which were attended by Chartist agitators armed with bludgeons and pikes. The Home Secretary told the House that the government had advised the Queen to issue proclamations to prevent the gatherings taking place from which 'the most salutary effects had been produced'.[424] Russell felt that the Home Office was doing everything in its capacity as it had taken measures 'to arrest, and if possible to repress' Chartists who had exhibited a desire to riot and cause harm to people and property.[425] He later said that the issue had been 'a frequent matter of consultation between himself and the Attorney-General', who had put the issue before the Cabinet in which they decided to pursue a sensible course of action, rather than propose measures of 'an extraordinary description'.[426]

The route that the Home Office eventually adopted was effectively a half-way house between the use of regular soldiers and auxiliary troops, in the shape of Armed Associations. Following an incident at a mill in Oldham where a man was shot, there were concerns about 'the assassination' of 'manufacturers' and 'destruction of manufacturing property'.[427] The factory owners in the town 'introduced arms for self-defence' and they wanted to turn places where the means of production were situated into 'fortresses'.[428] Having seen how the system operated, in May 1839 the Home Secretary wrote to the Earl of Harewood with this suggestion:

In case riots should take place, or if there should be good cause for apprehending that riots are about to take place, in any part of the county…and the principal inhabitants of a disturbed district should be desirous of forming an association for the protection of life and property, and offer their services to Government for that purpose their services will be accepted. In case of such an association being formed, I will give orders for providing such arms as may be necessary at the expense of Government.[429]

The creation of Armed Associations proved to be a popular measure with magistrates and was greeted with particular enthusiasm in places such as Bradford and Leeds.[430] The Justice of the Peace Abraham Horsfall told the Earl of Harewood that in response to the 'lawless attempts of designed men', he wanted to raise 'a corps of volunteers' comprised of 'respectable persons'.[431] He said that the men had shown a readiness to 'enrol themselves as a corps of riflemen' and were ready to 'assist in protecting the lives of fellow countrymen'.[432] However, in some quarters, major concerns were being raised about the use of 'undisciplined troops' who were 'infested by local animosities'.[433] The Duke of Wellington was highly sceptical of the measure. He warned that allowing groups of men to readily obtain arms in order to protect lives and property was dangerous. The Duke also felt that the associations needed a 'military officer' to 'command and control them' and was proved right, as suggested by later events in Bradford.[434]

The establishment of Armed Associations had very little effect on the activities of the Chartists. Whilst reports of arming and drilling continued to filter into the Home Office, another wave of mass political gatherings was held across the region. The Lord Lieutenant received a number of circulars from the Home Secretary who urged him to make these gatherings illegal. One of the biggest meetings was held at Peep Green on 21 May 1839. The episode revealed that when it came to preventing political congregations from taking place, the Home Office and local public order agencies were relatively weak. Many people just ignored their instructions and came out in force. One local newspaper reported that 'never did any public meeting create such a sensation throughout the whole Riding'.[435]

On the Saturday beforehand, twenty-four magistrates had convened at the Court House in Wakefield to discuss what to do about the proposed event. A caution was issued regarding the 'printing, posting and distributing' of materials in which 'the fourth commandment was utterly disregarded'.[436] Magistrates warned people not to attend any illegal meetings. Owners of public houses were ordered not to 'sell beer or spirituous liquids'.[437]

At a moment's notice, the army was put on standby in the event of a disturbance.[438] Initially, the Lord Lieutenant refused to allow the meeting to go ahead. In response to this development the Chartists produced a placard which advertised the Earl of Harewood's decision. The decision to ban the meeting was ignored by the many who defiantly attended. When the proceedings finally got under way, the army was kept out of sight and watched events from afar. Feargus O'Connor and Bronterre O'Brien were the only major Chartist leaders present and the former said that he was determined to gain universal suffrage or 'die in the last ditch'.[439] Despite the concerns of the authorities over the use of inflammatory language by some of the speakers, along with the danger of violence, the meeting was both a peaceful and tame affair.[440]

Throughout the summer 1839, the fear of severe unrest within the West Riding heightened following news of events that took place at the Bull Ring in Birmingham during July, from which major disturbances ensued. These incidents flagged up a number of issues over the deployment of the Metropolitan Police and its use as an agency for handling provincial disturbances. This episode revealed two sides to its behaviour, which later provided a major cause for concern within Home Office circles. The first incident revolved around the use of indiscriminate violence when the police force entered the town. Whilst the second confrontation revealed its impotence when civil control was absent.

Since May 1839, Birmingham had been the location for the Chartist Convention. The National Petition and the 'Sacred Month' were amongst many issues that were being discussed by the main leadership of the movement.[441] After a short break, the Convention reconvened throughout early July 1839, during which time the Bull Ring had become a nightly meeting place for the Chartists. On 5 July 1839, many people had turned up at the location to see the Birmingham delegate, John Fussell, deliver a speech. Local magistrates had tried to put a stop to the political gatherings but to no avail and they feared an outbreak of violence. Concerns about the 'inefficiency' of their own police force, especially its numerical strength, meant that they had very little option but to turn to the Home Office for assistance.

Russell sent '60 picked men' to the town. When the Metropolitan Police arrived in Birmingham by rail in the early evening, they headed straight for the Bull Ring. Their first task was to disperse a large mob that had gathered around a monument at the location. They were also ordered specifically to arrest any Chartists caught delivering speeches to a crowd.[442]

Antony Taylor has argued that this was one of many 'speakers' corners' in the country 'where all manner of political, social and religious views were expressed'.[443] Police constables, led by the mayor and two magistrates asked the crowd to disperse. When people failed to take notice of this request, the magistrates gave a signal to the police, who were at the end of Moor Street, to advance. The constables, who were filed four abreast, marched into the centre of the crowd and 'by the dint of their staffs', seized banners and flags from the Chartists. The crowd, which was clearly upset by the high-handed actions of the Metropolitan officers, broke their flag poles and used them as offensive weapons. After a 'furious assault', the police were 'beaten off to a considerable distance'.[444]

Once this attack had been withstood, the police rallied and attacked the crowd. In the ensuing battle, a constable, who had become separated from his colleagues during the melée, was surrounded by forty people who proceeded to beat him with their bludgeons and various other weapons. The helpless officer was later stabbed by a man wielding a 'large clasp knife'.[445] Two other constables of the 'A' Division of the Metropolitan Police were also stabbed and 'mortally wounded' in a 'deadly' battle that took place outside a liquor vault. By this stage, the Dragoons had arrived on the scene and they surrounded every thoroughfare that led into the Bull Ring in an attempt to prevent further violence from escalating.[446] When they attempted to clear the streets, the police and Dragoons drove the crowd back from Bromsgrove Street to St Thomas' Church, where another pitched battle took place. Protesters tore up iron palisades from the walls of the church and used them as weapons to attack the auxiliary soldiers and police. Many constables were seriously injured as their only means of defending themselves was through the use of their staffs. Once the crowd had been finally driven back beyond the church, order was gradually restored, despite their being a few minor incidents that occurred between troops and the Chartists.[447]

Malcolm Chase has argued that the main leadership of the Chartist movement viewed police actions as an attempt to destabilise the Convention, in which they claimed that the government had resorted to anti-democratic measures to silence its protest.[448] This was not only reflected by the failed attempt at suppression by Metropolitan Police constables of those Chartists gathered at the Bull Ring, but also through the arrest of key leaders such as Peter McDouall and Dr John Taylor; the latter was later suspected by the Home Office of being the mastermind behind the Bradford disturbances in January 1840.[449]

Following this first incident, the Metropolitan Police was instructed by the Birmingham magistrates and mayor not to take any course of action without the permission of a magistrate. This had major implications during the second major episode of unrest that took place on 15 July 1839. Without a Justice of the Peace to guide them, Metropolitan Police officers were impotent as they stood and watched rioting and the destruction of property.[450] The distrust that existed between the magistrates and the constables was such that from the moment they arrived until their departure, they were confined to the yard of the Public Office. Occasionally, they patrolled the vicinity of the building in fours but throughout the time that they spent there, the constables were given 'no opportunity' to know the state of the town, nor were they able to gather any intelligence.[451] The mayor gave the officers strict orders not to enter public houses and that if any gatherings 'worthy of notice' took place they were to be immediately reported to the Public Office.[452] Further to this, Metropolitan constables were not permitted to patrol the streets of Birmingham in plain clothes. The only action which the force could take revolved around cases of 'felony', when they were allowed to act in their 'usual capacity'.[453]

On the day of the second major confrontation, which followed the rejection of the Chartists' National Petition by Parliament, the chief constable and his men had intended to return to London. Until mid-evening, the Bull Ring had been peaceful. However, the situation changed when, in Superintendent May's words, 'a large mob' of around 10,000, decided to assemble below the church situated in the Bull Ring. The Chief Constable was told by the mayor 'not to allow men out' of the yard of the Public Office as it was feared that their presence would 'excite the mob'.[454] Those instructions were ignored and a Metropolitan constable was strategically placed at the 'outer gate' of the Public Office. The gate was kept half open, at the request of a senior officer, in order to avoid being 'shut in' should an incident occur.[455] At eight-thirty that evening, a large crowd 'armed with weapons of every description' decided to launch the 'most ferocious attack' on the Public Office.[456] This assault lasted five minutes, during which all the front windows of the building were 'demolished'.[457]

After the attack, the protesters retreated to the Bull Ring. The Chief Constable of the Metropolitan Police opposed the idea of pitching his fifty men against the rioters, because he knew that 'without the aid of the military' they could not force the crowd back 'further than the end of Moor Street'.[458] He believed that the constables would have been exposed to 'imminent danger' resulting in a major loss of life on both sides.[459] When the protesters retreated from the Public Office to the Bull Ring, they broke into shops and plundered the goods from them. Without a magistrate present, the Metropolitan Police could only watch and not intervene as a major disturbance broke out.[460] At twenty-past nine, a magistrate arrived at the Public Office and ten minutes later, after the Riot Act had been read, the Metropolitan Police tried to clear the streets. Many insurgents 'made off' after a number of houses had been 'fired'.[461] Twenty minutes later, the military arrived. They were followed by fire engines, which were used to extinguish burning houses and shops. Throughout the night, police and troops patrolled the streets as the disturbances eventually petered out.[462]

In the aftermath of those incidents, a Home Office report accused the Metropolitan Police of 'neglect of duty' for 'not suppressing the riot'.[463] The force was criticised over its failure to 'use due or proper means to quell and abate' the disturbance'.[464] It was also castigated over its refusal to 'hinder the mob from continuing the riot' which lasted for two hours.[465] Questions were raised as to why many of the offenders who went on the rampage and were described as 'evil disposed persons' had managed to evade capture.[466] The role of the Chief Constable, whose duty it was to 'marshal and organise his men', came under fire as he could not carry out this task.[467] He was later accused of failing to give 'proper orders' and directions in the suppression of the riot' as he refused to allow his men to act when riot and tumult broke out.[468] The issue of blame was stoked up by senior politicians and military figures such as the Duke of Wellington who questioned the role of magistrates and their inability to 'preserve the peace' in which the Home Office was accused of not controlling them properly.[469]

Following both incidents, many lessons were learned and later put into practice by the new police in Birmingham. Michael Weaver has argued that the disturbances gave rise to a consistent approach in dealing with Chartist gatherings and processions. Such tactics involved the deployment of plain clothes officers along the routes of marches; the use of additional men taken from night patrols; the employment of reserve constables that were deliberately positioned away from police stations to avoid confrontations and, more importantly, the occupation of public spaces where Chartist meetings were due to be held. The implementation of all those measures meant that there was no further repetition of the serious outbreaks of riots and disturbances that took place at Birmingham, especially during episodes of Chartist unrest which occurred throughout 1842 and 1848.[470]

Reflecting on how the Bull Ring disturbances affected the Home Office policy towards the West Riding, greater care was taken over the future use of the Metropolitan Police in the suppression of 'tumults'.[471] The controversy that surrounded the actions of the Metropolitan Police gave Russell a valid reason as to why major police reforms were needed in the provinces. The main debate that followed centred on whether such a force should be centrally controlled by the Home Office along the lines of the Metropolitan Police, or locally through magistrates. Russell was opposed to the idea of a 'migratory' force which could be transferred 'to any part of the kingdom' and favoured power being placed in the hands of the local authorities.[472] The Home Secretary's design for a provincial police force was met with opposition from Sir Robert Peel who believed that his proposals were 'audacious' as well as being the 'most stupid project thus coolly announced'.[473] The Tory politician was extremely concerned about the militaristic nature of a provincial police force in which he said that it was:

A project for the organisation of an army – of an army not controlled immediately by the Crown, and kept up by the consent of Parliament annually obtained, but a standing army at the disposal of the Minister, who may want, as in the late King's time, the confidence of the Parliament and the People.[474]

Despite Peel's concerns, the incidents that involved the Chartists in the West Riding and the Birmingham Bull Ring prompted Lord John Russell to take action and introduce police measures. In August 1839, three Rural Constabulary Bills were introduced for 'improving the police' in Birmingham, Manchester and Bolton. The key strands of this legislation placed power in the hands of Justices of the Peace who were given the authority to appoint a Chief Constable. This individual was responsible for the appointment of 'a sufficient number of fit and able men' whose duty involved preservation of peace along with the prevention of robberies and felonies. The magistrates were also given additional powers to levy and recover rates.[475] The cost of putting the force into operation, as in Birmingham, amounted to £10,000, the Home Office using money from the Consolidated Fund.[476]

The idea behind the creation of rural police forces came from the Constabulary Force Commission, which recommended that a paid force should be 'trained, appointed, and organised' on the principles laid down by the Metropolitan Police Act.[477] When it came to dealing with the after-effects of the Bull Ring incident, Lord John Russell opted to hand over control of the force to local magistrates. They were effectively allowed to create their own model for policing, independent of central control, as highlighted by later constabulary bills.[478] The decision to allow local magistrates to decide whether they wanted to adopt this legislation had far reaching effects for the Home Office and places such as the West Riding, where the matter was discussed at great length at Quarter Sessions and rejected.[479]

Following the disturbances in Birmingham, the attention of the Home

Office shifted towards the West Riding where major political unrest culminated in the 'Sacred Month' and a remarkable show of Chartist strength. In the two months leading up to this stand-off, the Home Office tried to suppress Chartist protestations through the adoption of various measures.

There was an attempted clampdown on the publication of seditious material. This was highlighted when Russell and the Attorney-General brought a case against Feargus O' Connor. Proceedings were issued against the Chartist leader, who had published 'a false and malicious libel' in the *Northern Star*. A few months earlier, under the heading 'Warminster Bastille', O'Connor had alleged that 'a little boy' was confined in a cell above the town's workhouse and had been 'literally starved to death'.[480] The allegations were challenged by the Warminster Union Guardians and the Chartist leader responded by saying that the statement was intended to be a joke. Justice Coltman and the Guardians did not find the allegation amusing and the Chartist leader was later found guilty of sedition.[481]

Literary censorship was also followed by an attempt to silence verbally the Chartist movement. Russell urged magistrates to clampdown on seditious speeches. A circular accompanied by a copy letter written by the Permanent Under-Secretary Samuel March Phillipps was issued by the Home Office and contained the following instructions:

> That in case any meeting should be held, attended by a large concourse of people with such circumstances of terror as are calculated to excite alarm and endanger the public peace at which any seditious or inflammatory speech should be addressed to the people, Lord John Russell advised the Magistrates to apprehend by warrant and commit to Prison, the persons who take the most active part – and Lord John Russell will support the Magistrates in the prosecution if a prosecution should be advisable.[482]

The attempt at repression did not have much effect as the number of illegal political gatherings increased. They coincided with an intensification of arming and drilling amongst Chartists across the West Riding.[483]

Paramilitary aspects of Chartist protest went hand in hand with the practice of 'Exclusive Dealing' which dated back to the 1820s and 1830s. It involved Chartists trading only with shopkeepers who showed support for their cause. Peter Gurney has argued that the Chartists resorted to this form of protest because they felt exploited by consumers and producers. This action was used as a weapon to undermine both what the Chartists saw as an oppressive state as well as middle men, who they felt were influencing market conditions at their expense.[484] Much of this activity centred upon Leeds which attracted the attention of the Home Office. The Chartists needed funds to further their political activities and activists went around asking 'shopkeepers and publicans' for money. Those who refused to give anything were threatened with 'serious injury'.[485] The money generated from this tactic was used to pay for a Defence Fund organised by Peter Bussey.[486] Local magistrates were determined to stop this type of protest. In doing so, they received support from Russell, who sent them a letter with clear directives:

> Having been informed that in some parts of the kingdom, attempts have lately been made to obtain money from shopkeepers, householders, and others, by means of intimidation (as by threatening them with personal danger, or with loss of business, or threatening to mark them down and report them as enemies, and by various other illegal means) and that persons have been combining and endeavouring to injure shopkeepers, householders and others, in their lawful business, representing them as enemies to the people, and persuading others to leave off trading with them, thereby to prejudice them in their business; having been also informed that persons, in pursuance of an illegal combination, have gone about among the working classes of people, exciting and endeavouring to persuade them to desist from working, and to desert their employers; I deem it to be my duty to call upon the magistrates to use their utmost endeavours to repress and put down such mischievous practices, which are contrary to law, injurious to trade, subversive of good order, and dangerous to the peace of the country; and to apprehend and bring the offenders to justice.[487]

Magistrates were ordered to take appropriate measures against those who were caught carrying out this type of criminal activity and urged that they should be charged with a 'misdemeanour'.[488] They were also ordered to suppress the 'unlawful proceedings' of persons who went around threatening 'members of the working classes' by causing both 'terror and alarm', which prevented them from going about their day to day business.[489] This led to immediate action in towns such as Leeds. On 1 August 1839, two local Chartist leaders, George White and John Wilson, were tried after being arrested for intimidating 'certain trades people'.[490] When they were caught in the act, they had in their possession two books, both of which, had a label stuck to them that read 'the bearers are authorised collectors of the Leeds Northern Union – George White, Secretary'.[491] The first page contained the following statement:

In compliance with the instructions of the National Convention, we take the liberty of waiting upon you to ascertain whether you will assist (by your subscriptions) in establishing a government whereby the labour of the poor may be protected, in the same manner as the wealth of the rich. We therefore take this as the only means of proving who are our friends and who are not; and are determined as far as in our power lies, to assist those who befriend us in the present struggle.[492]

Written inside the 'black book' were the names and addresses of several people who had refused to contribute to the Defence Fund. The other book contained details of four subscribers who had contributed six shillings after being threatened.[493] There was also a list of people who were due to be called on again. Several tradesmen and many other victims of the two men came forward and gave evidence. It transpired that White and Wilson had travelled around Leeds asking tradesmen and shopkeepers to read notices and state whether they were the 'friends or the enemies' of the Chartists. If the persons said that they were 'enemies', money was extorted from them. The apprehended were accused of being 'cowardly ruffians' who treated women in a similar manner. Justices of the Peace deliberated about what to do with the offenders as local Chartists threatened to use force to liberate them.[494] Russell later recommended that the magistrates should not take bail for White and Wilson and suggested that the printer of the placard, along with the people who had posted it, should also be prosecuted.[495] Both men were later committed for trial at York Castle.[496]

Whilst 'Exclusive Dealing' was, for most of the Chartist period, advocated by Feargus O'Connor as a weapon to be used by activists in an attempt to blackmail shopkeepers, publicans and businesses into supporting the movement and its goals, and often spoken about and adopted as a resolution at branch level, it was rarely put into action.[497] As a consequence, by 1842, 'Exclusive Dealing' was seen as a failure by supporters of the Chartist movement in the West Riding and in many places across the country.[498] This was despite later attempts by Feargus O'Connor to moderate its aims, by placing less emphasis on violent rhetoric and the threatening behaviour which often accompanied it.[499]

As well as the Home Office suppression of 'Exclusive Dealing', another major factor which hindered Chartist protest and the planned 'Sacred Month' was widespread economic distress. The Chartists were too poverty-stricken to mount a sustained challenge to the authority of the state, which was why the 'Sacred Month' was later reduced to three days of solemn protest. For example, in Great Horton the Chartists were 'nearly all in despair' and had to resort to desperate measures just to survive:

Many of them have pawned or sold their muskets – some of them as low as 4s 6d each, although their original cost was 15s. An effort is being made for a revival, the bellman having gone round yesterday, announcing that a meeting would be held in the evening at Lidget Green, at which Mr Peter Bussey, Mr Martin, and several others would attend on business of the great importance. We understand that of late, very little money has been received from the treasurer from Horton, and that some new scheme is about to be set on foot to remedy this evil.[500]

The Home Office left nothing to chance and a decision was taken to bolster the local machinery of public order with supplies of armaments that could be used in the event of an outbreak of violence. On 6 August 1839, the Earl of Harewood wrote to the West Riding magistrates with information concerning the 'supply of arms and ammunition for the protection of Bradford'.[501] Russell ordered 'three-hundred brace of pistols with ammunition'.[502] They were sent to the magistrate E.C. Lister, who was given the task of returning the weapons to the Board of Ordnance when they were no longer required.[503] The Home Secretary also ordered magistrates to use the 'greatest precaution' by distributing the weapons to individuals who could be trusted with them. They were only to be used in self-defence under the supervision of a magistrate.[504] The firearms were kept at Leeds Barracks and made available to the civil authorities on request.[505] A slightly smaller number of weapons were also sent to Barnsley.[506] The provision of firearms was followed by frequent magisterial requests for military assistance as they reported that the inhabitants of places such as Bradford became 'more and alarmed by the Chartists'.[507]

Before dealing with matters in the West Riding, Russell had to defuse a row that had broken out between Lord Hill and Napier over the way in which assistance was given to the civil authorities. The main significance of this dispute was that it revealed that at the very highest-level within military ranks, senior generals could not decide what the best course of action was in policing Chartist agitation. Napier was highly concerned about the safety of his troops. He believed that 'all detachments' when deployed, 'should be comprised of Infantry and Cavalry troops'.[508] Hill was critical of this stance and thought that there were cases when the use of either force was necessary to deal with disturbances. He felt that any decisions taken should be based on circumstances as they occurred. This brought about another issue of contention, which related to the way that soldiers were accommodated. Whereas Napier believed that detachments should be placed in barracks in the 'midst of houses in the centre of a town', Hill disapproved of his tactic.[509] He felt that it presented dangers as soldiers could be barricaded in by insurgents and access points blocked during a confrontation.[510]

Hill and Napier also disagreed over the use of small detachments and how they were situated and deployed. Hill believed that under no circumstances should a detachment be replaced or troops billeted at a distance from their officers. He asserted that the troops required by the civil power that were to be used against the Chartists should be kept as far from the insurgents as possible. Napier felt the need to 'press earnestly upon Lord John Russell' the necessity of keeping the soldiers together.[511] A problem raised by Hill over this tactic was that with Chartist 'disaffection' and insurgency being spread out over a broad territorial expanse, it was inevitable that the cavalry and other forces required to aid civil power would be 'comparatively small' and dispersed over a great distance.[512] Hill felt that it was ultimately up to the civil and military power to pull together and make joint decisions to secure places from widespread radical unrest, along with the violence that it threatened.[513]

Despite this infighting amongst the authorities, Russell retained the belief that military intervention was needed to deal with 'spirits of turbulence and disaffection' on the mainland as a whole. In a speech delivered in the House of Common, Russell launched a scathing attack on Richard Oastler and Joseph Rayner Stephens over their 'clamour against the Poor Laws'.[514] The Tory Radicals were accused of inciting working-class violence; he also warned the House that the Chartists had become a 'very formidable' force.[515] Its main leadership was accused of having 'a fixed design by means of terror and confusion to produce a general, total and entire change in the institutions of the country'.[516] In the immediate aftermath of this major outburst, Russell and the Home Office were confronted by three days of 'solemn processions' and political meetings centred on the West Riding.[517]

From the very outset, the organisation of this wave of protest was flawed as it was arranged at such a short notice. The decision taken by the Chartist leadership to proceed with its protestations was criticised at a meeting in Bradford, when one of the speakers made this perceptive observation:

Ireland was not prepared. Part of Scotland was not fully prepared. There was a difference of opinion amongst the Members of the Convention. The commencement of the Sacred Month must therefore be deferred a short time, and in the mean time everyone should supply himself with the necessary fireplace ornaments.[518]

Further to this, divisions between Feargus O'Connor and the Birmingham Chartist Thomas Attwood surfaced. There was a collision between the two radical leaders over whether violence should be embraced for the three days of protest. O'Connor, who favoured a moderate stance, denounced the ideas of his counterpart for a confrontation with the authorities as being 'a wild and visionary scheme'.[519] He feared that the working classes would end up being 'deserted' and 'sacrificed' by the upper and middle classes.[520] There were deep-seated fears amongst Chartist leaders that the event would become 'a revolution of blood'.[521] Those suspicions were also shared by the Home Office. In the days leading up to the wave of protest, it had received numerous reports from the West Riding that many mill owners had been anonymously threatened by a number of radicals. They were warned about the serious consequences that they faced if their premises were allowed to be opened during the three days of protest.[522] A reporter employed by the Lord Lieutenant and Magistrates told the Home Office that the Chartists wanted to 'destroy all the cattle and the corn' within the region to 'create a famine in the land'.[523] Russell was told that shopkeepers would be threatened if they failed to show any support for three days of defiance.[524]

The Home Office responded immediately to these threats by stepping up the military presence. The Metropolitan Police was sent into the West Riding to monitor the situation and watch potential troublemakers. At the time, the *Northern Star* reported that two 'vagabonds' were 'prowling about Huddersfield in disguise' and warned its readership to 'beware of all strange companions' and 'parties' that they didn't know who were 'excessively violent'.[525] In Chartist strongholds such as Bradford, local Justices of the Peace called upon pensioners to maintain order as 'one hundred and sixty-one' of them were sworn-in as special constables, largely as a precautionary measure.[526] The policing provisions were organised along military lines as Lord Russell and the Earl of Harewood took the precaution of appointing Colonel Angelo to supervise and train the special constables appointed by the magistrates.[527] Angelo was a high-ranking officer in the British Army, who was very briefly the first Commissioner of the Bolton Police – a post which he resigned from due to differences with the government over his salary.[528] He was later paid £40 by the Chief Clerk at the Home Office for his services in the North which included personal and travelling expenses.[529]

When the 'great national' and 'moral demonstration' got under way on the 12 August 1839, the Home Office and local public order agencies watched the West Riding grind to a halt.[530] A number of political gatherings were organised across the region. The largest one was held at Fairweather Green, Bradford where Peter Bussey and a number of other speakers addressed a crowd of around '9,000 to 10,000' people.[531] Local magistrates issued notices and warned people not to attend the meeting. Their pleas were ignored and throughout the duration of the gathering, the Justices of the Peace sat in the Court House where they waited for news of any unrest.[532]

All in all, the three days of protest passed off relatively peacefully. In Leeds, which was the 'capital of the clothing district', not a single mill was threatened by the Chartists, and the situation in Huddersfield and Halifax was similar.[533] The only town that experienced any skirmishes was Barnsley, where the Riot Act was read twice.[534] However, during the immediate aftermath of this protest, the local authorities became apprehensive about the safety of towns across the West Riding. Magistrates were particularly concerned about the role of Armed Associations in places such as Bradford. It was feared that as they had previously been given firearms to protect the town from unrest, those weapons could be used in a possible violent backlash against the Chartists. This development forced magistrates to petition the Home Office for a 'military officer' to oversee the affairs of Armed Associations and keep tensions in check for 'a short period of time'.[535] The presence of a military officer in the town 'would not only give confidence to the well-disposed inhabitants' but also aid civil power in dealing with any outbreaks of violence.[536] They believed that having a military officer stationed in the town would enable them to make best use of special constables, especially by letting them use pistols in the event of an armed confrontation with the Chartists.[537] The threat of an actual outbreak of violence occurring in the town seemed likely as a wave of clandestine meetings took place:

> Our large Parish Church was taken possession of by the Chartists & their followers on Sunday last, many, hundreds being unable to get in...The Chartists are fully aware that we have one eye upon them & of late, have and openly but not so numerously as formerly, they more generously collect in sections of from 12 to 20 in private houses & how, or in what manner they communicate with each other from their close meetings we have not been able to make out.[538]

In response to fears over the safety of the people and property within the town, on 23 August 1839 Russell sent in reporters to monitor the situation. At the same time, alarmed magistrates communicated with a member of the local Chartist society in an attempt to gather information about what was being plotted behind closed doors.[539] The episode was one of Russell's last acts as the Home Secretary. At the end of August 1839, he left the Home Office to become Colonial Secretary.

In summary, Lord John Russell used his diplomatic skills to extract the most in terms of the limitations of the public order apparatus when containing Chartist unrest. The next chapter will examine how his successor, the Marquis of the Normanby achieved the opposite, and presided over the rapid deterioration of relations between central and local agencies. This had long-term implications for the development of the state and the machinery of public order as a whole and its capacity to control the outbreak of violence.

4. MARQUIS OF NORMANBY: DISTURBANCE, DIVISION AND STAGNATION, 1839-41

In September 1839, the Marquis of Normanby, who had previously served as Colonial Minister, changed places with Lord John Russell to become Home Secretary as part of a Cabinet reshuffle instigated by Lord Melbourne. Very little has been written about Normanby's tenure at the Home Office. On being appointed as Home Secretary, he was described as a 'middle-aged dandy of little talent' and ridiculed as a 'statesman of acknowledged incompetency'.[540] His handling of Chartist agitation in the two years that he served as Home Secretary confirmed the latter assertion.

Normanby's appointment at the Home Office was unexpected. In searching for plausible reasons as to why he was handed the role of Home Secretary by Melbourne, evidence would suggest that he had a clear agenda to suppress Chartist agitation at any cost. This was reflected by his previous experience in such matters. During the early 1830s, when he served as the Captain-General and Governor of Jamaica, the Marquis quashed a rebellion against British rule in the colony. Further to his experience in the suppression of civil unrest, Normanby also had strong social skills and an ability to charm people, which endeared him to many, including Melbourne.[541] However, despite these attributes, in his previous roles within government Normanby was associated with a pattern of failure. This was evident during his stewardship as the Lord Lieutenant of Ireland and at the Colonial Office. This continued in the realm of home affairs. The Secretary of State presided over the deterioration of relations between central government and local public order agencies. His weak leadership and heavy-handed responses to Chartist unrest did little to suppress the radical movement, nor advance the development of the British state. As a result of Normanby's stagnant approach the operation of the machinery of public order and centre-local relations was almost plunged into a dangerous situation caused by division and neglect.

The weak stewardship shown by the Marquis of Normanby at the Home Office in the suppression of Chartism was reflected in his response to mass political gatherings. Whereas Russell commanded respect and exhibited a certain degree of authority in his handling of magistrates, his successor was feeble and allowed them to do as they pleased. An example of this occurred as early as September 1839, when a fairly peaceful 'silent meeting' in Sheffield turned violent. For two nights there was a disturbance in which 'a pistol was fired' and several windows were 'broken with stones'.[542] This incident highlighted the dangers in using the Dragoons to police crowds. On this particular occasion, they fought with Chartists who clearly responded to their violent provocation. The episode also started a train of events that culminated in an attempted uprising a few months later.

Before the incident took place, local magistrates displayed placards and urged people not to attend Chartist meetings. They warned that fierce measures would be taken to disperse the crowds. This heavy-handed approach was highlighted by the use of armed soldiers who were strategically placed at the Town Hall, whilst a 'whole force of policemen' and watchmen were 'mustered'.[543] The magistrates also enlisted the support of Colonel Marten and the Dragoons who appeared at the Town Hall during the evening, by which time around 2,000 people had gathered at the Town Square that was placed into total darkness as all the gas lamps were put out.[544]

Trouble began when the cavalry tried to clear the public square and from that moment onwards chaos ensued. The police chased crowds along avenues that branched off from the open area. Many Chartists took shelter in a neighbouring churchyard, where they let off 'tremendous vollies of stones'.[545] A pitched battle ensued which brought the town into a state of siege. Further skirmishes took place at the Doctor's Field near the Lead Mills, where troops and watchmen were assailed by a further 'volley of stones' thrown by a number of 'scoundrels' who had hidden in various passages and corners.[546] The military and the police managed to restore calm after the main battles had petered out.[547] The entire incident demonstrated that no lessons had been learnt from the way in which the Bull Ring disturbances had been handled by the Metropolitan Police. It also highlighted that when magistrates did not receive adequate guidance and instructions from the Home Office they were prone to adopt measures that were too aggressive. This was denoted by the overt use of the military as a measure of repression, which did more to incite than allay crowd trouble.

A few weeks into Normanby's reign as Home Secretary, the severe course of action was evident when magistrates tried to put an end to secret gatherings that had been frequently organised by Chartists. Following the incident at the Doctor's Field in Sheffield, local radicals were denied access to a Parish Church on 30 September 1839, where they had previously held clandestine meetings. The main entrances to the building were guarded by 'eight or nine policemen armed with cutlasses', who were ordered not to let anybody inside except legitimate church visitors. As the Chartists were prevented from entering the building, Dragoons were placed on standby, in case there was a riot. After a while, the radicals just waited outside and sang two hymns before quietly marching home.[548]

Following the attempted suppression of Chartist political gatherings, the Home Office attacked its main leadership in an effort to destabilise the movement at the top. The principal target was Feargus O'Connor who was arrested for 'conspiracy', 'unlawful assembly' and making 'seditious speeches'.[549] He was charged at Leeds Police Station on 20 September 1839 after the Manchester Borough Police had previously issued a warrant for his capture.[550] The apprehension and detention of the charismatic Chartist leader sparked fears amongst magistrates that there would be a violent backlash in many places across the West Riding.

Bradford was particularly vulnerable to attack from insurgents because it had minimal public-order apparatus in place. F.C. Mather made an observation that the magistracy was inefficient because there were not enough representatives in place to serve the parishes and boroughs.[551] On 10 October 1839, the Home Secretary received a request from Justices of the Peace who wanted a 'resident magistrate' to preserve the safety of the town, even though 'one or more' of them attended the court house on a daily basis.[552] In response to their request, on 16 October 1839 Normanby wrote to the Lord Lieutenant of the West Riding and told him that:

> I do not doubt that there is a sufficient attendance of magistrates daily in Bradford, but I am informed that there is no magistrate resident in the Town or nearer to it than about a mile. In a place of so much mercantile importance and where so large a population exists, this seems to be imprudent.[553]

Normanby urged Harewood to take the necessary steps to find a 'fit and proper person' who would be willing to take residence in the town to conduct those duties.[554] On 8 November 1839, the Lord Lieutenant wrote to the Bradford Justice of the Peace Matthew Thompson and told him that he had recommended someone for the role to the Lord Chancellor.[555] Later that month, a magistrate was appointed and following this development, the security of towns across the West Riding became paramount as

Chartist unrest intensified. This surge of activity was directly influenced by momentous events at Newport in South Wales.

The events in Newport on 4 November 1839 began when several thousand men from the Welsh mining and iron working valleys marched on the town and tried to take control of it.[556] The rebellion was led by John Frost, who was a linen draper and member of the National Convention. An armed battle took place between the Chartists and the military which opened fire at protesters from the windows of the Westgate Hotel.[557] This led to the loss of twenty-two lives and, more importantly, revealed the strength of the military and the state. Edward Vallance has argued that the attempted uprising was 'botched' as poor weather conditions hampered the marchers. On reaching Newport after daybreak, they were too visible for the authorities who picked them off at will, which led to a 'bloodbath'.[558] Vallance argues that this episode speeded up the judicial campaign waged by government against the Chartists', while John Walton believes the failed uprising 'provided dispiriting confirmation of the impossibility of taking on the army in an isolated campaign'.[559] One thing is certain: it 'exposed a myth' that the military would not open fire on its subjects 'under any circumstances'.[560]

When this episode occurred, the Home Office felt that the Chartist movement had 'assumed a more threatening character'.[561] Peter Bussey and Dr John Taylor were convinced that the Charter could not be obtained without resorting to violence. It became evident that these leaders wanted to destroy the government and set up their own administration. Their goal was a National Convention that would be elected by the population with responsibility for managing the affairs of the nation. The scheme was 'visionary' but many people in the West Riding who were swayed by this rhetoric believed in its viability; it proved to be too ambitious, as events later showed.[562]

In the aftermath of the Newport Rising, the Home Office and local public order agencies faced a wave of defiance from Chartists across the West Riding. The twenty-two men who were shot and killed by the army became martyrs and the fate of John Frost and other protesters seized by the state hung like a shadow over the Whig government. By explaining the link between the attempted uprising at Newport and later incidents that occurred in the West Riding in more detail, David Jones has argued that the events in South Wales were part of a wider plot to create a 'Chartist republic' and generate an insurrection at a national level throughout Christmas 1839.[563] The elaborate plan involved causing a number of simultaneous uprisings in Nottingham, Birmingham, Carlisle, East London, Trowbridge and the West Riding.[564] However, the scheme failed when the Welsh Chartists had 'jumped the gun'.[565] According to Jones, what followed afterwards were a number of 'belated expressions of solidarity'.[566] This later included the Chartists in the West Riding, prompting similar turbulence but on a far lesser scale.

The Chartist backlash against the Home Office which followed the failure of the attempted uprising at Newport began at Leeds in December 1839, when the Earl of Harewood wrote to the Home Secretary and warned him that he had received information from magistrates about the continuation of 'secret proceedings'.[567] Normanby was told that the activities of Chartist agitators were being conducted in a way that 'eluded the watchfulness of the authorities'.[568]

The Home Secretary's previous attempt to silence the main leadership of the Chartist movement proved ineffective as Feargus O'Connor continued to speak out against the government at will, and sustained a demand for electoral reform. On 19 December 1839, the Chartist leader addressed electors at Bradford near the Odd Fellows Hall. As O'Connor made his way from the Sun Inn, he was accompanied by, the report concluded, 'a promiscuous crowd of unemployed operatives' who escorted him to a piece of vacant ground opposite the hall.[569] From there, he spoke and called upon those in possession of the franchise to hold up their hands – only nine were raised. He turned to those who lifted their hands and said that he was very 'pleased to see such hands as them as they were better than a white hand with a kid glove on'.[570] In his main speech, O'Connor blamed economic distress on 'Whig misrule' and also asserted that the Cabinet was divided over the issue of John Frost's trial. The Chartist leader suggested that 'Lords Russell and Normanby wanted a conviction but Lord Melbourne did not'.[571]

The misery that Feargus O'Connor alluded to in his sermon was an indirect cause of political tension within the West Riding. The region was affected by an economic depression. This was caused by a monetary crisis in the United States that severely impacted upon local trade. One third of woollen goods produced in the county were exported to the American markets and the impact of a downturn in trade was felt in all major towns which specialised in those particular industries. In Sheffield the 'sufferings of the working classes' reached the 'summit of endurance' as 'tens of thousands of well, able hands' were denied the chance to earn a living.[572] In Halifax, the sale of fewer woollen goods meant that prices became lower and local businesses were hit by a sharp downturn in profits. This worsening situation forced manufacturers to cut back on production, which shortened the working hours of spinners and forced them to take on smaller labour contracts than ever.[573]

Deteriorating economic conditions coincided with an increase in the number of secret Chartist meetings. The defiant stance of its main leadership prompted the authorities to put in place preventative measures, in case there was a serious outbreak of violence. The Marquis of Normanby's weak leadership at the Home Office was illustrated by his decision to allow Sir Charles Napier to dictate military tactics and make his own arrangements across the West Riding. A stronger and more effective Home Secretary would have reined in Napier, yet he was allowed to continue to establish his own system of *surveillance militaire* in which he outlined:

> My men should be in three masses, one around Manchester to watch the manufacturers; one around Newcastle-on-Tyne to watch the colliers; one around Leeds and Hull to watch the other two: but such an arrangement cannot be effected in time; it would take a month ere the Secretary of State would understand it, and then he would have a host of magistrates on his back![574]

On 29 December 1839, Napier told troops serving in the Northern District about 'a widely circulated report' that he had received.[575] This warned him that the Chartists were about to organise 'a general outbreak' as a show of support for John Frost who was 'under trial for high treason'.[576] Taking the threat seriously, various commanders of regiments and detachments of the entire Northern District Army were placed on alert. The order which Napier sent to commanders across the district read as follows:

> That such a general rising should take place, the Major-General deems to be so wild a scheme that he does not place much belief in the truth if the report; but should so great a misfortune to the country take place, he has the fullest reliance upon the troops which he has the honour to command, and that they will display the same steady courage and humanity that was exhibited by the detachment of the 40th Regiment in the lamentable riot at Newport, when honourably supporting the integrity of the Civil Authorities, the Laws of the land, and the honour of Her Majesty's crown.[577]

The threat of a serious outbreak of violence amongst the Chartists in the West Riding was echoed to a lesser extent by its main leadership on 10 January 1840, after the dissolution of the National Convention, which had been held at the Arundel Coffee House, Strand. Delegates from Nottingham, Bradford, Hull, Newcastle, Bolton, Birmingham, Bristol and Scotland had attended over a period of three months to discuss tactics for obtaining the Charter. The leadership had plotted a course of action that they hoped would defeat the government and put in place the 'Six Points'.[578] The trials of those captured at Newport were discussed at great length and delegates adopted the following resolution:

> Seeing that the exertions of the working classes to form a General Convention, representing the whole country, are for the present marred by the contrances of the open persecutors of our cause, and their allies, the false friends of the people, together with the apathy of some portion of the people themselves, we feel it our duty to dissolve; and, returning to our respective constituencies, exert ourselves to the utmost or our power in counteracting the above mischievous influences.

A memorial to the Queen was later read and passed. When it went to a vote which outlined 'the distresses of the labouring population', this document was sent to the Home Office.[579] The day after the announcement was made, serious rioting broke out in the West Riding.

Throughout January 1840, a series of attempted uprisings occurred across the West Riding, affecting the towns of Dewsbury, Sheffield and Bradford. The incidents clearly demonstrated the strengths and weaknesses of the machinery of public order in the region. Whilst military intervention was quite effective in the suppression of those incidents, by contrast the magistracy and the police were relatively weak in the discharge of their duties.

In the build-up to this watershed episode, on 1 January 1840, the clerk to the Dewsbury magistrates wrote a letter to the Home Secretary and warned him that 'considerable harm' was being caused in the town due to 'the arming of the lower classes'.[580] A wave of political gatherings had been held on 'a nightly basis' for the 'purpose of organisation and offensive operations'.[581] The Clerk of the Peace told the Marquis of Normanby that magistrates could do nothing to suppress the meetings, because they could get 'no legal information' to 'justify their interference' in the affairs of the local Chartists.[582] As no crimes or breaches of the peace had been committed, the insurgents could not be arrested.[583]

The worsening fears over the safety of the town prompted magistrates to demand 'military assistance without delay' from the Home Secretary and Sir Charles Napier.[584] They also requested the Home Secretary and the military to build 'temporary barracks' to house a 'sufficient force' that would secure the town from Chartist unrest.[585] The magistrates sent a letter which contained statements taken from 'two respectable individuals' – Police Constables Thomas Oldroyd and Henry Cullingworth. They claimed that 'secret meetings' had taken place between the 'Chartists and delegates from several towns in the kingdom' at the Wellington Tavern in Dewsbury.[586] Those gatherings were held behind a guarded door to prevent intrusion, which suggested that intrigue was involved.[587]

The request made by the clerk to the magistrates at Dewsbury for military assistance was dismissed by Normanby who did not think that an outbreak of violence would occur in the town. As the person who was ultimately responsible for the placement of troops to deal with riots and disturbances, Normanby felt any civil unrest would take place at Leeds or Halifax where the troops were stationed.[588] His refusal to act upon the warnings given to him by the Dewsbury magistrates coupled with the weak nature of the machinery of public order that was in place, provided an opportunity which the Chartists exploited. On 11 January 1840 a crowd marched into the town and occupied it for a number of hours without any resistance. At two a.m., the Deputy Constable of Dewsbury, John Hirst, saw a number of people together on the Bradford New Road. The officer then heard firearms being discharged from the direction of Wakefield Road. When both he and his colleagues attended the scene, they saw a crowd of 'around a hundred people' that was 'four deep' assembled before them.[589] The Chartist Joseph Page, who was at the very front of this group, told the band of protesters 'March, Death or Glory – The Town's our own'. The insurgents headed to the town centre and discharged their firearms.[590]

The police provisions in the town of Dewsbury were so weak that magistrates had to call out the 7th Dragoon Guards. When they arrived from Leeds, there were violent clashes between soldiers and Chartists. Although 'considerable alarm' had been caused to the town and its inhabitants, very little damage was done to property.[591] The Lord Lieutenant told the Home Secretary that only 'two or three squares of glass and a few gas lamps had been broken'.[592] In the aftermath of the major skirmishes, local magistrates feared a further outbreak of violence and sent for an additional troop of Dragoon Guards. When the regiments arrived, the situation had calmed down considerably and peace was restored.[593]

From the evidence, it can be safely asserted that the incident in Dewsbury was not a revolutionary act because if it had been, the insurgents would have attempted to take control of strategic outposts such as the Court House and the Army Barracks to secure their grip of the town. The episode bore all the hallmarks of symbolic protest which was inter-connected with the earlier attempted uprising at Newport, along with the outcome of the trial of John Frost. This would explain why the insurgents marched into town and discharged their weapons as a show of defiance against the authorities, and stayed there until they were moved along.

On the same night that the Dewsbury disturbance took place, there was a contrasting episode in Sheffield, where tensions had been running high since September 1839. Whereas the incident in Dewsbury can be seen as a largely spontaneous and symbolic response to the trial of John Frost, the attempted uprising in Sheffield had been organised well in advance. The main ringleader was Samuel Holberry who had previously served in the army and wanted 'a general rise to gain the Charter'.[594] He organised the local Chartists along military lines into classes in which there were eight in total. Armed with pikes, grenades and a whole array of other weaponry, their aim was to capture the Town Hall and Tontine. Once the insurgents had achieved that goal, their intention was to set ablaze the town and its army barracks. This involved the assassination of any watchmen and policeman who dared to cross their path. The Sheffield Chartists were quite considerate about their aspirations: before the planned uprising they had all unanimously agreed not to set fire to any places of worship or stores that contained any provisions, and this may have aided their cause.[595]

The motives behind this attempted insurrection are not particularly clear.[596] Treasury Solicitor's papers written at the time, which contained various witness statements, suggested that the unrest had nothing to do with the liberation of John Frost but was, instead, an over-ambitious scheme to bring about the downfall of the government.[597] If this was the case, it had very little chance of success as the Chartists were no match for the military forces that were deployed across the Northern District. Further to this, during the run-up to this rebellion the local radicals had played directly into the hands of the authorities. They used watchmen and reporters to monitor nightly gatherings which frequently took place at the Fig Tree Lane meeting room. The intelligence that they had gathered over a period of time was crucial in the suppression of this attempted insurrection.[598]

The episode revealed two sides to the Sheffield Police as they tried to suppress the Chartists. First of all, the strength of this agency as a preventative detection force was clearly evident. Intelligence, which they had acquired by observing various political gatherings, ensured that they could suppress the planned uprising at birth through the arrest of Samuel Holberry. The intelligence that the police had gathered was so accurate that they knew exactly where to look for weaponry when they searched his house. A number of firearms and grenades were found inside his loft, which may have been used against the authorities had the Chartist ringleader not been seized. When he was arrested by the Sheffield Police, Holberry told one of the constables that his main intention was to take lives in the 'defence of liberty' and that his goal was to 'obtain the Charter'.[599]

Following the capture of Holberry, the attempted uprising became a rudderless plot. Normanby was very concerned about the disposition of 'hordes of armed men' who wanted to attack Sheffield, despite the number of them being 'very inconsiderable'.[600] The clashes that followed between watchmen and insurgents revealed another side to Sheffield Police, showing the force to be relatively weak when it came to the suppression of riot and tumult. Many watchmen armed with little more than staves patrolled the vicinity in single file and were subjected to vicious assaults by angry mobs. A number of them sustained serious injuries, which highlighted that the police could not control armed mobs without the assistance of the military. For instance, following a clash with a number of insurgents, the watchmen Samuel Howe was 'fired upon' and received severe wounds from a sword that left him covered in blood. In the melée, his hat was almost cut to pieces and he received severe cuts to his head.[601] Shortly after this incident, another officer who was ambushed by a force of '20 to 35 men' had a lucky escape when a ball cartridge fired from a blunderbuss went clean through his helmet! With very little means of protection from assault, the deficiencies of the Sheffield Police were there to be seen as they tried to contain the rioting Chartists. Their defective organisation meant that Dragoons had to be called upon to restore order.[602] Normanby described the civil force in Sheffield as being 'not adequate' in dealing with the emergency situation. To boost its strength, Metropolitan Police were deployed with immediate effect.[603]

An additional weakness with the machinery of public order in Sheffield was demonstrated by the failure of local magistrates to secure the convictions of insurgents arrested for their involvement in the disturbances. This was despite the accumulation of pikes and various firearms by watchmen and Dragoons as evidence to secure convictions. The situation was succinctly summed up by the Lord Lieutenant in a letter written to the Home Secretary on 13 January in which he stated:

It is much to be regretted that in consequence of the inefficiency of the local authorities, none of the parties could be arrested at the time; and the magistrates have not yet been able to obtain sufficient evidence to justify the committal of any person implicated in the disturbances.[604]

The circumstances were not helped by the fact that some agitators had managed to evade capture by the authorities as they fled the town. A paucity of internal communications and the failure of borough and parish forces to share intelligence meant that many Chartists were effectively beyond arrest.

Despite these difficulties, the main ringleaders were tried for their involvement in the attempted uprising. On 15 January 1840, Samuel Holberry, his wife Mary Holberry, Thomas Booker, Samuel Foxhall, William Booker junior and Samuel Thompson were all charged with high treason at the Session Room, Sheffield Town Hall. A large table inside the room was filled with articles taken from prisoners and the houses of Chartists including hand grenades, two large balls and a large quantity of other combustible materials. There were also 'great numbers of large pikes, daggers, swords, spears, guns, pistols, "cats" and ball cartridges'.[605] One alarmed observer pointed out that the exhibits which were displayed, gave 'a fearful idea of the horrible nature and extent of the proceedings of the physical force Chartists'.[606]

On the same day that the Sheffield Chartists were charged, magistrates in Dewsbury informed Normanby that an insurgent called Joseph Page had been rearrested and committed to the House of Correction at Wakefield, where he was later charged with riot offences. The magistrates in Dewsbury proved to be just as weak as those in Sheffield, as the Home Secretary was notified that they too had failed to succeed in 'taking any others' who were caught up in the violence.[607] The Secretary of State was told by the local Justices of the Peace that they scarcely expected to arrest anybody else for the disturbances, primarily because they did not have the means to do so.[608] Normanby recommended that £100 should be paid by the Lords Commissioners of the Treasury for any information or evidence concerning those involved in rioting who had evaded capture by the authorities.[609] Similar rewards were also offered for the capture of Chartists involved in the Sheffield disturbances.[610]

A few weeks after major disorder in Dewsbury and Sheffield, the attention of the Home Office shifted to Bradford, where local and central authorities thwarted another attempted uprising. This plot involved the Scottish Chartist leader, Dr. John Taylor, who had sent his colleague Robert Peddie to Bradford to organise a scheme, with the aim of engulfing the entire West Riding in a state of rebellion.[611] Chartist cells in Bradford had forged links with similar factions in Halifax and Leeds. Taylor looked to their support for an overly ambitious and broader rebellion. This involved 'fifty thousand men' who would march on London and eventually take 'possession of the nation' after capturing a number of key towns.[612] However, Peddie and his associates were totally unaware that six months previously, the Bradford Police had paid James Harrison, an unemployed brickmaker, to infiltrate the local Chartist organisation and uncover their intentions, which he did so with a relative degree of success.[613] In fact, William Brigg, the Head Police Officer at Bradford, had spent £45 6s in trying to gather information about the 'plans and proceedings of the Chartists'.[614] This sum of money was later reimbursed by Normanby's office.

The plot that Harrison uncovered revolved around the Low Moor Iron Works and the home of 'Old Kit' Dawson who owned the industrial plant. Both were to be set ablaze as part of a decoy operation organised by the Chartists. Whilst people were tending to both fires, the insurgents intended to steal cannons from the works and then move them by horses and carts to the centre of Bradford, where they would be used to bombard the town. The carts were to be retained in order to move baggage and cannons from one town to another. After Bradford had been taken, the Chartists designed to capture Dewsbury and other places across the West Riding such as Barnsley.[615] Once those goals had been achieved, Robert Peddie told his fellow conspirators that he would 'have all the law in his own hands'.[616] The main ringleader later claimed that within the space of a few days, he would 'shew Yorkshire' and 'alter the opinion of tyrants'.[617] He also boasted about becoming the 'Full Commander' of the country.[618] Peddie's ambitions were thwarted by Harrison whose information about the plot enabled local magistrates to alert the Home Office, which sent a military force to Bradford. A trap was set into which the insurgents fell.

The attempted insurrection highlighted the weaknesses of the Bradford magistrates and police as vehicles of suppression. The military was heavily relied upon to keep the peace. On 26 January 1840 this incident began at two o'clock in the morning when the head of police and a band of special constables patrolling the area passed the Green Market and noticed a light shining from a shed. When the constables investigated the scene there was a scuffle. Two watchmen were taken prisoner and later guarded by two Chartists, armed with pikes. Those taken hostage had their rattles taken from them and it became clear that the insurgents intended to seize and disarm all the watchmen and police in a similar manner.[619] Throughout the night, magistrates were based at the Court House that was guarded by special constables. Whilst the regular army was deployed, infantry and cavalry troops patrolled the town and its surrounding areas in an effort to control the potential insurgency.[620]

When the revolt began, small groups of men armed with pikes, guns and pistols assembled at the Green Market. They were ambushed by the forces deployed at the scene and later dispersed by constables, who took sixteen people into custody, eight of whom were armed. Those captured were sent to York Castle, whilst the remainder were either sent home or discharged due to a lack of evidence. It was estimated that around 200 to 300 armed men were involved in the plot. This was easily suppressed by the military and civil forces. Ten pikes, several guns and pistols were seized by the authorities, along with a quantity of bullets, ball cartridges and bottles of gunpowder. A printed book that contained detailed instructions of how the Chartists could resist the cavalry was found in the possession of one of the captives, along with other inflammatory publications.[621] Robert Peddie was later caught and arrested at a public house in the Pottery Fields area of Leeds and placed in custody at York Castle.[622] Many others were also arrested for high treason and charged with rioting. However, some of those who were involved in the Bradford disturbances evaded capture, including George Flinn, a wool comber who fled to Kidderminster, and Isaac Holloway, a tailor, John Turner, a weaver and James Marsden, who managed to disappear. The government offered huge rewards for their apprehension.[623]

In the aftermath of the revolt, the civil authorities in Bradford adopted precautionary measures. A number of lessons were learnt from this incident, especially by the police. For instance, whereas previously watchmen had taken to the streets as 'solitary wanderers', they later carried out their patrols in companies of 'two and two'.[624] Each night, thirty special constables were called out and divided into six companies to tour the town and its suburbs. At the end of every hour, the specials were ordered to return to the Court House and report their progress to Chief Constables of the Metropolitan Police or their deputies, whilst army pensioners armed with large pistols were placed on duty at the Court House each day.[625] However, despite these minor changes to the way in which the civil forces went about their duties, there were still many questions left unanswered about the ineffective nature of the machinery of public order in the West Riding and its ability to suppress future Chartist unrest.

The failed uprisings and the need to secure the West Riding from further Chartist agitation prompted two parallel discussions. The first involved magistrates who could not decide amongst themselves whether or not to put in place a constabulary force across the region. This was based upon amended legislation that stemmed from the 1839 Rural Police Act. The second debate revolved around Sir Charles Napier, the Commander of the Northern District Army, who at the time believed that the military presence in the region should be strengthened. The general came up with a number of alternative proposals to rebuild and construct army barracks in order to accommodate an expansion in troop numbers. Both measures were costly to implement but more worrying was the lack of intervention in the separate debates by the Home Office, especially by the Marquis of Normanby, who offered very little guidance. More worryingly, Normanby allowed both the magistracy and military to pull in different directions. This neglect later had very serious repercussions, especially when a second wave of violent Chartist protest occurred during 1842.

The idea behind the creation of a constabulary force for the West Riding was first discussed at a meeting of county magistrates, at the Pontefract Quarter Sessions, in April 1840. This matter was debated for an entire year until April 1841. The discussions were chaired by Lord Wharncliffe who later became the Lord Lieutenant of the county. During that period, the cases both for and against the adoption of the proposed force were put forward. The scheme entailed giving magistrates the power to appoint a Chief Constable who would have the authority to appoint a force of police constables that would not exceed 'one in a thousand of the population', at the cost of £60,000.[626]

At the beginning, there was some agreement amongst magistrates, particularly those who served densely populated towns within the region that the system of parish constables was unsuitable. Lord Wharncliffe believed that it would be difficult to suppress further Chartist unrest 'without an increase in the police force'.[627] These views were shared by the Whig Justice of the Peace Francis Wood, who felt that the parochial system was beyond repair. The magistrate likened it to an old steam engine that 'could not be mended' and was in need of replacement by 'a new one' made 'by Boulton and Watt', which at the time was state of the art technology.[628] However, despite there being some support for the measures from magistrates in the larger towns, a number of dissenting voices objected to the proposed force. For instance, the Justices of the Peace who represented Sheffield wanted the town to be excluded from the scheme on the basis that it already had an organised police force. The Tory politician John Stuart-Wortley, who spoke on behalf of town's Police Commissioners, argued that its 'body of 110 Gentlemen' elected by its citizens was 'rated at not less than £7' and sufficient to maintain order.[629]

The issue of cost and its effect on the county rate proved to be the main stumbling block to the proposed constabulary force. This problem dictated whether the measure would succeed or fail. Randall Gossip, who presented petitions from Wighill and Heslaugh, argued that under the proposals the rate in those areas would double to support one constable for every 2,000 persons. He suggested that because they were thinly populated places, the scale of the measure meant that there would only be 'three constables for seventeen townships' and such a force would be 'totally inefficient'.[630] He then questioned whether ratepayers would be happy to 'contribute twice or thrice' for rates, in order to pay for the cost of three constables.[631] The arguments both for and against the proposed constabulary force led Edwin Lascelles to assert that the magistrates did not have enough information at their disposal to make a snap decision about the measures. He felt that there was a huge raft of measures which needed broader consideration. These included the number of constables that were needed, their salaries, the choice of chief constables and, more importantly, the cost of the force in real terms. When the sessions ended, Lord Wharncliffe agreed with the concerns that were raised and decided to put off the adoption of a constabulary force until the next sessions, which were held at Wakefield on 22 September 1840.[632]

Throughout the intervening months, doubts emerged over the constitutional and potential long-term effects of the proposals. At the forefront of this debate was Richard Oastler whose opinions on the matter generated a wave of opposition. The leader of the Factory Reform movement was highly suspicious of the plans that were afoot. He argued that the discussion was over whether 'the principles of the English Constitution', which included 'local government and jurisdiction', were 'sound or not'.[633] Oastler said that at stake was the 'existence or non-existence' of 'an unpaid magistracy', along with the fate of the 'old parish constables'.[634] He questioned, whether the 'power' of local taxes and expenses should rest with the 'sessions and vestries' or be 'transferred to the 'Queen's Council'.[635] He said that the people of the West Riding had the choice to retain 'the old English system of local government' or the opportunity to replace it with 'a new French system of centralisation'.[636] This was a major issue in the national debate over policing generally during the nineteenth century. Oastler believed that the long-term effects of the measure would be the formation of a centralised police force. Thus control would be gradually transferred from the local magistrates to the Home Office.[637]

Richard Oastler's opinions on the idea of police reform for the West Riding acted as a catalyst for a number of anti-Rural Police meetings and demonstrations. These were held across the region during the run-up to the Quarter Sessions in September 1840. In Huddersfield and Bradford, opposition to the police proposals cut across class divides. Tradesmen and shopkeepers attached themselves to the working classes. They voiced their disapproval of the proposed force because it was 'unconstitutional in principle'.[638] Bound up with this view was the burning issue of cost. Opponents continued to argue that the measure would place 'a heavy expense upon the ratepayers'.[639] For instance, if the proposals were adopted in Bradford, it was argued that ratepayers would be charged in the region of 'three thousand pounds a year'.[640] This equated to 'nearly ten times' the cost of the force that was already in existence within the town.[641]

At the Quarter Sessions, held at Wakefield in September 1840, magistrates raised further questions about the unconstitutional nature of the measure. For instance, Tory magistrates feared that the proposals would 'rip up ancient and domestic' institutions in the parishes.[642] They were seen as a direct assault on their powers, particularly over the ability to appoint constables through the Courts Leet system, the power to read the Riot Act and certain police functions that were bestowed upon them, such as the right to call out the military when needed.[643] Even though local magistrates had much to gain by adopting this measure, it was clear that they also had much to lose politically if it succeeded.

Those divisions were also worsened by changes that had been made to the laws concerning the creation of constabulary forces since the Pontefract sessions. Whereas previously county magistrates could not divide the region so that a police force could be applied in some urban but not rural places, a House of Commons Bill ended this anomaly. This measure made it possible for the creation of districts that were most in need of police provisions.[644] However, magistrates could not decide amongst themselves whether a force should be created in the agricultural or manufacturing areas, or across the entire region. Whilst Whig magistrates wanted to safeguard towns from the threat of further Chartist agitation, their Tory counterparts felt that due to the size of villages and hamlets they presided over, a police force was not necessary.[645]

Another issue that was raised at the sessions concerned the composition of the proposed force. Some magistrates feared that adoption of the proposals would create 'a standing army of police armed with bludgeons and cutlasses'.[646] They were also worried about the prospect that the new officers would have more powers than ever before. Those anxieties were alleviated by Lord Wharncliffe who suggested that the force would be made up of the best parts of the Metropolitan and Sheffield models of policing. For instance, Wharncliffe admired the way in which the Sheffield police force was managed and how its handling of angry mobs during the Chartist disturbances was coordinated by a 'Head of Police' who was always 'on the spot'.[647] He felt that if the measures were adopted, a head officer, accountable to a superior officer, would be appointed to act as a 'Superintendent of the

West Riding'.[648] Wharncliffe also advocated the creation of a daytime police force that had proved popular in London. He felt that this measure would reduce criminal activity. After much deliberation amongst the magistrates over the various issues raised in this discussion, there was an agreement that the police force should be put into operation on a trial basis. This involved the creation of a police district that encompassed the densely populated towns of Dewsbury, Huddersfield, Halifax, Bradford and Batley.[649] The Justices of the Peace also agreed to form a committee to look into the viability of the proposals put forward at the meeting.

At the Quarter Sessions held in December 1840 and February 1841, the discussions centred upon the boundaries of the proposed constabulary force and whether the legislation should be 'extended throughout the whole Riding' with 'each district' subsidising its own expenses.[650] Doubts were raised by some magistrates over the legality of the February proceedings. Out of 220 magistrates, only forty-eight had attended, yet at this meeting a committee was appointed to examine the merits of a constabulary force. What followed was an 'animated discussion' about the cost of the proposed scheme which resurfaced as a major area of contention.[651] For instance, magistrates such as Colonel Tempest examined how the police reforms affected neighbouring counties, in particularly Lancashire, where its magistrates regretted the hasty adoption of the measures. Tempest discovered that the cost of putting the force into operation in the region was much more than the magistrates had initially anticipated. The magistrates in Lancashire had received fifty-five petitions calling for its 'total abolition'.[652] Some wanted a reduction in the size of the force because the cost of its implementation had doubled the county rate.[653] From this evidence, it was suggested that in the West Riding 'some districts would pay less and others probably more' for a county force.[654] Critics of the scheme such as Tempest argued that the key issue was whether to give magistrates the power to tax 'ratepayers of the whole Riding' in order to pay for the force.[655] Despite these serious concerns, a vote was taken to consider whether the region's policing provisions were 'sufficient for the preservation of peace' and the 'protection of inhabitants, as well as the security of property' in which twenty-eight of the forty-eight people present said that they were not adequate.[656] The main driving force behind the discussions was the fear of disorder and how it could be averted. The Chartist disturbances proved that the parish system could not cope under such pressure. Yet despite wanting reform, the issue of cost, as ever, remained a highly contentious issue; it would later prove to be a massive stumbling block.[657]

In April 1841, the county magistrates gathered at the Quarter Sessions to discuss the findings of the committee appointed to examine the viability of putting in place a constabulary force across the county. With 181 magistrates at the meeting, this was the largest attended gathering on the matter.[658] When the committee produced its findings, it recommended the appointment of 475 constables to police the entire West Riding. They also suggested that a Chief Constable should be paid £500 a year to oversee the entire operation of the force.[659] Other recommendations included the appointment of an assistant Chief Constable who was to be paid £100 a year, the payment of Inspectors on a wage of four shillings a day, Sergeants, three shillings a day, and the division of constables into three classes who would be paid between sixteen to eighteen shillings per week for their duties.[660] When put to a vote, magistrates voted fifty-one to thirty-eight to reject the report and its findings.[661] There was an additional blow to the adoption of this measure when Justices of the Peace rejected the committee's recommendation that a certain number of constables should be appointed to work in the agricultural districts.[662]

These major setbacks had severe implications. Whilst there was unanimous agreement amongst magistrates that the system of parish constables was inadequate, at the same time a number of them presented signed petitions that bemoaned the cost of the new scheme. As an alternative measure, there was a feeling amongst some of those present that the 'existing force' could be 'gradually absorbed' under the new regulations. The dissenting magistrates believed that this would be a much more cost-effective compared to the way in which the forces had been expensively introduced in Lancashire.[663] For instance, J.A. Rhodes argued that the parish system could be improved by paying constables better wages and offering incentives for their 'preventative efforts'.[664] It was under this huge weight of opposition that Lord Wharncliffe decided to postpone the introduction of the proposed force. This decision was clearly swayed by the effects of its implementation in Lancashire.[665] The issue was later put to a vote and magistrates voted 45 to 40 against the introduction of a constabulary force for the entire West Riding.[666]

Whilst animated discussions took place over the introduction of a constabulary force in the West Riding, at the same time there was a debate over whether the military presence should be stepped up in order to secure the region from further Chartist rebellions. In May 1840, Napier commissioned a report which looked into the state of barracks across the Northern District (See Map 2). The troop stations based within the boundaries of the West Riding were by and large, in a state of neglect and disrepair. His report said that the small barracks within growing new towns were inadequate for the containment of unrest. They were also unfit for the military to use in order to train the soldiers in confrontational situations. Napier wanted new buildings placed near recently constructed railway stations so that troops could be rapidly moved from place to place. He also wanted the barracks to be situated on the periphery of towns to ensure that the military presence had a sufficiently low profile.[667]

Map 2: The location of army barracks in the Northern District, 1840

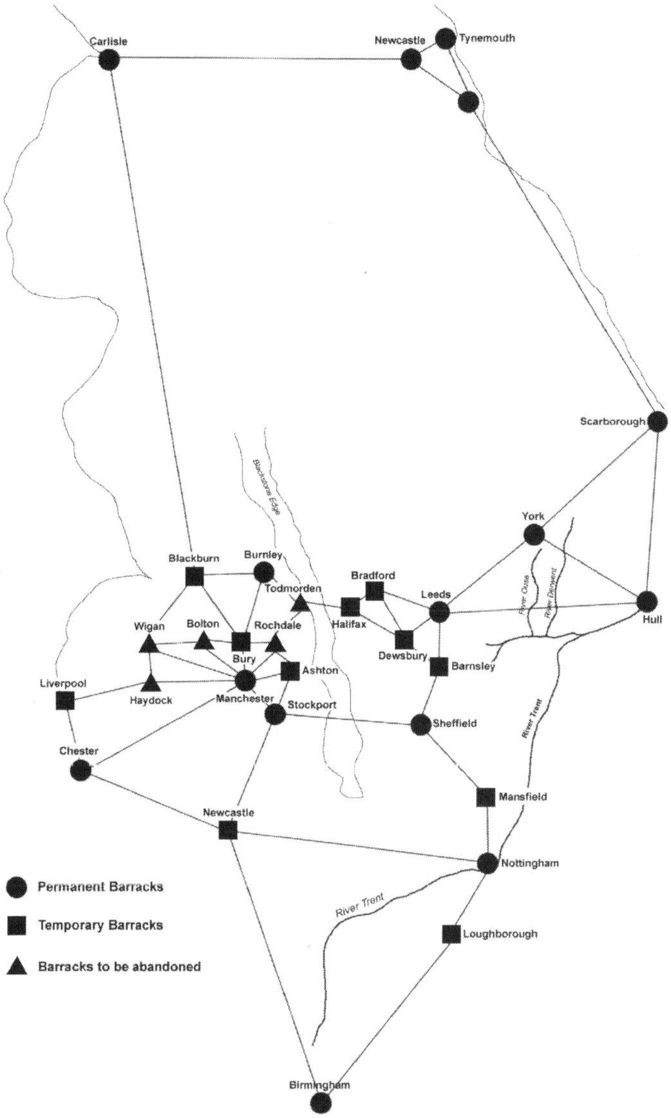

Map taken from HO 50/451, Sir Charles James Napier's Report into the state of the Northern District Barracks, 23 May 1840

The West Riding contained barracks that were situated at Brighouse, Leeds, Sheffield, Halifax, Barnsley and Bradford (See Map 3). During the build-up to the disturbances of January 1840, Napier had been involved in a running battle with Justices of the Peace over the issue of poor troop accommodation. As a result, the Commander of the Northern District Army elected to take matters into his own hands. The report that he compiled was later presented to the Home Office. However, this was not fully acted upon due to the problematic relations between central and local agencies and the cost of this vast scheme.

Map 3: The location of army barracks in the West Riding, 1840

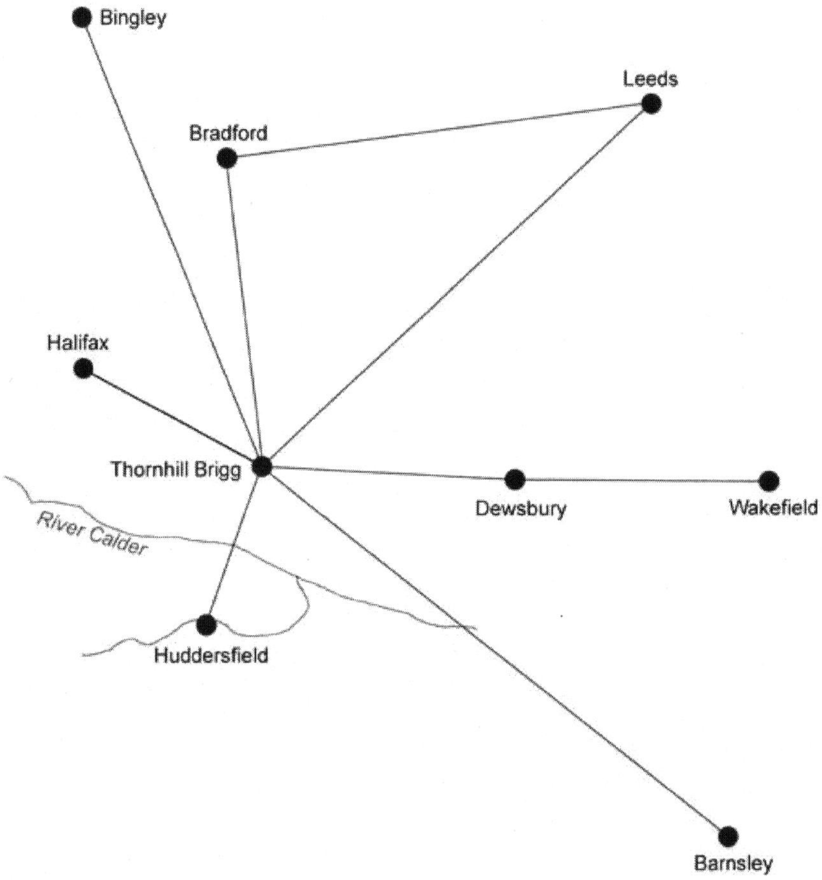

Map taken from HO 50/451, Sir Charles James Napier's Report into the state of the Northern District Barracks, 23 May 1840, p. 4.

In an effort to secure the region from further revolts and guarantee the safety of troops, Napier came up with a number of fresh recommendations. First of all, he wanted barracks built at Thorn Hill Brigg near Brighouse that would house a battalion of 800 men. With the exception of two companies that were based at a temporary barracks in Halifax, the entire West Riding did not have an infantry force. Secondly, Napier wanted the cavalry to be supported by a strong infantry. The motive behind this tactical arrangement lay in the harsh terrain:

> On the Yorkshire side, the Forces so occupied are chiefly among the roots of the hills before they blend into the Yorkshire plains. They are built on the mountain streams, and most of their streets are narrow and steep. To protect these towns with Cavalry…very well against ordinary rioters, but now the nature of disturbance is changed, and Cavalry becomes less sustainable. The Chartists have openly expressed their belief in the inefficiency of Cavalry among the narrow streets. It is, therefore to be apprehended that unless the Cavalry be supported by Infantry, the Chartists of these towns may be tempted to try their strength.[668]

Napier's main aim was to secure those towns that were affected by serious Chartist disturbances during January 1840. For instance, Sheffield was seen as a central location within the Northern District that was used as a key outpost for the security of the West Riding as whole (See Map 4).

Sheffield being a 'large and rich' urban centre, had 'a dense population of about 70,000 inhabitants' and was connected by road to Manchester, Leeds and Nottingham. It also had roads which fed from the town to the hills of Cheshire and Derbyshire. Napier saw Sheffield as being a major communications hub for the military from which information and intelligence could be channelled between its surrounding areas and troops moved rapidly by rail:

> Sheffield is also placed upon the line of the North Midland railway which passes through Rotherham, a distance of only 6 miles, and to which… from Sheffield, a railroad is now open. Sheffield is also the point where the mail coach road from the North / through Leeds / is carried by the transverse mail coach roads and railroad which run from Liverpool and Manchester eastwards. It is also but 18 miles from Doncaster through which the other great Northern mail coach road from York passes, and is, in like manner, cut by the transverse road from Manchester & Liverpool which road there ends, thus Sheffield may be said to command the great

mail coach and railways communications of the centre of England, towards the north, south, east, and west.[669]

Map 4: The location of Sheffield in relation to the Northern District military zone, 1840

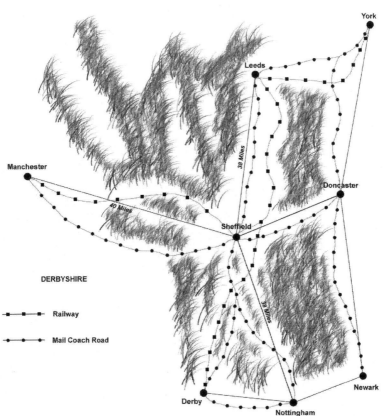

Map taken from HO 50/451. Sir Charles James Napier's Report into the state of the Northern District Barracks, 23 May 1840, p. 14

The main drawback that the army faced in using Sheffield as a base for its operations in the suppression of the Chartist movement was the neglected state of its cavalry barracks. They were 'very old' and in need of reconstruction. The hospital wing was 'bad, inadequate, ill-arranged and cold'.[670] With the barracks being situated on the 'back of the river' and constructed from 'only nine-inch brick work', they were prone to damp.[671] Napier's intention was to add an 'officer's quarters' plus a new hospital wing to the building.[672] He also wanted the barracks to 'be prepared for the headquarters of a cavalry regiment' and an infantry depot.[673]

In relation to Bradford, Napier wanted to build a new troop station. A temporary garrison had been erected in 1839 which housed sixty men and forty horses but this was insufficient. Napier wanted a 'considerable' infantry force in place to keep the peace amongst its 'great and discontented' inhabitants.[674] The estimated cost of building a permanent barrack for three companies of foot soldiers and a horse troop was put at £17,000. Napier wanted to purchase the temporary barracks and the land on which it stood, for a fee of around £2,000. This scheme attracted much support from local magistrates who were willing to pay the government £500 to put in place barracks that would accommodate the cavalry. In 1841, the construction of new premises began, although this proved to be a problematic exercise as it again revealed flaws in relations between central government and local agencies which immeasurably slowed the pace of building work.

Clearly under the Whigs' stewardship at the Home Office, and its suppression of Chartist unrest in the West Riding, the British state and the machinery of public order did not progress. This was despite an attempt made by Lord John Russell to reform civil arrangements through the introduction of the Rural Police. The main hurdle that both Whig Home Secretaries had to overcome was the problem of poor internal communications. This meant that the deployment of police and troops, along with the processing of information between the centre and localities, remained slow. Furthermore, the two-tiered system of governance stayed intact as local agencies remained resolute in the face of encroachment by the centre in which they did their utmost to preserve their identity, customs and finances.

The gulf in relations between central government and the magistracy meant that in order to maximise the limitations of the machinery of public order when dealing with Chartist unrest, strong leadership and a skill for diplomacy was needed at the Home Office. In this respect the two Home Secretaries contrasted in style. Lord John Russell cultivated good relationships with local agencies and showed a firm and authoritative stance in his dealings with magistrates and military leaders. This played a major role in ensuring that dangerous episodes such as the 'Sacred Month' passed off peacefully. By contrast, the Marquis of Normanby proved to be a weak and dilatory Home Secretary. His lack of leadership skills and guidance allowed both the magistracy and military to dictate their own terms and eventually pull in different directions. This ineffectiveness was highlighted by their diverse responses to preventing further Chartist unrest following the 1840 disturbances.

From a very early stage, Russell realised that the civil and auxiliary forces in the West Riding were relatively weak. It forced him to turn to militaristic measures in order to secure the region from Chartist unrest as arming and drilling took place on an unprecedented scale. Whereas Russell fully understood the limits to which military force could be applied to the suppression of the movement and its activities, his successor failed to acknowledge this detail. Under Normanby's stewardship, the military got carried away with its own authority. The use of excessive force at Newport did more harm than good as tensions became inflamed rather than suppressed. In turn, they spread directly to the West Riding where a wave of symbolic disturbances and minor insurrection attempts took place that could so easily have been averted.

In addition, the role of magistrates was a major cause of Chartist turbulence. They did their very best to take advantage of the lack of direct control that the Home Office could exert over their activities, and abuses were commonplace. Whereas Russell showed firm leadership and created boundaries within which they could operate, his successor was feeble and exerted very little control and guidance over their actions. The disturbances that took place at Sheffield in September 1839, when magistrates used heavy-handed tactics to violently suppress Chartist meetings, tested the resolve of the Home Office. Those incidents became the prelude to a more concerted plot that was later organised by Samuel Holberry. This could so easily have been avoided if stronger leadership had been shown by Normanby and those magistrates had been reined in.

The Chartist plots organised in January 1840 demonstrated that police forces were ill-equipped to deal with civil disobedience and disturbances which later impacted on the role of the West Riding magistracy. Russell was quick to grasp that the failings of the system of parish constables, along with those of the Metropolitan Police as a riot squad, required the need for an overhaul of provincial policing via the introduction of a rural constabulary. As well as being an attempt at securing the Industrial North from Chartist agitation, the reason behind this measure was political. In a sense, it was designed to cement the Whig magistrates in the boroughs and generate new support within the parishes by granting them extra powers. However, the measure backfired as Normanby failed to sway magistrates in the West Riding with concessions to offset the cost of its implementation. The permissive nature of the Constabulary Acts meant that magistrates could determine their own fate, which is what they did. Their rejection of the measure was a decision which had serious consequences as demonstrated by the difficulties experienced by Sir James Graham, Normanby's Tory successor, during the handling of the 1842 Plug Plot riots.

5. SIR JAMES GRAHAM:
BARRACKS, PLUG PLOTS AND REFORM, 1841-46

The Tory response to Chartist unrest in the West Riding was more centralised and more repressive than that of the Whigs. Many decisions were taken from the top downwards and there was little consultation with local agencies. Under the newly elected government, Home Office policy was largely shaped by two factors. First, from an ideological perspective, it was based upon Sir Robert Peel's famous Tamworth manifesto.[675] This was delivered on 18 December 1834 and showed a strong commitment to uphold the principles set by the 1832 Reform Act. The manifesto was created to broaden the support of the Tory Party and win over middle-class voters who had become newly enfranchised.[676] Peel asserted that the 1832 Reform Act was 'a final and irrevocable settlement of a constitutional question' and an agreement by which 'no friend to the peace and welfare of this country would attempt to disturb, either by direct or insidious means'.[677] The measure had created 'a vortex of agitation' which culminated with the advent of Chartist unrest. This prompted Peel to undertake a 'careful review' of civil institutions that entailed 'the firm maintenance of established rights, the correction of proved abuses and the redress of real grievances'.[678]

As the Chief Secretary for Ireland from 1812 to 1818, Peel had oversight of the establishment of a uniformed and paid police force for 'disturbed' counties that was initiated through the Peace Preservation Act of 1814. This force came under the authority of the Lord Lieutenant. A further act of 1822 established police forces in each Irish county which were later merged into a single constabulary in 1836.[679] Peel's early development of policing in Ireland continued when he later became Home Secretary on two occasions from 1822 to 1827 and 1828 to 1830.

Peel had seen for himself the challenges that the Home Office faced domestically in dealing with law and order in the new industrial age. Whilst serving in the role of Home Secretary, Peel made major alterations to the Bloody Code.[680] This brought about a reduction in the number of offences which came under the death penalty. He also made significant changes to consolidate statute laws, as well as to introduce prison and penal reforms. During Peel's second stint at the Home Office from 1828 to 1830 his most significant reform was the creation of the Metropolitan Police, which unified district and parochial police constables and magistrates under one body. The new force came under the control of the Home Office and was paid out of the general rate. As well as detection, the constables were deployed to patrol the streets of London and maintain order by curtailing activities such as theft, drunkenness and prostitution.[681] The success of the force later raised questions about the state of provincial policing. For example, Chartist unrest during the 1830s and 1840s in densely-populated urban-industrial centres not only highlighted the need for better provisions to be put in place, but also the kind of changes that were needed to the machinery of public order as a whole. It was under the auspices of Peel that a serious review of policing was later undertaken. This had major consequences for both central and local relations as well as for the Chartists during 1842-6.

The second factor in the Tory suppression of Chartist agitation in the West Riding was the personality and attributes of Sir James Graham. The Home Secretary had excellent administrative abilities which made him 'an upright and able statesman'.[682] Graham forged a strong working relationship with Sir Robert Peel who was reputed to have controlled 'each and every government department with great intensity'.[683] The Prime Minister's leadership skills combined with Graham's administrative acumen helped suppress Chartist unrest in 1842. These actions also explain why, according to Malcolm Chase, 'history failed to turn' for the Chartists.[684] Under Graham's stewardship, the Home Office's handling of civil and industrial unrest brought about sweeping changes to the machinery of public order which enabled the British state to emerge stronger and more cohesive.

The Peel administration was handicapped by a number of problems in the suppression of Chartist unrest in the West Riding. There was the issue of a sizeable trade deficit of £7,500,000, which meant that a lack of funds at the government's disposal limited what it could spend.[685] The Tory Party was also confronted by the grievances of a number of political movements the Whigs had failed to handle and which continued to remain active issues of contention. The Factory Reform question, disputes over the Corn Laws and Free Trade agitation, along with increasing poverty and unemployment amongst the working classes within the manufacturing districts, all posed hazardous problems for the authorities.[686]

Further tension was caused by the release of Feargus O'Connor from gaol. This led to a resurgence of the Chartist movement. On 17 September 1841, the radical leader spoke to a room full of his supporters at the Montpellier Tavern, Camberwell and complained that Sir Robert Peel had not been totally clear about the intentions of his government. O'Connor said that the Tory Prime Minister had been silent on every topic 'save one', which was the Poor Law Amendment Act and he went on to state:

> And what had he said on that subject? Why, he said that he would re-enact that law till next July'. (Cries of 'Shame!') Shame, they cried shame. Yes, but whose was the shame? It was the people's, who allowed the first blow to be struck (Cheers.) The tale of the man with the glazed hat was repeated amidst the loud groans and cries of shame. He had also seen the case of the conviction of Peddey at Yorkshire, who had been convicted on the sole evidence of an infernal conspirator and villain, named Harrison, who confessed that he had been 40 times in gaols and prisons, and that he had received 30*l.* from the high constable, and expected to receive 25*l.* more; the same man was now in prison for horse stealing'.[687]

O'Connor used the remainder of his speech to demand the repeal of the Act of Union between England and Ireland and said that he would do all in his power to achieve that goal.[688]

In response to the threat of renewed mass Chartist agitation and the various difficulties that presented themselves at the very beginning of his stewardship at the Home Office, Graham promised the general public that 'every exertion' would be made to ease the distress that existed in the country.[689] To achieve that aim, he promised 'to extend the resources of the state' which he believed would 'protect its mighty interests and give satisfaction to every class in the community'.[690] It is clear that the Peel administration looked to adopt a top-down approach towards achieving its aims.[691]

In the West Riding, Sir James Graham responded to the recommendations made by Sir Charles Napier requesting the construction of new and rebuilding of existing barracks. During the period 1841-5, the ambitious scheme cost £212,000 to implement, but it revealed many weaknesses in the relationship between central and local government, and it was marred by a number of petty disputes as well as a great deal of incompetence by both sides.[692] Bradford's experiences typify the problematic relationship between the Home Office and various other agencies as they sought to achieve this goal locally.

From the very outset, the conversion of Bradford's temporary army barracks to a permanent arrangement was fraught with many difficulties.

The overall scheme dated back to 1839, when local magistrates agreed, in principle, to purchase premises on Bradford Moor for £2,250.[693] An additional sum of £1,300 was raised by public subscription to pay for alterations and on 1 December 1839 the military took possession of the property. [694]

The first major dispute to affect the project erupted over who should pay for the scheme. The local magistrates, who later refused to adopt a constabulary force for the West Riding on the basis that it was too expensive, wanted the Home Office to carry the burden of the cost. In April 1840, an agreement was made to sell the property to the government on terms which were specified by local magistrates but this was not carried into effect. Following Chartist disturbances that had taken place in the town in the early part of the year, the Bradford magistrates made a proposal to the Home Office in which they offered £500 towards the conversion of the barracks. This was recommended by Sir Charles Napier, and in return for this, the magistrates wanted the Home Office to settle the purchase costs that were still owed to the owner of the property. The magistrates and local inhabitants tried to assist the process by raising £250, which reduced the overall amount still owed to £2,000.[695]

A year later, a further demand for financial assistance from the Home Office was made by the magistrates, who at this stage stressed the need for both infantry and cavalry soldiers to be permanently stationed in Bradford because of concerns for public safety. At the time, they had become embroiled in a dispute with the owner of the property who demanded £100 in rental arrears to cover the period leading up to April 1841, along with a further £50 to pay the rent for the rest of the year. The Bradford magistrates told the Home Secretary that they did not have the money in place to pay this deficit and they requested the Home Office to clear the debt or buy the freehold. The demand was again reiterated in October 1841, as the Home Office was told by the town magistrates that the debt had still not been paid. In response to this request, a month later Henry Manners Sutton told the magistrates that a permanent barrack could not be built until 1842, largely because central government did not have any money in place to fund such a scheme.[696]

In January 1842, there was a major development when the Board of Ordnance told the magistrates in Bradford that they were willing to step in and buy the property but only if certain conditions were met.[697] One of those demands involved the magistrates raising £500 towards its cost. This matter was discussed at a meeting which included residents and was chaired by the Tong Hall magistrate and Deputy Lieutenant of the West

Riding Colonel John Tempest at the local Court House on 16 March 1842.[698]
Whilst the money to fund this demand was raised by 'many respectable
people', the meeting attracted severe criticism from some quarters such as
an anonymous individual called 'Common Sense' who wrote a letter to the
Bradford Observer in which he said:

> But what a sublime idea (could we the brutes, but see it) is presented to us
> in the prospective view of these new barracks on Bradford Moor! The art
> military has been brought to a high degree of perfection in these modern
> times – so much so that a Colonel Tempest, for instance, might demolish
> such a place as Bradford quite easily in a morning before breakfast,
> without being in the least fatigued. It seems that the magistrates and other
> responsible inhabitants think it absolutely necessary that the elements
> of an artificial earthquake be got in readiness to be put in operation as
> regards this our old town, so soon as the civil power is not competent to
> prevent excitement becoming too excited.[699]

The author argued that money used for building the barracks would
have been better spent on building 'a number of handsome schools'.[700]
He mentioned that this scheme clearly demonstrated how much the local
ruling elites distrusted 'the unrepresented'.[701]

As the parties involved looked to broker an agreement to convert
the barracks, the problematic relationship that existed between central
government and the local agencies continued to delay the project. Disputes
had arisen throughout 1842 over the development of the land and the titles
of the property. One dispute with the Lord of the Manor concerned the
development of three acres of unenclosed land that adjoined the barracks.
Underneath the ground were minerals. The landowner was willing to allow
the Home Office and Board of Ordnance to use the surface territory but
unwilling to permit any excavation of the soil for construction purposes.
After many disagreements amongst the parties concerned, in July 1842, an
agreement was reached with the Lord of the Manor that 'any quantity of
wasteland adjoining the Barrack site, not exceeding three acres' could be
enclosed to 'exercise and train the troops'.[702] This permission was granted
on the basis that the land would be returned to its previous owner, once the
barracks were no longer needed.[703]

A further disagreement that ran parallel to this had erupted over the
titles to the property. When the temporary barrack was erected in 1839,
the textile manufacturer and Bradford Justice of the Peace, J.G. (John
Garnett) Horsfall, who had chaired a public meeting on the issue, assumed

responsibility for its purchase. Horsfall was an Anglican mill owner who in 1826 had established Bradford's first power loom factory.[704] Confusion raged when his solicitor failed to send key documentation to the Board of Ordnance, concerning the property and its true ownership, which caused a major delay. The Bradford magistrates pointed the finger of blame at the Home Office and the Board of Ordnance who retaliated by threatening to remove troops from the town and build the barracks elsewhere.[705] The mix-up surrounding the completion of the title was not rectified until June 1843, by which time Horsfall had come clean about his role and the Board of Ordnance finally paid the £2,000 purchase money that was outstanding.[706] The matter of rent that was also owed to the magistrates was later settled in November 1844 when the Treasury paid £300.[707]

As late as 1848 the issue of providing adequate troop accommodation had not been properly resolved. This was particularly evident when a third wave of mass Chartist unrest hit Bradford. It also proved to be a major problem during the summer of 1842 when Chartist unrest spread across the West Riding.

In his book *Chartism: A New History*, Malcolm Chase devotes an entire chapter to the events that occurred throughout 1842. He asserts that the summer of that year was 'a momentous phase in the history of Chartism'.[708] Chase argues that the industrial action associated with Chartist unrest 'constituted one of the most serious threats to social stability'.[709] Whilst his book offers an interesting narrative, it only touches upon the importance of government suppression. In order to address these gaps, we need to examine in broader terms why history failed to turn for the Chartists in the West Riding.[710]

Following the failure of the National Petition in May 1842, radical associations were reinvigorated and the Charter was seen as a solution to the economic difficulties which affected the manufacturing districts as a whole. Leading Chartists in Halifax issued this rallying cry to their supporters:

When a country like our own, with all her resources already developed, continues for year after year to grow worse and worse – and every year adding fresh miseries to the woes of its predecessor – the continuation of a state of things like this, proves that this accumulating misery is only the result of some deep-seated cause – and that cause is the present legislative system. To remove that cause is our object.[711]

In June, there was staunch political opposition in the West Riding to the 'proposed new Corn Law Bills' which were blamed for an increase in the price of bread, particularly in places such as Sheffield. Further, there was a slump in the woollen and worsted trades as manufacturers complained that business was being lost to 'more favourable climes'.[712] The gathering economic crisis meant that more operatives were made redundant on a daily basis.[713] The situation became so dire that many were left without the basic means of survival, which caused widespread resentment. The combined effects of an economic downturn and political turmoil intensified to such a fever pitch that by August 1842 a wave of strikes which began in Manchester, Stalybridge and Ashton-Under-Lyne had spread across the Pennines to the West Riding. The operatives struck because their wages were reduced.[714] This resulted in 'men begging in large bodies' and extensive criminal activity that involved theft from shops and private houses being broken into on a widespread scale.[715] The plundering turned into severe rioting which magnified both the defective nature of the machinery of public order and the fractious relationship between central government and the local agencies that it supervised. The initial response to the disturbances across all levels was reactive rather than proactive as the authorities did not know what to do about the situation in hand.

In describing the events that occurred during August and September 1842, this information cannot be taken at face value as the sources contain both strengths and weaknesses. There are many hidden connotations behind the statements written by the Home Secretary and Home Office staff, along with their exchanges with the military and magistrates. For instance, some of the magistrates, who were also factory owners, would on occasions exaggerate the nature of a disturbance to force the Home Office to send in the troops. They were alarmist because they knew that central government would act on their requests, as well as shoulder the burden of cost instead of bearing the responsibility themselves. However, aside from such ambiguities, the sources offer unique insights into how the Home Office interaction with various public order agencies in the West Riding was often fraught with tension. This arose from disagreements on the spot between the military and local magistracy over tactics when dealing with unrest. Furthermore, the many incidents which occurred in the West Riding revealed the difficulties which the authorities faced in containing flashpoints, especially when there were no organised policing provisions in place. The situation came to a head when the Home Secretary, Sir James Graham, aided by the Duke of Wellington, decided to take matters into his own hands, after which the disturbances gradually petered out.

The trouble began on 13 August 1842 when 'a large body' of working-class strikers, estimated to have been in the region of 3,000 men, crossed the Pennines and visited Huddersfield.[716] They arrived from Saddleworth and the borders of Lancashire, and when they descended on West Yorkshire the local operatives were encouraged to join their crusade. The strikers divided into smaller groups and within a very short space of time they had brought the mills in Huddersfield to a standstill. The ringleaders of this dispute demanded 'a fair days wage for a few days work'.[717] Whilst there was no violence attached to the actions of the striking operatives, local Justices of the Peace warned the Secretary of State that 'a single spark' could 'set the whole town in a blaze'.[718]

The Home Office responded in the West Riding by sending troops to quell the unrest. The department took full advantage of changes that were gradually being made to the growth and development of internal infrastructure across mainland Britain through the advent of railways and later the telegraph. The former had been expanding since the 1830s. The first main railway line to link the capital with the manufacturing districts was the London to Birmingham line, built in 1838.[719] In theory, the expansion of the railway network which radiated outwards from the capital meant that soldiers and police could be deployed much more quickly to deal with disturbances. This development also allowed information between the Home Office and civil power in the localities to be relayed much faster. However, there were dangers as Sir James Graham warned Major-General Sir William Warre, the Commander of the Northern District Army to provide alternate lines of communication across the West Riding in case the railways were 'broken up or obstructed'.[720]

The Home Office remained undeterred by this problem and whilst the Lancashire workers caused unrest in Huddersfield, a few hundred miles away 'in the terminus of the London to Birmingham railway', two special trains were provided by the railway authorities and used to move troops to Manchester, along with 'other disaffected manufacturing districts'.[721] The railway companies made necessary preparations for the military as they provided carriages so that soldiers could be transported to the scene of unrest in greater numbers. As the troops entered Euston station and boarded the trains, a crowd of around '1,000 to 2,000' gathered with several shouting 'don't go and slaughter your fellow countrymen'.[722] When ammunition was being loaded onto the first train, the crowd jeered the troops in 'the most vociferous manner' and whilst artillery was being placed onto another carriage, one observer at the scene warned of a Chartist plot to prevent the train from reaching its intended destination.[723] As the troops set off on their journey to the West Riding, people lined bridges along the route and hurled 'large stones' at the train carriages as they expressed their disapproval of their deployment.[724]

For the first few days, the decision to send troops to the affected area did very little to remedy the situation. The military response, which was coordinated by local magistrates, was met with huge resistance. Many operatives openly defied the reading of the Riot Act. An example of this occurred in Huddersfield on 14 August 1842 when the military used excessive force to put down a disturbance. Justices of the Peace from Huddersfield told the Home Secretary about a meeting that was organised and supposed to be joined by flying pickets from Lancashire. When the strikers failed to show up, the meeting went ahead. The magistrates turned up at five o'clock in the morning and told the protesters to disperse. When the Riot Act was read, some of them dispersed, whilst others continued to walk the streets in defiance of the authorities. As a diversionary tactic, the men from Lancashire went to Meltham and Holmfirth where they stopped the mills. After visiting those places they later turned out woollen operatives at Crosland, near Huddersfield.[725] The crowd, which was heavily armed with bludgeons, marched into Huddersfield and discharged their guns into the air. Magistrates, along with the troops and a group of special constables, arrived at the scene where the Riot Act was read again but the crowd stood firm. At this stage, the troops and special constables followed the protesters. As they threatened to close Brooks Mill, there was a stand-off in the yard of the premises. One man who managed to get into the boiler house was arrested and several other strikers received injuries inflicted by soldiers armed with sabres.[726]

In the attempted suppression of Chartist unrest, tensions between the magistrates and the army reached boiling point. The two were at loggerheads with each other over tactical arrangements. The dispute between these agencies of repression meant that the response to civil unrest was disjointed. Moreover, the Home Office was directly caught in the middle of their conflict. Matters were not helped when Major-General Sir William Warre complained to Sir James Graham about the 'inadequacy of the staff' who served under his command. This prompted the Home Secretary to ask Lieutenant-General Lord Fitzroy-Somerset to send additional officers to the Northern District.[727]

As a further measure, the Home Secretary contacted the Earl of Harewood in relation to the 'acts of outrage and violence' and the 'repression of tumult' across the West Riding.[728] Graham told the Lord Lieutenant that 'all Justices of the Peace and other magistrates' had a duty to impose the law in order to protect people and property from 'violence and threats'.[729] He warned Harewood that 'no mine, mill or factory' should be 'closed by force'.[730] Graham said that the factory owners were entitled to the aid of civil power in the defence of property and the restraint of anyone who attempted to invade their premises. He also warned that if the civil power was unable to overcome any violent assault on the businesses, military assistance would be given. The Lord Lieutenant was left in no doubt that magistrates had a duty to prevent any 'riotous assembly' from 'venturing into a town'.[731] However, one of the problems Sir James Graham faced in imposing those measures was that with police provisions across the West Riding being relatively weak, the magistrates had no other option but to rely heavily upon military aid. As a consequence, the Home Office and the Commander of the Northern District Army were inundated with requests for troops from Justices of the Peace.

In Bradford, such were the fears over the safety of the town that magistrates demanded additional cavalry troops. They told Sir James Graham that although the situation was relatively tranquil, their constabulary force was 'insufficient' to deal with an urgent situation, should it arise. Six hundred special constables were sworn in to preserve the peace and protect inhabitants and their property.[732] Despite these measures, the protesters were not deterred from both defying and overriding the authority of Justices of the Peace. When the magistrates in Bradford attempted to stop the insurgents they were often outnumbered and overpowered. In one incident, three magistrates accompanied by two troops of cavalry followed several thousand people.[733] They tried to dissuade them from protesting but their efforts were largely 'in vain'. The Riot Act was read but the agitators, who were told about the 'consequences' that they faced if they did not disperse, refused to do so.[734]

Disorder was allowed to escalate within the West Riding and there were clearly weaknesses within military circles. Major-General Sir William Warre who now commanded the Northern District Army, made a number of serious tactical errors. The biggest mistake made was the failure to distribute troops evenly across the region. Too many soldiers were concentrated in and around Leeds. The reason why Warre made this tactical decision was the town's central location within the West Riding, along with its strong effective rail connections with London via Birmingham. As a major commercial centre within the manufacturing district with links to Manchester and Liverpool, Leeds was also seen as a place that could potentially come under attack from Chartists. The concentration of so many troops in one place directly affected the safety of other towns such as Bradford and Halifax, which were exposed to the threat of violence. The deployment of so few troops in those towns meant that they were highly vulnerable to Chartist attack. The weakness was highlighted by two separate incidents that occurred at Elland and Salter Hebble, near Halifax.

These incidents proved to be an important watershed in the Home Office's suppression of Chartist unrest. Not only did it reveal the weakness of the local machinery of public order but it also stressed once again the need for greater central control to prevent agitation from escalating out of hand. The incident began on 15 August 1842, when the mayor and the magistrates of Leeds received information from Halifax that armed soldiers had been involved in a confrontation with 'huge numbers of people'.[735] As they were moving prisoners to a nearby gaol, the troops had been assaulted at two different points'. It was claimed that the outcome had been 'disastrous'.[736] The first report they received stated that soldiers passing through Elland Wood near Halifax had been attacked. Two officers were seriously wounded and several other people were injured by the soldiers. This episode was followed by details of a second major incident at Salter Hebble. An omnibus returning from the train station was met by thousands of protesters who were positioned on a hill. They hurled stones at the vehicles and its passengers. The driver of the omnibus who was unable to control the horses was severely injured. Some soldiers became entangled with the horses. Stones, weighing from 5lbs to 20 lbs, rained down on the passengers of the omnibus! Five soldiers were dismounted from their horses; three of them were kicked and beaten by the crowd, who wanted to kill them, whilst a corporal was also shot at the scene. Those wounded were yeomanry troops of the 11th Hussars from Barnsley.[737]

Following the ugly incidents at Elland and Salter Hebble, the situation went from bad to worse for the magistracy and military as they had potentially lost control of public order. In Huddersfield, the aptly titled Plug Plot disturbances took place when 'eight thousand' people marched through the town and stopped the mills by removing plugs from the boilers of steam engines.[738] Without a military force at their disposal, the helpless magistrates could not offer any resistance.[739] The previous day, the Huddersfield Postmaster William Moore had written to Sir James Graham and told him that several thousand men had turned off the steam and water which powered the mills. The Home Secretary was informed that the local magistrates were powerless and did not know what to do.[740] This pattern of confrontational behaviour spread to neighbouring towns and villages. In Holmfirth, a 'lawless mob'; which consisted of '2,000 people armed with bludgeons and sticks', forced the closure of mills and 'compelled the workpeople to discontinue their work'.[741] Magistrates and special constables followed the crowd to different mills. They tried in vain to apprehend some of the ringleaders.[742] One Justice of the Peace claimed that the proprietors of forty mills in the district were known to be 'in a state of alarm'.[743] The magistrates refused to endanger he lives of workers by allowing them to operate.[744]

On 17 August 1842 even worse followed as disorder spread to Leeds. Throughout the day, magistrates discussed how to prevent 'bodies of rioters' from entering the town. They received news that the mills at Stanningley had been stopped by 'a large number of the rioters'.[745] It was also reported that a group of them had entered Bramley where they carried out similar actions.[746] The Leeds magistrates told Sir James Graham that throughout the morning groups of people, many of whom were total strangers, had entered the town in 'twos and threes from the West' and 'congregated in the streets'.[747] They reported that the crowd, which showed a huge 'disposition to be turbulent', was dispersed 'without difficulty' by the borough police, who were out in force to protect the neighbourhood.[748] The events that took place in and around Leeds that day showed the merits of deploying the borough police and how the machinery of law and order, when coordinated and organised properly, could effectively suppress Chartist unrest with ease.

During the afternoon, protesters forced the mills at nearby Holbeck, a 'populous part' of the town, to close.[749] At three o'clock, Captain Burdett, a 17th Lancer, assisted by a troop of the 17th Troop of Royal Horse Artillery and armed with one gun, along with twenty men of the 8th Regiment and a party of constables led by three borough magistrates, marched to Holbeck. They met 'a very large' group of people who were in the process of stopping Messrs Latham's Mill.[750] When the crowd saw the army, a number of people fled from the scene out of fear from being involved in a violent confrontation. The Riot Act was read and the striking workers who remained at the location 'would not disperse for sometime'.[751] A person was arrested for throwing stones as the mill was closed. Throughout the evening, violence continued when the strikers returned and attacked the mills. Constables were deployed at the scene and later assisted by the army which was pelted with 'showers of stones'. In total, twenty people were arrested and taken into custody for various offences.[752]

The military embarrassments at Elland and Salter Hebble, along with many other incidents that had occurred within the West Riding, clearly showed that the local machinery of public order could not keep the peace. Graham feared that the threat which the rapid spread of unrest posed to the stability of the nation was more severe in 1842 than the previous episode of Chartist agitation during 1839-40.[753] With this belief, Graham, aided by the Duke of Wellington, decided to by-pass the authority of the military and local magistrates by directing affairs from Whitehall.[754] The Home Secretary's decision to bring the Duke of Wellington onboard was clearly a master stroke. The Duke was by now an elderly statesman and decorated military general. His most notable achievement was the defeat of the Napoleonic Army at the Battle of Waterloo in 1815. In the suppression of Chartism, his experience and expertise was beneficial to Graham. As a successful military warrior, the Duke exuded a fear factor which may help to explain why some discontented radicals decided to pull back from causing further turbulence. In doing so, they clearly made the right call. The seizure of the reins of power by the Home Office and the Horse Guards in 1842 meant that inter-government relations would never be the same again. From this point the centre gradually assumed hegemony over local governance and, therefore, over the handling of the serious Chartist unrest that had affected the West Riding.

The first decision that Graham and Wellington took in this new approach to dealing with Chartist agitation involved the restoration of order and leadership to the Northern District Army. Graham wanted to appoint a Lieutenant-General to take charge of all the troops across the disturbed district. In addition, the Home Secretary particularly wanted the appointment of Major-General to be stationed in Yorkshire.[755] One of the first decisions taken by Graham and Wellington was to dispense with the inept Sir William Warre, who was immediately replaced by Lieutenant-General Sir Thomas Arbuthnot.[756] A very close friend of the Duke of Wellington, he was both experienced and adept at dealing with industrial disturbances. Whilst serving as a Colonel of the 52nd Light Infantry, Arbuthnot had played an active part in the rout of colliers at Clifton.[757] This made him a more than suitable alternative in dealing with not only striking protesters but also local magistrates whose interference in military affairs during the week-long dispute was shown to be counter-productive. Graham had received numerous demands from magistrates for troops, many of which exaggerated the familiar theme of danger to public safety and property. He later warned magistrates across the region that the 'services of the military in aid of the civil force' would not be called upon 'unless absolutely necessary'.[758]

Given the shortage of police across the West Riding, the Home Office had very little option but to increase significantly the military presence within the region. Once the presence of regular troops began to be felt, the disturbances petered out within a matter of days. On 18 August 1842, a detachment of the 87th Fusiliers consisting of forty men under the command of Colonel McGuiness arrived in Leeds from Hull.[759] The arrival of this force generated so much fear amongst protesters in places such as Holbeck Moor that they took flight 'when the police and military arrived'.[760] This meant that none of the mills were closed.[761] That same day, '600 rank and file of the 73rd Infantry', under the command of Colonel Love, travelled from Woolwich and arrived in Leeds by railway.[762] From there, they went to Bradford and took with them a 'cannon', along with a 'troop of artillery' from the Leeds Barracks.[763] The following day, another 638 of the 32nd Infantry Regiment under the command of Colonel Maitland travelled by railway from Portsmouth to Leeds. The force remained in the town until further notice. It was stationed at the Assembly Rooms and a warehouse on Trinity Street which had been converted into a temporary barracks.[764] The formidable presence of such heavily-armed troops acted as a deterrent to further riot and turmoil. From that moment onwards, a potentially dangerous situation was avoided.

At the same time that the military presence was stepped up across the West Riding, Graham tried to encourage people to return to work. The Home Secretary persuaded Justices of the Peace to do their utmost to protect scab workers at any cost.[765] In order to prevent factories and mills from being assaulted any further, the Home Secretary received demands from magistrates in places such as Halifax for firearms to be given to army pensioners. Graham did not agree with this course of action and refused to accept those requests. The Home Secretary thought it was the ultimate responsibility of magistrates to suppress disturbances.[766] By 19 August 1842, it would appear that many of the workers in the factories and mills across the region in towns such as Huddersfield had returned to work, some of them being sworn-in by magistrates as special constables.[767]

Following the Plug Plot disturbances of 1842, both Sir James Graham and the Duke of Wellington held their own inquest over what went wrong with the machinery of public order and why it malfunctioned in the way that it did. The first point of attack was the magistracy, who came in for very severe criticism. Many incidents during the Plug Plot disturbances occurred in towns where Whig magistrates served. Predictably, Graham rounded on them for failing to carry out their duties properly. He believed that their poor handling of the disturbances was a deliberate ploy designed to both embarrass and bring down the Tory government. The Home Secretary further accused them of being too reliant on military assistance and warned that government could not 'provide troops for every town and village' in the event of further unrest.[768]

Graham then moved to attack their power base, particularly at county level. The Home Secretary wanted to appoint stipendiary officials to assist Justices of the Peace at Quarter Sessions. The issue attracted huge opposition from both Tory and Whig magistrates, who saw the measures as being a direct assault on their powers. This hostility left Graham with no alternative but to shelve the proposal on the insistence of his Prime Minister, Sir Robert Peel, who had previously given his full backing to this measure.[769] However, despite this about turn, Graham's decision to attack the power of the magistracy did much to alienate them, especially at a time when he needed their support more than ever in order to carry out necessary improvements to the machinery of public order. The magistrates' distrust of the Home Secretary later proved to be a major obstacle to the introduction of much-needed reforms to the public-order apparatus.

The Home Office assault on the failings of the magistracy was followed by an attack launched by the Duke of Wellington on the state of the armed forces. Firstly, he bemoaned the lack of leadership that was shown in the suppression of the Plug Plot riots. It had resulted in embarrassing episodes at Elland and Salter Hebble where troops had been ambushed by the Chartists. The Duke cited problems dating back to the point when Sir Charles Napier gave up the post of Commander of the Northern District Army. A succession of generals had followed in his footsteps but none measured up to the standards set by the erstwhile leader.[770]

The Duke of Wellington went a stage further in his assessment of the failings of the military. He questioned the defence policy of various governments since the French Revolutionary wars. During thirty years of peace, the number of troops had declined. For instance, from 1820 to 1842, the total number of soldiers serving the Northern District Army had fallen from 7,524 to 4,990.[771] Furthermore, the armed forces had received very little investment in terms of kit and armaments. This state of affairs was also magnified by the fact that the military had failed to embrace industrialisation and the mechanisation of weaponry.[772] In order to instigate reform after the Plug Plots, Wellington reprised his role as commander-in-chief of the British Army, in succession to Lord Hill in August 1842. He accepted the role on a '*pro tempore*' basis from the Queen, largely due to his age and 'delicate state of health'.[773] However, within military circles, the Duke was still held in great esteem. Both officers and men looked up to him as their 'great captain' and a 'considerate though strict and disciplined friend'.[774]

The joint criticism of the magistracy and the military as agencies of repression prompted the Home Office and the Horse Guards to forge closer ties through which they attempted to effect improvements to the machinery of public order. In deciding whether the state 'softened' or 'hardened' its approach towards the Chartists, the evidence overwhelmingly supports the latter argument. Historians of the 'linguistic turn' such as Gareth Stedman Jones have argued that reforms introduced by the Peel administration during the period 1841-6 in the shape of mines, banking and factory legislation, signified a sea change over the way in which the government and the state operated. Jones suggested that a softened approach towards the working classes through direct intervention in economic affairs and the removal of the abuses of the *laissez-faire* capitalist system weakened the Chartists as it took away the focus of their protest. Their protestations had revolved upon attacks on the corrupt nature of the state.[775] On the other hand, the counter-argument put forward by Dorothy Thompson and Neville Kirk argues that Stedman Jones overlooked the repressive measures introduced by the Home Office as a possible reason the movement fell into decline, especially in places such as the West Riding.[776] Thompson in particular argued that the state cranked up its coercive approach towards the Chartists and the working classes. This was demonstrated by the events that took place throughout 1842, about which she claimed:

> More energy was hurled against the authorities than in any other of the nineteenth century. More people were arrested and sentenced for offences concerned with speaking, agitating, rioting and demonstrating than in any other year, and more people were out on the streets during August 1842 than at any other time. It was the nearest thing to a general strike that the century saw.[777]

The view put forward by Thompson and endorsed by Kirk is that the government and state became more repressive towards the Chartists, especially during the final wave of agitation in 1848. This was highlighted when Lord John Russell's administration used a combination of militaristic and police measures to drive the movement into decline. In making a judgment on this debate, it can be argued that during the period 1842-6 the state did not soften at all, but actually stiffened its resolve as the Home Office under Sir James Graham tried to remedy defects with the machinery of public order. Those deficiencies were critically exposed by the Plug Plot disturbances, which led to a number of reforms in the areas of policing, communications and prisons.

Sir James Graham felt that he could impose reforms on the localities in an autocratic fashion.[778] However, as he later discovered, his initiatives needed the support of local agencies such as magistrates in order for them to be fully enacted. His decision to criticise them publicly over their failings in dealing with the 1842 Plug Plot disturbances was a major error of judgment, and it meant that many reforms were never implemented properly. The magistrates did not take too kindly to being criticised openly in public, as well as being dictated to in public.[779] However, this hindrance did not deter Graham from trying to stamp his own authority on the system that was already in place.

The reform of the machinery of public order began when borough councils decided to scale back the costly scheme of building military barracks and elected to remove troops from towns across the West Riding. For instance, in Leeds during 1843 the infantry was removed because the mayor and local magistrates did not see the need for their 'continued presence'.[780] At the same time, the temporary barracks were dismantled.[781] The council had received a number of complaints from the general public about the 'annoyance' caused by troops, which prompted their removal.[782] Further, the town had adequate police provisions that it could draw upon. The police force that existed in and around Leeds consisted of one chief constable, one superintendent, a police clerk, five inspectors, fourteen sergeants, one hundred and three police constables and two thousand special constables. Roughly two to three hundred special constables were appointed annually in October 1842, under the provisions of the Municipal Corporations Act.[783] This strong police presence meant there were sufficient means to protect commercial and industrial interests from further radical unrest without recourse to the deployment of the military. It would also explain why the town remained largely immune from violence associated with the Chartists throughout 1842.

In many smaller towns and parishes, the decision taken by magistrates to petition the Home Secretary for the removal of the army and dismantling of temporary military barracks following the Plug Plots, stressed the need for a greater police presence. Following the disturbances, Sir James Graham had spoken of the 'inadequacy of the permanent police force in towns across the West Riding.[784] The Home Secretary told the Lord Lieutenant that if the police was 'placed on a more efficient footing', troops stationed in many towns across the region would be dispensed with.[785] Lord Wharncliffe was told by Graham to rectify the 'deficiency' immediately.[786] This was evident in places such as Bradford, where the police force within the town consisted of only two constables and three deputy constables.[787]

In a further attack on the state of affairs within the region, Graham was particularly scathing in his assessment of the 'proprietors of large towns'.[788] The Home Secretary felt that they were 'greatly mistaken' in their supposition that their 'existing civil force' could be 'called a force'.[789] In an attack on those places which had refused to adopt the 1839-40 Rural Police measures, the Home Secretary wanted 'every large town' to have 'an adequate constabulary force for the maintenance of public peace'.[790] At the time, Graham felt that the improvement of policing within the West Riding could only be effected through the provisions of the 1833 Lighting and Watching Act. The Home Secretary rounded on magistrates across the region for their continued request and use of the military as a substitute for civil power. They were warned that it should only be used as an 'auxiliary measure'.[791] Graham said that it was the duty of the principal inhabitants of the incorporated towns to provide their own civil defence and that it was the role of central government to 'protect and support' civil power through military force only in 'emergency cases'.[792]

In Huddersfield, the provision of troop accommodation and the amenities required for the military force stationed in the town proved costly. Sir James Graham told magistrates that they also had a responsibility to put in place 'an adequate and properly organised civil force'.[793] The Home Secretary suggested that if such a force had initially been in place during the Plug Plot disturbances, the magistrates would not have incurred 'unnecessary' expenses through the construction of temporary barracks and payments to inn keepers.[794] Graham later told Lord Wharncliffe that the cost of temporary accommodation for troops should not be paid for by individual magistrates but by the owners and proprietors of the factories and mills who had received protection.[795]

The failure of the magistracy and military to protect the peace during the Plug Plot disturbances led directly to the introduction of the 1842 Parish Constables Act.[796] The legislation entailed the payment of constables, the 'enlarging and improving' of lock-up houses and the appointment of superintendent constables within various 'divisions and districts' of the region.[797] The aim was to 'increase the security of persons and property', and in doing so magistrates were charged with drawing up yearly lists of people who could be liable to serve as constables.[798] The persons chosen had to be between twenty-five and fifty-five years of age, resident in the parish, and 'rated to the relief of the poor or to the county rate'.[799] Clive Emsley has pointed out that this system appealed to ratepayers on the basis that it was an attempt to rectify the failings of the Constabulary Acts regarding the cost of implementation.[800] The measure also gained approval from the Lord Lieutenant of the West Riding as it sought to put in place a system of paid policing.[801]

Before the 1842 Parish Constables Act was implemented, questions were raised over the key points of the legislation, in particular, the twenty-first section of this Act, which stated:

That after the passing of this act, no Petty Constable, Headborough, Borsholder, Tithingman or Peace Officer of the like description under any name of the office shall be appointed for any parish, township, or village within the limits of this act, except for the performance of duties unconnected with the preservation of peace or with the execution of this act, at any Court Leet.[802]

Magistrates across the region were suspicious that the new legislation would remove the Courts Leet of their 'most important powers and functions', even though they would retain the right to appoint officers.[803] When the law came into operation in November 1842, these suspicions were confirmed as some of the community powers of the vestry were removed. The responsibilities stipulated that no constables could be appointed by the Courts Leet 'except for the performance of duties unconnected with the preservation of peace or with the execution of the Act' (Sect. 21) and that 'all newly appointed constables' were to have:

Within the whole country and within all liberties and franchises, and detached parts of other counties situated therein, and also in every county adjoining to the county in which they are appointed, all the powers, privileges, and immunities, and shall be liable to all the duties and responsibilities of a constablewick. (Sect.15).[804]

The Permanent Under-Secretary at the Home Office reassured the magistrates that although they had the power to appoint constables for a parish which had partially adopted the provisions of the Lighting and Watching Act – in relation to lighting only – they could put in place lock-up houses under the twenty-second section of the Act without having to pay compensation.[805] The significance of this measure was that for the first time, the West Riding had professionally paid police forces employed in many of its towns where none had existed previously.[806] In a departure from the 1839 Rural Police Act, this measure was far more cost effective to implement and justices and parishes could make decisions over how the forces operated in each town.[807]

On 3 April 1843, a committee made up of eleven magistrates was appointed at the Spring General Quarter Sessions held at Pontefract. It considered how this measure would be adopted.[808] At a later meeting held on 5 May 1843, the group received a number of applications for the appointment of superintendent constables and lock-up houses from magistrates across the region, in particular places such as Huddersfield, Bradford, Halifax, Dewsbury, Barnsley and Knaresborough.[809] The magistrates gave various reasons why they were needed. These ranged from the absence of a police presence to lock-up houses that were either non-existent or in need of major repair and enlargement. This was the case with the application made by the Barnsley Justices of the Peace.[810] At a further gathering the committee agreed to requests from the Bradford and Knaresborough magistrates to build lock-up premises underneath their town court houses.[811] In order to put in place all of those structural arrangements, the magistrates in charge of the scheme approached the Home Secretary for financial assistance. They estimated that the creation of each lock-up house and superintendent constable would cost £850.[812]

On 9 June 1843 the committee overseeing the enforcement of this measure produced detailed plans of the lock-ups at Dewsbury, Huddersfield, Barnsley, Halifax, Bradford and Knaresborough. The buildings were designed on the principle that each prisoner would be secured from all 'external communications and violence'.[813] In addition, the cells contained the 'best ventilation and light' to ensure their personal safety.[814] The overall purpose of the lock-up house was that it was to be used by the superintendent constable to extract information from prisoners in the 'prevention and detection of crime' to preserve the peace within a given place.[815] Furthermore, the person appointed to the role was also entirely responsible for the security of the prisoners. The salary of the superintendent constable was set at £160 with accommodation, and £120 without any housing provisions.[816]

Following their construction across the region, questions were raised by magistrates and the superintendent constables about the quality of the lock-up houses and their amenities. The committee received complaints that the locks on the doors of the cells could be 'easily picked' and there were incidences of offenders absconding.[817] Questions were also raised about the lack of stables for horses and running water for the prisoners to drink.[818] In Barnsley, the magistrates also made an observation to the committee that the lock-up houses had no provisions for female detainees. As a result, they needed a separate cell. [819]

In May 1846 the magistrates' committee tried to address the concerns and it came up with a number of recommendations that were gradually implemented. For instance, to protect passage ways between the superintendent house and its cells, wrought iron-grated doors with secure locks and bolts were installed.[820] The locks on the cell doors were strengthened by using iron plates. These contained openings so that prisoners could be adequately incarcerated when a constable was absent from the building.[821] Cell and passage windows were reinforced with wrought iron or wrought iron-gratings that were fixed outside the windows. This meant that prisoners could not escape but received adequate ventilation. Iron beds and bedding were also placed inside the cells as a basic form of comfort.

When all these improvements in security were introduced, the committee boasted that the only way in which a person could escape from a lock-up house was if a crowd attacked and took control of the premises. Ironically, such an incident occurred during the 1848 Chartist disturbances.[822] However, despite some of the difficulties in enforcing the act on a national scale, this measure was relatively successful. During 1848, when reforms designed to develop the scheme were introduced in the West Riding, it was estimated that 368 Parishes and Unions within 21 English Counties had adopted this method of control. As a consequence, 2,817 paid constables were created.[823]

The policing of the West Riding was also bolstered by the creation of Detective Forces, an initiative which originated in London. There had been a number of cases where criminals had escaped custody. This called for better detection methods.[824] One of the problems of policing Chartist agitation was the fact that some insurgents who had damaged property and caused violence towards individuals had evaded capture. This was due to some extent to the failure of the police in gathering sufficient evidence in the face of community silence. A good example was the case of Peter Bussey, the famous Bradford Chartist, who played a part in the organisation of the disturbances that affected the town. The radical orator fled from the West Riding to the United States and escaped the clutches of the authorities.[825]

The Detective Force was the forerunner of the Criminal Investigation Department (CID) which was created in 1878. On 20 June 1842, Metropolitan Police Commissioners took the decision to create the force. Two inspectors were appointed and they each received a wage of £200 per annum. Beneath them, six sergeants were recruited with a wage of £73 per annum.[826] The Commissioners wanted 'a certain number of men' who would specifically concentrate on 'following up cases'.[827] They appointed officers with 'experience' and 'superior intelligence' and recruited the 'most competent men' to perform the task of suppressing larger criminal activities.[828] This was done through surveillance and the acquisition of information by communicating with lesser-known criminals.[829]

Aspects of Chartist agitation such as 'Arming and Drilling', along with 'Exclusive Dealing', which had previously proved difficult for the local authorities to police, pinpointed the need for a specialist branch of policing to work above parish and borough constables. Commissioners of the Metropolitan Police published a memorandum, which was later forwarded to Sir James Graham, that outlined a number of reasons why a Detective Force was needed. One of those stemmed from a murder case of the 'most shocking barbarity'.[830] This revealed 'a want of skill', along with defects within the force, when it came to the detection of crime.[831] The weak investigation of this crime meant that the perpetrator, who was later found guilty of the murder, was allowed to abscond after assisting constables at the scene. An innocent person called David Good was then arrested for the murder and later executed for a crime that he did not commit![832] At an inquiry, embarrassed Metropolitan Police Commissioners discovered that there was a breakdown in communications between the C and D divisions of the force. Critical leads concerning the whereabouts of the actual perpetrator were not acted upon by the sergeants and inspectors who handled the investigation.[833]

As well as deficiencies within the Metropolitan Police, another major factor prompting the creation of the Detective Force was concern over the 'immense' number of people living in and around London. The capital contained a huge 'amount of moveable wealth' that needed protection from the 'habits of the community at large'.[834] Rising criminal activity and official returns which measured 'the general operations of bringing criminals to justice' showed that during the period 1829-42, in London alone there were 22 murders. Fourteen people were convicted and seven had either escaped or could not be prosecuted due to a lack of evidence. In terms of general felonies, the number of people who had been apprehended by the Metropolitan Police and committed for trial from 1831 to 1841 totalled 38,057. Out of this number, 397 individuals received the death sentence, eleven of whom were executed, and 8,515 were transported for various felonies. Those weak statistics in one area of the country alone stressed the need for the Home Office to take action to rectify the problem nationally.[835]

When the Detective Force was put into operation in November 1842, it proved effective. However, there were concerns about the pay and conditions of the branch, in particular, its rewards scheme.[836] Whilst some commissioners believed that a results-based system would lead to greater efficiency and better detection levels, others were concerned that it would cause 'great dissatisfaction' within the ranks of the Metropolitan Police but more importantly, the general public.[837] When employed outside of the

Metropolitan Police district, inspectors were given an extra fifteen shillings a day and sergeants eight shillings, excluding travelling expenses and lodgings.[838] An example of its deployment beyond its normal boundaries occurred in 1848, when the force was sent to Bradford and Halifax to monitor the extent of Chartist 'arming and drilling' taking place within those towns.[839]

As well as police reforms, the suppression of the final stage of Chartist unrest would not have been possible without certain improvements that made it easier to move police and troops from one location to another. They also spawned other innovations that speeded up the movement of information between the centre and localities. During the period 1843-8 a 'railway mania' led to a major expansion of a new form of communication. Harold Perkin asserted that it 'played an important part in the rise of class and social pacification'.[840] The growth of railways allowed the Home Office to see for itself how the machinery of public order functioned in the localities. It also meant that the department did not have to resort solely to the use of spies and postmasters for intelligence, and allowed the Home Office to directly coordinate the tactical deployment of troops and police from the centre. However, the Chartists also benefited from this technological advance because it enabled them to use it to send activists and newspapers to places and canvass support in areas that had been largely untouched by their influence.

In the suppression of Chartist agitation, the movement of troops from other parts of the country to the West Riding had been slow. The region had remained relatively untouched by railways due to its geographical isolation. In order to forge links between Yorkshire and Lancashire, civil engineers had to navigate through the Pennines. Tunnels were built and four major rivers, the Wharfe, Aire, Calder and Don, along with 'a number of tributary valleys', had to be circumnavigated.[841] During the first wave of railway construction in 1835-7 the region was only served by four main lines. These included the Leeds to Manchester route that was the very first to penetrate the Pennines.[842] In 1842, the situation had remained the same and it was only through a second wave of railway building that the Home Office gradually gained access to towns across the region.

Communications between the centre and localities were further enhanced when negotiations took place between the Home Office and the railway companies who agreed on set costs. This made it cheaper to move police and troops to areas within the West Riding affected by unrest. In December 1844, the Metropolitan Police commissioners attempted to secure 'reduced rates' for the transportation of officers who were 'on duty' as they sought to amend Parliamentary Acts that regulated the railways.[843] A few months later, in February 1845, the Home Secretary, Sir James Graham, came to an arrangement with the people in charge of the railway companies. They agreed with the measures that he proposed, although the responsibility for the movement of police on each line later became the task of the Secretary of War.[844] This development had major implications for the suppression of future Chartist disturbances in the West Riding as the Manchester, Leeds, Hull, the Eastern Counties and Manchester and Birmingham Railway Companies were all directly affected by this measure.[845]

The flow of information between the Home Office and the West Riding was further enhanced by the advent of the electric telegraph, invented in 1837 by William Fothergill Cooke and Charles Whetstone. The innovation meant that messages could be transmitted via 'electric currents' which gave off 'signals' and 'sounding alarms'. This permitted information to be sent and processed between the centre and the localities much more quickly.[846] The Home Office saw the benefits of this form of communication and believed that it could be used for other purposes such as the maintenance of public order. The breakdown in communications between the centre and the localities during the 1842 Plug Plot disturbances heightened the Home Office demand for the electric telegraph to be used as a weapon of control, not only against the Chartists but also as a means of directing magistrates and the military when outbreaks of violent unrest occurred.

The need for its use became more pressing, particularly in 1844 when the Home Secretary, Sir James Graham, came in for heavy criticism as a result of the Mazzini affair.[847] This scandal occurred during the spring of that year when Giuseppi Mazzini, hitherto a little-known Italian radical exile, started posting letters to himself which contained bits of sand, poppy seeds and hairs.[848] When he discovered that these elements had been removed from the envelopes in which the letters had been sent, it led Mazzini to believe that his mail had been tampered with. Following a House of Commons investigation led by the radical Whig politician Thomas Duncombe, it was confirmed that Mazzini's mail had been opened by the Home Secretary at the request of the Austrian Ambassador. The incident raised many questions about the use of espionage by central government as a means of safeguarding internal security. The matter caused much tension for the government as it came at a time when it appeared to be making tentative moves towards a more open state. As a consequence, the episode led to the closure of the Secret Department of the Post Office which had carried out this practice since 1703.[849]

However, despite this development, David Vincent has argued that whilst the Mazzini affair was effectively the first attempt by government to control the flow of information, it began a culture of state secrecy in Britain.[850] This trend gathered pace in 1846 when Sir James Graham put forward a Parliamentary Bill which both formulated and regulated 'the use of the Electric Telegraph'.[851] Under the terms of this legislation, the Electric Telegraph Company was created and placed under the direction of its creator Sir William Fothergill Cooke and the politician John Lewis Ricardo. The business was given the power to purchase land and granted a licence that gave it the sole right to lay down telegraph poles. This company was granted a monopoly by the state to put in place telecommunications equipment.[852] It was estimated that by 1848 over 1,800 miles of the railway network had telegraphic apparatus. The machinery linked London to many major towns and cities across England and Wales, including Leeds and Manchester.[853] In doing so, this complementary form of communication to the postal service provided the Home Office with a far more cohesive and centralised means of carrying out the surveillance of its own subjects than ever before.[854]

Whilst the growth of policing and telecommunications would play a major part in the later suppression of Chartist disturbances, so too did the way in which the government treated state offenders in prisons. An added cause of radical unrest throughout 1842 was the death of Samuel Holberry from tuberculosis at York Castle in June. His death and the incarceration of other leading radicals such as Robert Peddie and Feargus O'Connor caused uproar amongst the working classes as reports of their maltreatment were circulated in the *Northern Star*. Some of those who died in captivity became martyrs for their cause.[855] The situation forced the Home Office to re-examine its approach in dealing with the effects of political unrest, especially the way in which Chartist prisoners were treated through the use of harsh punishments such as the tread wheel.

Throughout the last year of Samuel Holberry's life, his condition had deteriorated to such an extent that there were a number of campaigns led by many sympathisers to prompt his release. Holberry was initially imprisoned at the Northallerton House of Correction. In September 1841, a few months before his death, he was moved to York Castle on the grounds that the discipline of the Northallerton gaol had become 'too severe for him'.[856] The Home Secretary ordered his transfer. When Holberry arrived from Northallerton, he was in such 'a weak and enfeebled state' that the last two months of his life was spent in the prison hospital at York Castle. He was treated by a 'surgeon every day and sometimes twice a day'.[857] In a letter dated 30 April 1842, Holberry said that he was 'reduced to a skeleton'.[858] Such was the state of his health that he could barely crawl. Holberry said that 'the Castle' was 'a worse place for a man in sickness than the House of Correction at Northallerton'.[859] During his last days, Holberry was practically starved to death to the point where his eyes had sunk into his head. On 19 May 1842, Holberry wrote another letter in which he stated that his condition had deteriorated so significantly that he suffered from 'dyspepsy'.[860] He could not digest food without the assistance of medicine due to the poor state of his lungs.[861] His death forced the Home Office to look at how it could prevent similar incidents in the future.

Throughout the late-eighteenth and nineteenth century, changes had taken place over the way in which the state punished its offenders. There was a shift away from the use of torture as a form of public spectacle towards more humanitarian and corrective forms of punishment such as separate prison cells.[862] During the ten years of Chartist unrest, there had been no public executions carried out for treasonable behaviour. However, inmates such as Peddie and Holberry had been subjected to cruel punishment by mechanisms such as the tread wheel which clearly induced torture. These methods of control appeared to be out of keeping with the ideas of prison reformers, yet they were still being commonly used. This prompted demands for changes. The main protagonists at the heart of this call for reform were the prison architect Sir Joshua Jebb and the Home Office prison inspectors William Crawford and Whitworth Russell. The latter were described by Donajgrodzki as being 'two of the most radical theorists in the country' within this field.[863] Jebb, who was responsible for the construction of Pentonville Prison, published a report in which he stated that there were 'valid objections' to the use of tread wheels.[864] He wanted to prevent prison governors from putting in place new machinery and stop the continuation of those that were already in use. The architect demanded the abolition of the tread wheels on 'a very large-scale' and told the Home Office that a 'substitute' form of punishment should be put in place.[865]

Both Whitworth Russell and William Crawford argued that the tread wheel was 'the worst form of hard labour'.[866] They believed that it had 'no moral or reformatory influence'.[867] The prison inspectors claimed that this particular system of hard labour was 'unequal in its operation'.[868] On the one hand, it was 'severe and trying' to anyone who was 'tall and heavy', whilst alternatively, it was 'little more than exercise' to anyone who was 'short, light and active'.[869] Russell was of the opinion that the prisoners who suffered most from this brutal form of punishment were those 'unaccustomed' to prison conditions, along with less frequent offenders.[870]

He went on to assert that the tread wheel was 'injurious to health' because it required 'the largest amount of diet' in order to sustain the strength of the prisoners who were subjected to it.[871]

The criticisms came at a time when the Home Office under Sir James Graham had tried to enforce a strict dietary regime in prisons. As a deterrent, the Home Secretary advocated that the amount of food prescribed to a prisoner should be based on class. This measure was initially put into practice at Devon Prison. Meat was substituted for gruel and individuals in their 'second and subsequent imprisonments', were given less food than those in their first stint at the jail.[872] Potatoes, 'the greatest preservative against scurvy', were removed from the diet. An even worse feature of this measure was the treatment of prisoners in solitary confinement who received no food at all.[873] The combination of a poor prison diet and the use of the tread wheel proved to be major factors in the deaths of Samuel Holberry and other Chartists. The reforms also prompted questions about the use of 'solitary confinement' as a means of housing prisoners, particularly as cases of 'lunacy' and maltreatment were revealed by the press.[874] This led Whitworth Russell to argue that the systems of 'separate confinement' and tread wheels were incompatible with each other.[875]

The search for an alternative form of punishment to the tread wheel proved difficult and raised two key questions. First, there was the definition of hard labour to consider. With no uniform system of punishment in place, it varied from prison to prison. It led to calls from Crawford and Russell for the Home Office to adopt uniform regulations and create a legal meaning of the term.[876] Secondly, in finding a replacement for the tread wheel, there was a difference of opinion amongst prison architects and inspectors. Whereas Sir Joshua Jebb believed that that 'hard labour' was 'essential' for 'a sound system of penal discipline', Russell and Crawford wanted a balance between 'hard labour' and 'separation'.[877]

The solution that Jebb came up with was for the tread wheel to be replaced by a form of punishment operated by 'crank machinery' which ran 'through a line of cells'.[878] The equipment revolved around four wheels that were attached to an axle. When turned by hand, for each revolution of the axle, the first wheel moved one tooth. Punishment was based on the number of revolutions turned by the wheels. This could potentially run into the thousands.[879] Whitworth Russell opposed this system because he felt that it could be abused by prison governors and medical officers.[880] The inspector was concerned that 'such a powerful instrument' could be used to exercise 'oppression or favouritism'.[881]

As an alternative form of punishment in some institutions, certain classes of prisoner were placed 'under instruction'.[882] At Pentonville Prison, which was opened in 1842, a penitentiary system was adopted. Inmates were both 'instructed and assessed' for a treatment period of eighteen months.[883] Sir Joshua Jebb was highly sceptical of the use of 'reforming discipline'.[884] He questioned whether a 'permanent moral effect' could be produced on 'a great mass of criminals'.[885] As an example of its failings, Jebb cited an experiment that had been conducted in Scottish prisons where 'concessionary hard labour' combined with 'separation' was tried.[886] The prison architect argued that the combination of 'moral and religious instruction' failed to work because it did not deter inmates from re-offending.[887]

A major obstacle to the reform was the magistrates who effectively controlled the regime in prisons through their capacity as governors. Because the system in place was not fully state-controlled until 1877, it was at their discretion whether or not reforms were implemented.[888] Graham's criticism of magistrates and his attempted assault on their powers meant that initiatives such as those proposed by Jebb, Russell and Crawford were unlikely to succeed. This was despite the fact that the Home Office had introduced twenty-one pieces of legislation during the period 1835-48.[889] It would be some time before major reforms were enacted to rectify the abuses of the harsh and brutal system that killed Samuel Holberry and other Chartists,.

The Home Office under the guidance of the Tories brought about significant changes to both the British state and the machinery of public order in the 1840s. In relation to the state, under Sir James Graham's tenure at the Home Office it is clear that there was a shift towards the development of an integrated police state with an emphasis on greater central control. The origins of this change stemmed from the inept handling of the 1842 Plug Plot disturbances by local magistrates, the military and police. Various incidents revealed how ineffectual the machinery was in relation to the handling of crowds and the control of riot and disorder. When the apparatus began to fail, particularly following the rout of the army at Elland and Salter Hebble, along with the damage wrought by insurgents to the means of production in the West Riding, the Home Office was given an opportunity to seize some power from the magistrates. From this point onwards, the make-up of the state began to change. The decision jointly made by Sir James Graham and the Duke of Wellington to take control of the situation at the behest of the local public order agencies was the first major sign that the two-tiered structure of governance had started to disappear. The power vacuum was further eroded by the rapid expansion of internal communications through the building of railways and the electric telegraph. This led to greater interconnectivity that enabled the Home Office to direct responses to unrest from its base at Whitehall.

Secondly, there was clearly an attempt to remove many abuses and address the failings of the system. Many of those occurred after the 1842 Plug Plot disturbances but the reforms in areas such as policing and prisons did not go far enough. This was largely due to political opposition from Whig magistrates who clearly objected to being blamed for the poor handling of the 1842 Plug Plot disturbances. As a consequence, initiatives designed to improve the efficiency of the apparatus were either watered down or never implemented.

With regard to the military apparatus, many questions were raised by the Duke of Wellington about its role in the handling of civil and industrial unrest. Following the incidents in the West Riding throughout 1842, there were signs that the government and state wanted to move away from quasi-military responses towards the widespread adoption of greater police measures. This was reflected in the removal of troops and dismantling of military barracks in major towns such as Leeds, where a borough police force existed on a substantive scale. Such a development went alongside a decision taken by magistrates across the region to adopt the 1842 Parish Constables Act. It made up for the absence of police provisions that stemmed from the failure of county magistrates to put in place constabulary forces during 1840-1. Policing arrangements were further bolstered by the creation of Detective Forces which were used to check widespread criminal activity.

Throughout 1842 Chartist unrest was suppressed largely because the Home Office managed to take control of the situation. The number of arrests that followed, along with the extreme measures that were used to secure the region from further violence, effectively drove the movement into relative decline. As a consequence, the Chartists were later forced to moderate their protestations against government and the state, a response that had many implications, especially when it came to the final stage of mass activity throughout 1847-8.

In the final analysis, the state had too much coercive power in reserve and easily checked the protestations of the Chartists as a whole, and this explains why, according to Malcolm Chase, 'history failed to turn' and also, as suggested by Miles Taylor, that from 1842 onwards mass support for the Chartists declined.[890] More importantly, the evidence from the West Riding overwhelmingly suggests that Dorothy Thompson was correct in her interpretation that the state toughened its stance towards radical protest.

The reforms that stemmed from the 1842 Plug Plot disturbances directly put in place a more centralised and cohesive police force, as well as effective communication mechanisms of control for dealing with civil unrest.

6. SIR GEORGE GREY:
THE CHALLENGE OF CHARTISM, 1846-8

The Home Office suppression of Chartist unrest in the West Riding during the period 1846-8 took place against the backdrop of rising foreign tensions. This prompted the government to both tighten and step up mainland security in response to the threat from invasion and the later internal insurgency that stemmed from it. The person charged with this task was Sir George Grey, who replaced Sir James Graham as Home Secretary. His appointment followed the return to government of the Whigs, who were now led by Lord John Russell. The move proved to be a successful appointment; it may even be regarded as a masterstroke.[891]

At the time, Grey's appointment was described as being 'judicious' but, in the final analysis, proved inspired.[892] There were fears within press circles that the new person filling the role would not live up to the standards set by his Tory predecessor. Prior to his appointment, Grey had held a number of only minor government roles and rarely participated in House of Commons debates.[893] As a major landowner, the Home Secretary believed that the power of the state should rest in the localities and not at central government level. However, as a result of the unique situation that the Russell administration found itself in, Grey was reluctantly forced to deviate from that position. This change of policy was highlighted by the Home Secretary's response to the renewed threat of Chartist agitation in 1848.[894]

In examining how Chartism was suppressed in 1848, this chapter will demonstrate how much of the evidence supports James Vernon's argument that the political system became closed and disciplined.[895] It is clear that throughout 1848 the Home Office imposed limits on what could be written or said, along with restraints on the movements of the Chartists to prevent revolutionary activity from gaining a foothold.[896] In doing so, the government was able to claim control of the sphere in which political protest was conducted. This subsequently led to what John Belchem has described as the collapse of the mass platform.[897]

The state theorist David Storey has asserted that a 'political elite can invoke nationalist rhetoric in order to maintain its own hegemonic control within its territory'.[898] During the period 1846-8, the British government resorted to this tactic by using the threat of a French invasion and possible revolution in Ireland in order to win over sections of the population to legitimise its control of the nation.

Throughout the 1840s, a series of incidents made war between Britain and France seem likely, since Louis Philippe's regime was weak and subject to social unrest. In 1844, the French annexation of Tahiti, a former British colonial possession, was seen in press circles as being an act of aggression.[899] Also, in 1844 there was a diplomatic dispute that was caused by Prince de Joinville who had written a pamphlet which called upon the French government to build a navy of steam boats and attack Britain. Sir Robert Peel thought that this statement was highly provocative and, along with senior naval and military generals, deliberated over what action should be taken.[900] Ties between both Britain and France were eventually severed by a dispute over the marriage of the Queen of Spain and her sister. The French Foreign Minister Guizot and Lord Palmerston collided over the prevention of a British-supported Coburg marriage. The latter was deceived by a counter-arrangement that had already been made for Louis Philippe's youngest son to marry the Queen's youngest sister.[901] The outcome of this agreement was a feud between Britain and France in which Lord Palmerston became highly suspicious of French naval and military capabilities, the threat of war and an attempted invasion.[902]

The Irish situation added to the strain. Throughout 1846-7, potato blight had resulted in famine, the mass migration of inhabitants and many deaths. The episode generated huge bitterness and was a major factor behind the emergence of the Irish Confederate movement inspired by William Smith O'Brien, who led the Young Ireland Party. The radical political organisation wanted to overturn the Act of Union and end the exporting of grain from Ireland.[903] John Fox Burgoyne, the Chairman of the Board of Works, warned his military and political associates in Westminster about the dangerous situation that was rapidly unfolding. He said that a 'maxim' had been set into the minds of the Irish populace who wanted to revolt. Burgoyne felt that such action would lead to the 'extreme subversion of all existing order of government'.[904] There was also an added danger that if a rebellion occurred in Ireland, it would spread to the mainland. Kay Boardman and Christine Kinealy have argued that the British government stood firm in the face of such threats, since had it shown any sign of weakness by allowing revolutionary activity to gain a foothold, the problem of political and social unrest could have spread further a field, severely endangering the security of its colonial empire.[905]

The difficulties that had arisen over external threats to both colonial and mainland security came at a time when the Whig administration wanted to improve the efficiency of the military. The boom caused by 'railway mania' was followed by a major economic downturn which forced the Whig administration to cut back on state expenditure.[906] One of the areas where the government looked to reduce its budget was defence spending. As a cost-cutting measure, Sir George Grey wanted to discontinue the practice of enlisting soldiers for unlimited service. What he proposed was a system of limited enlistment in which an infantry would serve a maximum of ten years whilst cavalry and ordnance officers would serve twelve years. On completion of their duty, the infantry soldiers would be given an option to re-enlist for another eleven years, whilst cavalry and ordnance troops were offered an additional twelve years service.[907] Grey believed that the new system would not only produce 'a better class of recruit' but also 'diminish desertion'.[908] He was also of the belief that the measures, which also included a mandatory retirement age of fifty-five for all classes of soldier, would encourage more people to join the army, especially those 'who otherwise would never enter it'.[909]

The Duke of Wellington greeted the proposals with disquiet. He felt that the legislation would severely weaken rather than strengthen the armed forces, with the immediate loss of 12,000 men from all regiments.[910] At the time, there was a decline in the number of men enlisting for the army. This meant that in relation to the security of the mainland and the colonies, the soldiers would be very difficult to replace. Another consideration was the pressure that the measures would place upon a labour market which was already under very severe stress through high unemployment caused by the economic downturn. In a later memorandum on the subject, Wellington noted that theoretically under threat were 21,000 infantry soldiers who had served between ten and fifteen years, and a further 3,000-4,000 cavalry troops who had done twelve to sixteen years service. The implications of Grey's proposals meant that those 25,000 soldiers in total were entitled to a free discharge.[911]

The Duke also alerted the Home Secretary about the wider effects of this measure. He suggested that if the troops were pensioned off it would be difficult for them to find immediate employment at a time of economic depression. In turn, this would lead to greater social unrest.[912] On the basis of these arguments, Wellington told Grey that he did not want to be associated with any of the measures that he had proposed. In order to protect the military from further reductions in its strength, the Duke took matters into his own hands.[913]

In January 1848, Wellington tried to force the Home Office to pull back and retreat from its position by leaking a letter that had been written to John Fox Burgoyne, the Inspector-General of Fortifications, to the *Morning Chronicle*.[914] The letter, written a year earlier, was a response to a document that Burgoyne had produced in November 1846 which painted a poor picture of the state of Britain's defences. He warned that a war with France carried the 'risk of invasion' and the possibility of one of the 'most frightful disasters'.[915] In summarising what needed to be done to ward off the threat of an invasion, Burgoyne stated that there should be an increase in the size of the regular army to 60,000-70,000 troops and the creation of a reserve force. He called for the immediate preparation and the constant maintenance of military equipment and the organisation of a militia force during peacetime.[916]

The decision taken by the Duke of Wellington to leak a document that warned the general public about the failings of the British Army and its navy had a two-fold effect. Firstly, it put immediate pressure on the Russell administration to reverse its policy and to invest state money into the armed forces, along with much-needed ordnance provisions. However, the supposed political about-turn that the Duke tried to bring about never materialised. As foreign tensions subsided, the government reversed its policy and continued along the economic path that it had intended from the very beginning of its stewardship.[917] Secondly, the leaking of the Burgoyne memorandum clearly injected fear amongst British subjects. Those fears were deepened by the resurgence of the Chartist movement which – since the end of the Plug Plot disturbances – had been in the doldrums.

The Chartists had been severely weakened as many of their main leaders and activists had been arrested and imprisoned for their involvement in the mass unrest throughout 1842.[918] During the intervening years, the movement had tried to renew itself by creating a space through which it could conduct its protest against the government.[919] The Chartist Land Plan of the middle 1840s, which was an attack on industrialisation and its system of organisation, attempted to liberate workers from the factories and the mills and, instead, to provide them with opportunities as small holders on the land as an alternate way of life.[920] The emphasis was on providing labourers with the means to earn a 'fair day's wage for a fair day's work'.[921] It was an experiment which involved 2,000 men chosen by ballot. Each of them subscribed £2 10s to purchase land that was later sub-divided into two acres each, upon which cottages and farm buildings were erected. The subscribers to the scheme were given £15 each to develop plots of land that were allocated to them. The profits generated from their investment were later used to buy more property and recruit additional members and subscribers to the system.[922]

This scheme was certainly popular within the West Riding. Chartist Cooperative Land Societies were set up in all of the major towns across the region including Leeds, Bradford, Sheffield, Barnsley and Huddersfield.[923] Meetings were held and members joined the societies, in which they paid subscriptions, obtained shares and took part in conferences, along with the lotteries for plots of land.[924] The first major scheme was created in 1846 at Heronsgate, which was a village situated two and a half miles from Rickmansworth and was later aptly named O'Connorville.[925] It was followed by further schemes at Lowbands, Snigs End, Minster Lovell and Great Dodford.[926] From a territorial perspective, land ownership permitted the Chartists to exist independently from state interference. This meant that the leadership could freely promote its culture upon those that had signed up to the scheme. However, the growth of the venture created problems in itself. Questions were raised about its status as a friendly society and joint stock company.[927] Those issues were not helped by Feargus O'Connor's lack of business sense, along with a number of legal and political challenges initiated by the Russell administration.[928] The combination of those factors caused speculation and a fall in the share value of the Land Company, and many people lost money that they had invested in the scheme. This decline reflected badly upon Feargus O'Connor, whose popularity and leadership of the Chartist movement suffered as a consequence.[929]

The Land Plan masked another problem for the Chartists: their ability to mobilise enough support to openly challenge the authority of the government and its state machinery. During previous peak periods of mass activity in 1838-40 and 1842, the Chartists had taken on the Home Office and the local public order agencies, but mainly in isolation. The circumstances that rapidly unfolded throughout the latter part of 1847 prompted the need for a change in policy. Strategically, the main leadership of the Chartist movement forged a close alliance with the Irish Confederate organisation.[930] From a political standpoint, this decision was driven by extremist elements on both sides. On a short-term basis, the two radical movements had a shared aim which was to unseat the British government and generate enough unrest to make Ireland ungovernable. From a long-term perspective, the move towards political violence which was later carried into effect in towns and cities across the Industrial North throughout 1848 alienated some elements within the movement. The alliance between the Chartists and Irish Confederates also alarmed the Whig administration and was perceived as an open declaration of civil war. The alliance made the government more determined than ever to stamp out radical unrest. Matters were not helped by events that had unfolded across the English Channel. From the moment when Louis Philippe fell from power as the King of France in February 1848, the Chartists became reinvigorated as revolutionary movement. The provisional government which replaced Louis Philippe's regime introduced universal suffrage and a number of social and economic reforms that were designed to appease various class divisions. Fabrice Bensimon has argued that following the fall of the regime in France the ruling elites in Britain became highly concerned about the impact that it would have on the working classes, along with the spectre of Irish Nationalism.[931] In so doing, the British government took the initiative in denying the space in which the Chartists conducted their protests. The first part of this process involved waging a propaganda war against the Chartists in an attempt to sway sections of the population from engaging in revolutionary activity.

Kay Boardman and Christine Kinealy have argued that the demise of the Chartist movement in 1848 was a huge propaganda victory for the British government.[932] Railways and the electric telegraph, as noted, enabled the spread of ideas and information outwards from the centre to other parts of the country far more rapidly than ever before. James Vernon has pointed out that these technological developments enabled the ruling elites to use print culture in order to shape the 'political sphere' to suit their own 'aspirations'.[933] From the mid 1840s onwards, the growth of a mainstream national press centred upon Fleet Street led to the decline in popularity of the Chartist press. Newspapers such as *The Times* made greater use of the growth of communications and were better resourced. Furthermore, the increase in circulation of national newspapers meant that the messages put out by the Home Office attracted a wider audience. This clearly had an effect in swaying many people away from engaging in revolutionary activity during 1848.

The use of the electric telegraph meant that by the mid-1840s, the coverage of news events such as parliamentary proceedings could reach its readership by the early hours of the next day.[934] For example, in June 1846 following a debate over the Corn Laws, the newsagent W.H. Smith 'despatched 4,000 copies of *The Times* to all parts of the North' less than an hour and a quarter after the House of Lords had risen.[935] Once the paper had been 'made up' and 'sent to press', copies were despatched from its headquarters to Euston station, where they were loaded onto trains.[936] The trains departed at ten o'clock at night and delivered the newspapers to provincial outlets in Manchester, Birmingham and Liverpool. In 1848, this service was extended further north to Carlisle, Edinburgh and Glasgow.[937]

The impact of railways on the sales of the The Times in the provinces was such that whereas in 1837 it only accounted for 16 per cent of the London dailies sold in Manchester, by 1846 that figure had risen to 48 per cent.[938] In turn, the circulation of the newspaper grew during the period 1834 to 1847 from 10,000 copies per day to 40,000.[939] Hannah Barker has maintained that the electric telegraph and railways enabled the The Times to become 'the most prominent English newspaper'.[940] Nevertheless, despite a general increase in circulation and sales (see Table 3), newspapers still remained fairly expensive to buy. As a consequence, within provincial areas such as the West Riding, the working classes continued to rely heavily upon reading rooms at Mechanics' Institutes for news.[941] The advent of the Trans-Pennine Telegraph network which linked Manchester to Leeds, Wakefield and Halifax meant that the inhabitants of the region learnt about domestic and foreign affairs much more quickly and on a broader scale than previously.[942]

Table 3: Selected Newspaper Stamp Returns, 1843-8[943]

Title	1843	1844	1845	1846	1847	1848
Morning Post	1,090,000	1,002,000	1,002,500	1,045,500	990,100	964,500
Morning Chronicle	1,784,000	1,628,000	1,554,000	1,356,000	1,233,000	1,151,304
Morning Herald	1,516,000	1,609,070	2,018,025	1,752,500	1,510,000	1,335,000
Sun	1,098,000	868,000	1,098,500	1,105,000	909,000	893,312
Times	6,250,000	6,900,000	8,100,000	8,950,000	9,025,230	11,021,500
Manchester Guardian	761,800	859,000	967,000	1,002,000	1,009,000	968,000
Bradford Observer	55,500	48,000	54,000	54,000	54,000	55,598
Halifax Guardian	59,000	74,000	69,000	82,000	117,450	109,000
Leeds Intelligencer	190,000	200,000	210,000	208,480	201,480	220,174
Leeds Mercury	459,006	464,190	489,250	500,000	500,000	521,000
Leeds Times	176,000	204,000	241,000	234,650	254,000	281,500
Northern Star	454,500	384,000	337,500	322,000	455,000	626,000
Sheffield Independent	134,600	131,999	156,000	174,000	168,500	170,000

In October 1844 the Chartist movement tried to take advantage of changes within the newspaper industry, when Feargus O'Connor and the editor of the *Northern Star* decided to relocate the newspaper from Leeds to London. They did this in order to boost its effectiveness as a journal and organ of 'Democratic Movements'.[944] For twelve months previously, the topic of relocation had been widely discussed amongst the Chartist leadership. They felt that the newspaper had outgrown its 'little sphere of Yorkshire' as the movement had become 'the only National Party of the day'.[945] While the newspaper was published in Leeds, the paucity of communications that existed between London and the West Riding meant stories from the capital were often published twenty-four hours after the event. The Chartist leadership believed that by positioning the newspaper nearer to the seat of government, 'state secrets could be learned' from the 'clubs and coteries'.[946] This in turn, would give the radical organisation the power to influence legislation that affected the working classes.

From an organisational perspective, the decision to relocate the newspaper gave the Chartists a more cohesive look as the propaganda wing of the movement became tightly bound to its main executive leadership.[947] As London also had a far bigger population than Leeds, the Chartists had the potential to mobilise more support for their cause than ever before. However, the decision backfired as a newspaper that was rooted in Northern radical traditions did not have the same impact and appeal in the South. In addition, the spread of the railways meant that this once-provincial radical journal struggled to compete with mainstream newspapers such as *The Times* and *Manchester Guardian*.[948] The readership of both expanded and so too did their resources. For instance, there was an increase in sales of the *The Times* which generated advertising revenues of between £4,000 and £5,000 per week during 1847-8.[949] Some of this money was invested in an Applegarth Steam Printing Machine that produced 10,000 copies in an hour.[950] Pitched against such competition, the *Northern Star* could not compete and its sales gradually declined.

The cause of the Chartist press was not helped by the raised expectancy of political violence that followed the fall of the regime in France. This prompted the Home Office to impose a blockade on the information which the Chartists received by expanding the new infrastructure. On 9 March 1848, Sir Thomas Arbuthnot, the Commander of the Northern District Army, was told by the Home Secretary, Sir George Grey, about the 'importance of providing for the security of different lines of railroad' within the West Riding.[951] Further instructions were given to the civil authorities to 'prevent any injury to the railroads by riotous assemblages'.[952] Those instructions were followed by orders given to mayors and commanding officers to take possession of the 'stations and machinery of the Electric Telegraph Company'.[953] The superintendents of the stations were told not to forward any messages unless they were delivered to them in person with a copy of the authority enclosed.[954]

During the week of the presentation of the Chartist National Petition, Sir George Grey issued a warrant to take control of the Electric Telegraph Company, which he was permitted to do in a state emergency.[955] This enabled the Home Office to dictate the flow of information from the centre outwards. However, the measure failed to deter the Chartists from challenging the authority of the British state. The new crisis came in the shape of a head-on confrontation with the Home Office in an attempt to claim control of public space. The battle initially centred upon London and then shifted to the West Riding, where the Chartists were subsequently defeated.

The suppression of Chartism in London centred mainly upon the presentation of the National Petition on 10 April 1848. In preparation for that day of reckoning, the Home Office went to extreme lengths to ensure that the event would pass off peacefully. The tactics used for dealing with the handover of the Petition and the procession that accompanied it were framed to the finest detail. Some years ago, John Saville argued that Sir George Grey made all of the arrangements that secured the capital from unrest.[956] However, a fuller examination of contemporary materials would suggest important figures such as the Duke of Wellington and the Metropolitan Police Commissioner, Sir Richard Mayne, also played significant parts in putting in place the public-order arrangements for the events of the 10 April 1848.

A report sent by the Duke to the Home Secretary makes it clear that from the outset, the main aim was to prevent Chartist protest from gaining a foothold. Antony Taylor has argued that this involved the government restricting the Chartists' right to congregate by using the military and police to curtail their freedom of movement.[957] As a further ploy to secure the capital from unrest, the Chartists were kept at a distance from the vicinity of government buildings that could be harmed or potentially fall into their hands. For instance, the Houses of Parliament, the Bank of England, Buckingham Palace and Somerset House were occupied and heavily-guarded by a mixture of police and soldiers. Buildings of strategic importance such as railway stations and military barracks were also tightly secured by troops, who were told to keep a low profile.[958]

The Home Secretary and the Duke of Wellington tried to control public space by preventing the Chartists from marching in and around the capital. The sophisticated level of organisation that was put in place involved the banning of processions and gatherings both on and near bridges which were heavily guarded by two levels of security. The first was special constables and, if they failed in their duty, the second was armed regular soldiers. Heavy carriages were prevented from crossing bridges and circulating near state buildings, largely because of fears that vehicles carrying explosive equipment could be detonated as an act of terrorism.[959]

The limitations placed upon the Chartists and their freedom of movement were further extended to parks, which were closed at particular times both day and night. Taylor has argued that the parks were seen by the authorities as major focal points in securing the capital from civil unrest.[960] To prevent crowds from gathering illegally, notices were posted on the gates and when they were opened no more than five people were allowed to enter at once. Those who gained access had their behaviour monitored continually by cavalry soldiers on horseback. Any incidents of note were immediately reported back to their superior officers.[961] Notices issued by Commissioners of the Metropolitan Police also made it illegal to hold public meetings at Kennington Common on the day that the Chartist petition was due to be presented. The restrictions were later extended to towns and cities right across the country, including those in the West Riding.[962]

To further shore up the capital and mainland as a whole against violent and revolutionary assault by the Chartists, the Home Office introduced the Crown Government and Security Bill. This was a 'gagging act' that made it illegal for people to incite through speech direct action against the state and its institutions.[963] The measure made it a treasonable offence for people to speak out against government. It also gave magistrates the power to issue proceedings against anyone caught making seditious speeches.[964] To enforce this law, the Home Office recommended that two shorthand typists or confidential writers should be sent to political gatherings to monitor the content of the speeches that were made.[965] Whilst Prime Minister Russell felt that the government did not have any means of preventing 'machinations against its rule', the law enabled his administration to steer between 'two great dangers': sedition and treason.[966] Passed within twelve days, the Bill is described by Edward Vallance as 'a far reaching measure that redefined the offence of treason' which included 'open and advised speaking'.[967] The legislation was supplanted in May 1848 by an Aliens Act which gave the Home Office the power to deport those people who posed a threat to national security.[968] The new measure was intended to guard against 'any revolutionary attempts' that could undermine the constitution and state institutions, and keep a lid on radical tensions.[969]

On 10 April 1848, the day that the National Petition was presented to

Parliament, the Chartists planned to assemble at Kennington Common and march towards the House of Commons. This plan was thwarted by the strisecurity arrangements that had been put in place. In the morning, before the petition was due to be handed over, the Commissioner of the Metropolitan Police, Sir Richard Mayne, met Feargus O'Connor. He warned him about the wide-ranging preparations that had been put in place for the event. The Chartist leader had very little option but to agree to his demands. O'Connor was told that the National Petition would be sent to the House of Commons in three Hackney cabs. Both he and two other Chartist leaders were ordered to travel in the same vehicles as the petition. When Mayne told O'Connor about the security preparations, he said that he had never seen a man look 'more frightened' than the Chartist leader.[970] Subsequently, O'Connor was accused of succumbing to the wishes of the police. This led to an even greater loss of face amongst his supporters.[971]

When the presentation of the petition revealed much about the weakness of the Chartist movement. The Duke of Wellington and the Home Secretary had made arrangements in preparation for a crowd of around 200,000 people to descend on the capital and protest against the Government.[972] According to Metropolitan Police sources, the number of people who turned out on the day for the procession and presentation of the Petition was estimated to have been from around 14-15,000 to a more generous figure of 20,000.[973] David Goodway has suggested that around 80,000 people had gathered at the location.[974] Whilst a few foreign people at the scene bore arms, the event passed off fairly peacefully, despite there being a few skirmishes later on between disheartened Chartists and the police.[975]

What was striking about the day of the presentation of the Petition was the number of people who turned out in force to protect the state and its national institutions from succumbing to potential revolutionary turmoil. Many had randomly volunteered their services to magistrates and were sworn-in as special constables.[976] The impressive show of force was a major factor in the suppression of Chartism, not only in the capital but also in many other towns and cities across the country. The development also signified how much opposition there was towards the Chartists and the Irish Confederate organisations. Furthermore, it would support an assertion made by John Belchem that 1848 was about the protection of 'English freedom and constitutional liberty' from Chartist agitation at Kennington Common, which was seen as 'criminal, unconstitutional, un-English and most damning of all, Irish'.[977]

In examining how Chartist agitation was policed in London, Roger Swift has argued that it has become accepted wisdom to suggest that recruitment of special constables was a largely among the middle classes.[978] Whilst this argument is difficult to prove, as very few records exist, it may not have been entirely the case, as highlighted by an observation made by the Leeds magistrate William Dawson. In a letter written to Sir George Grey on 15 April 1848, Dawson said that the majority from this social class refused to act as special constables in Leeds.[979] However, the Home Office was quite clearly taken aback by the number of people who were sworn-in by magistrates as specials in the capital. The Home Secretary looked to take advantage of this development as he sought to change the way in which they were organised. Instead of being appointed by magistrates on an ad hoc basis, Sir George Grey wanted to regulate their use through the creation of a permanent 'Loyal Volunteer Police'.[980] He drafted an outline proposal for its organisation. It was based on the appointment of three honorary commissioners charged with the regulation of the force, along with an acting commissioner who would be responsible for its operation. Further down the chain of command the intention was for a treasurer and clerks to oversee the administration.[981]

The Home Office wanted to organise the special constabulary into two separate classes – those who would serve the immediate area where they resided and a migratory class that could be moved from place to place within a given parish or district. Grey wanted each class to be made up of twelve special constables, with a section head or leader. From those, two sections would be formed to create a sub-division, and two of these would make up a division that consisted of 48 special constables and a leader. In relation to drilling, each class/sub-division would assemble at a given place to receive instructions that concerned the discharge of their duties. As a further measure of organisation, Sir George Grey wanted the parishes to be divided into divisions in relation to the number of specials based on their locality. The Home Office looked to put in place plans to unite the parishes to form districts with a given point of assembly. The forces would be overseen by a district leader who would assume responsibility for the entire moveable class of special constables. The scheme further entailed the removal of one hundred sergeants from active police duty who would be used to train this force. Each special constable who volunteered their services would receive a basic reprint of the constabulary laws, along with a book of police instructions that they could use as a guide in the discharge of their duties.[982]

Whilst critics felt that the proposals were too complicated to put into action, it is clear that the Home Office and Metropolitan Police Commissioners, respectively Sir Richard Mayne and Sir Charles Rowan, supported this scheme. They also wanted additional measures that included the payment of special constables for their duties.[983] From what was being suggested by Grey, the policy seemed a serious attempt by the Home Office to remove control of the appointment of special constables from the magistracy. How extensively those proposals were implemented across the country is a subject for a separate discussion. However, what is clear is that the response by many people to volunteer as special constables in London to suppress Chartist unrest was followed elsewhere in Britain, particularly the West Riding where radical protest again took root.[984]

The suppression of Chartism in the West Riding took place against the backdrop of economic depression affecting the plight of handloom weavers. Theodore Koditschek has said that the events in the region, particularly those in Bradford, represented 'the last gasp of the economically moribund handcraft stratum' which had been created during the early stages of industrialisation, but had become obsolete.[985] The cause of their dissent throughout 1848 was structural unemployment brought about by the mechanisation of production techniques in the woollen, worsted and cotton industries through the introduction of power loom machinery.[986] Both factory and mill owners profited from the application of technological advances that resulted in 'the largest body of workmen' being 'thrown out of employment'.[987] As a consequence, weavers' wages were reduced to their 'lowest ebb' and they were forced to turn to 'security sums allotted to them by the Poor Law Guardians' as a means of subsistence.[988]

Across the West Riding many towns affected by worsening unemployment and trade conditions became renewed Chartist strongholds for unrest.[989] For instance, in Bradford it was estimated that around 10,000 people suffered from economic hardship. The effects of the introduction of machinery on the labour market was such that one firm, Messrs Walken and Co., which had previously employed in the region of 1,700 combers, reduced its workforce to under 400. The owners of the company boasted that the machines could do the work of 'a thousand men'.[990] The poverty that emanated from this massive wave of unemployment hit the region extremely hard. Chartist speakers such as George White called upon the Whig government to alleviate the conditions of both starving and dying people. At the time, White believed that much inspiration could be taken from the events that occurred in revolutionary France:

The French Government were using their best endeavours to make man happy. They had opened workshops where a man could go, and after ten working hours could go home with his wages in his pocket; and the government meant to pass a law that all men who arrived at 65 years of age should receive a pension, not as a pauper, but as a free citizen of the French nation. Government should act as a father acted towards the children of a family. It was time indeed they sought out some government to treat them properly and humanely.[991]

The idea that the Whig administration should adopt a paternalistic role was not, of course, shared by every Chartist. For instance, in Bradford local leader David Lightowler, who spoke at a political meeting held on 30 March 1848 at Peckover's Walk, believed that 'corrupt government' was a central reason why the Charter should be adopted.[992] The delegate for the National Convention told the crowd that the points of the People's Charter were necessary to secure faithful representatives, along with 'good and cheap government'.[993] In response to the problem of starvation amongst the displaced textile workers, Lightowler suggested that a more representative political system was needed. He felt that had the working classes been given the vote, the Corn Laws may not have been introduced. Lightowler told the crowd that the landed classes had adopted the earlier measure in order to secure 'a monopoly of the staple of life, at the expense of the great mass of the people'.[994]

The Chartists also tried to encourage support among the Irish immigrant population many of whom had taken residence within West Yorkshire following the potato famine. The plight of the migrants was tied in with the disenfranchised working classes, with both groups looked upon as 'slaves'.[995] It led to calls from Chartist leaders for unity amongst 'Englishmen and Irishmen in a league to obtain freedom and equality for their respective nations'.[996] The slavery issue had two sides to it. The huge influx of Irish migrants placed huge pressure on local government infrastructure in many towns and cities across the country, particularly within the Industrial North. This meant that there were not enough resources to go around in terms of poor relief. The situation bred huge middle-class resentment towards the Irish as a race. *The Times* made the observation that 'we send over our relief and get back the pauper'.[997] The newspaper also bemoaned the fact that the nation had become the 'workhouse and hospital for the Irish'.[998] Secondly, tensions on the mainland were not helped by the outcry that stemmed from the arrest of John Mitchel on 22 March 1848. The Irish radical writer, who had published seditious material under the Treason and Felony Act, caused further resentment to build up amongst Irish communities against the British government. Many politicians believed that his incarceration would elicit a violent response from the Irish Confederate movement.[999]

In examining how the Home Office suppressed Chartist agitation in the West Riding, it is clear that many lessons had been learned both from the handling of the 1842 Plug Plot disturbances and the recent London experience. The prevailing tactic was to deny the Chartists space to manoeuvre and to protect property at all cost. As in London, the closure of space involved the protection of state buildings such as court houses and military barracks from potential assault by the Chartists. In Bradford, out of a total of 82 infantry soldiers and 26 dragoons, 20 were used to protect the army barracks on Bradford Moor.[1000] Magistrates across the region also wanted to extend the protection of property by securing the factories and mills from assault through placing enrolled pensioners inside them to prevent any vandalism.[1001] The Home Secretary refused the plan and told magistrates to speak to Sir Thomas Arbuthnot about using other forces as an alternative measure.[1002]

Despite this objection, another lesson from the handling of the Plug Plot riots concerned the role of the magistrates. Whereas previously, they had played a major part, along with the military, in policing riots and disturbances, during 1848 they were largely confined to making judicial decisions. The advent of better internal communications meant that closer ties were forged between the Home Office and magistracy, especially in the application of laws on a national scale. The growth of consultation between the centre and localities meant that legislation such as the Crown and Government Security Act could be widely enforced. An example of such cooperation in the suppression of Chartist unrest can be seen in an incident that took place in Leeds. Two individuals, Jonathan Wilkinson and Alexander Murdoch, went around the town posting hand bills on walls. The posters had been written by the local Chartist leader Joseph Barker, who called upon people to refuse to be sworn-in as special constables. As Wilkinson and Murdoch went about their business, they were followed and arrested.[1003] Whilst in custody, they refused to divulge the details of the person who had printed the hand bills. A reward was later offered to reveal the identity of the culprit. In an attempt to apply the law, the Leeds magistrates sent for scrutiny three of the posters to the Attorney-General, who decided that prosecutions could be carried out under the Printer's Act.[1004]

Despite the forging of closer ties between the centre and localities in the judicial handling of Chartist protest, there were still a number of difficulties in relation to putting in place public order arrangements. Although lessons had been learned from the handling of the Plug Plot disturbances, as the military presence was considerably stepped up, Sir George Grey was told by Sir Thomas Arbuthnot that there was insufficient accommodation for the number of troops stationed in the Northern District.[1005] Such was the shortage of space to accommodate soldiers in Halifax that the unoccupied part of the Northgate Hotel had to be used. The town's magistrates also arranged for the construction of makeshift stables for their horses.[1006] The situation in Bradford was equally bad. Despite having had a permanent barracks built on the outskirts of the town, its Justices of the Peace were forced to hire buildings to station troops. As a result, the Dragoons ended up being lodged and stationed at the New Inn public house.[1007] As a subsequent measure, the local magistrates and some of the inhabitants of the town had to put their resources together towards building a temporary barracks. A sum of £400 was raised towards fitting the premises, whilst the Board of Ordnance also subscribed £350 towards the rental of a property scheme. The move was later approved by Major Thorn.[1008]

The stationing of both regular and auxiliary soldiers at town centre public houses and hotels carried inherent dangers in that they attracted much unwanted attention from angry and hostile crowds. This was highlighted by the presence of the yeomanry at the George Hotel in Huddersfield. On 28 May 1848, a number of people gathered outside the building and greeted the cavalry with 'yells and execrations'.[1009] The hatred of the military as an instrument of oppression was such that greater emphasis was placed on policing than ever before. Unlike his Whig predecessor Russell, Sir George Grey would not allow or encourage the formation of 'Armed Volunteer Corps' as a half-way measure in the repression of internal disturbances'.[1010] He told the Earl of Harewood that civil power should rely on 'a well-organised police force' which should be supported in emergencies by special constables and in the event of any serious disturbances, the military.[1011]

The police forces within the West Riding continued to be divided along borough and parish lines. Whilst Leeds already had a borough force in place, growing towns such as Halifax and Bradford had recently adopted such forces as a result of changes to their municipal status. Smaller towns and villages, such as Barnsley and Bingley, continued to use the 1842 Parish Constables Act which revolved around the superintendent constable and lock-up house. In the suppression of Chartist unrest within the West Riding, the main difficulty with both types of forces was that despite having greater numerical strength than ever before, they were largely ineffective in dealing with disturbances and riots. This was due to the lack of weaponry and personal protection provided for constables dealing with violent assault. As a result, the police had to rely on the military for assistance even though they were for the most part, in the frontline of duty.

In Barnsley, the deficiencies of the 1842 Parish Constables Act as a measure for dealing with riot and disorder were clearly evident. The local superintendent constable refused to disrupt Chartist meetings that were held each Sunday on the basis that such action would lead to severe unrest.[1012] The police were powerless to prevent not only the continued arming and drilling that accompanied political gatherings, but also the mass-production of pikes. It was estimated that somewhere in the region of 300-400 weapons had been sold for one shilling and a penny each. The magistrates sought guidance from the Home Office about what to do in this worrying situation.[1013] Having learnt many lessons from the handling of the Plug Plot disturbances, the Home Secretary initially refused to send in the military. Instead, Grey urged the magistrates to use legal measures to put an end to the illegal activities of the Chartists.[1014] There was also the preference for magistrates to 'swear in and organise an efficient body of special constables'.[1015] When those measures failed, the Home Secretary and Sir Thomas Arbuthnot decided to send a detachment of infantry to the town in order to secure it from unrest.[1016] As a further precaution 900 men were later sworn in as specials, despite the fear of bloodshed if a confrontation with the pike-wielding Chartists ensued.[1017]

The situation in Bingley was just as fraught since local Chartist cells had organised themselves into National Guards and Life and Protection Societies.[1018] Throughout April and May 1848, clandestine arming and drilling was rife and the insurgents frequently marched in military array. The individuals at the centre of this activity were accompanied by colourful brass bands and iconic tricolour flags that were designed in support of the French cause. Members of the local Chartist organisation went around calling themselves the 'Fraternity'.[1019] Much of the unrest within the town was co-ordinated by the Chartist Executive Council in London and the drilling was organised by a discharged soldier.[1020] Sir George Grey told the Bingley magistrates to punish anyone caught carrying out this activity under the Unlawful Drilling Act of 1819.[1021]

When two of the ringleaders were captured by the civil authorities as a result of good detective work, their arrest led to a major incident. It revealed much about the deficiency of the police in the town. On 26 May 1848, as police constables escorted the prisoners to the railway station, where a train was waiting to transport them to York Castle for trial, an angry mob gathered at the scene and ambushed them. The police were forced to turn back to the Court House with the prisoners in tow. As they retreated the crowd followed and grew in size. The emboldened crowd then broke into the Magistrates Office and liberated the prisoners, from where they were later spirited off to Bradford.[1022] According to General Thorn, this was 'the first act of important aggression' that had been 'committed by the Chartists'.[1023] Grey told Bingley magistrate William Busfield Ferrand to forward the names the people who were rescued to the magistrates at Bradford so that they could be apprehended.[1024] At this point tension was so high that any form of action would result in confrontation. This is precisely what happened in Bradford; it became the epicentre of the 1848 phase of Chartism in the West Riding.[1025]

The suppression of Chartist unrest in Bradford fell largely on the shoulders of the newly-created Borough Police. This was problematic for a number of reasons. The force in place still had the same lock-up house and superintendent constable created in 1843 when the town magistrates adopted the 1842 Parish Constables Act.[1026] Throughout 1848, the lock-up house could not cope with the wave of Chartist agitation that swept Bradford as 1,020 supporters were taken into custody for various public order offences. The building was designed to cater for only ten people, yet it housed roughly twenty prisoners per week![1027]

In the battle to control public space, following the presentation of the National Petition, the police could not cope with the growth in the number of illegally-held political meetings in and around the town. More worryingly, the arming and drilling of Chartists intent on direct action was rife. Bradford's population contained a number of Irish immigrants and magistrates feared that 'the Chartists would rise if there was an outbreak of violence in Ireland or anywhere in England'.[1028] On 7 April 1848, a 'large body of bankers, merchants' and 'manufacturers' to the number of 1,500, were sworn-in as special constables.[1029] The specials – recruited here from largely middle-class occupations – were arranged into companies with a captain for each division, whilst the 'command and control' of the entire force was entrusted to the superintendent constable.[1030] At the same time, the ordinary police were armed with cutlasses instead of staves and were trained on a daily basis in the use of this 'destructive weapon'.[1031]

In response to the illegal meetings, the Bradford magistrates initially wanted Sir George Grey to send a reporter to the town to take notes of Chartist speeches. The Home Secretary refused to adopt this course of action on the grounds that 'more specific information' was needed about the language that was being used at the meetings.[1032] The main spark that ignited tensions occurred on the 13 May 1848, when a plain-clothes off-duty constable, who was walking towards a barber shop on the Manchester Road, noticed a group of men marching in military array.[1033] They were armed with dual staves that were six-feet in length and led by an 'ancient soldier' who had 'drilled them in military-manoeuvres'.[1034] The constable went up to the person at the head of the procession and asked for his name. Several of the party attacked him. As he called out for assistance, more police arrived at the scene and arrested a member of the group. When the captured prisoner was being escorted along the Manchester Road 'an unruly crowd' followed the police. The plain-clothed officer who had earlier been assaulted tried to capture another member of the party. In response, the police had brickbats and stones thrown at them. Many constables, who by this time had retreated from the scene, sustained injuries and the persons that they had captured were taken from their grasp.[1035]

When news of the incident reached the Borough Police office, a group of constables were sent to the New Inn where they kept a low profile and watched the crowd until the early hours of the morning. By this time, it had gathered at the bottom of Sterling Street on the corner of Manchester Road. The majority of those assembled were women who sang Chartist hymns and declared the 'near advent of liberty'.[1036] Two to three Chartist orators were also present, one of whom, Isaac Jefferson, announced himself as the 'Yorkshire Wat Tyler'.[1037]

After this street confrontation with the police, tensions in and around Bradford escalated. The biggest gathering that caused the greatest concern within Home Office and local circles was held on 23 May at Peckover's Walk in the centre of the town, where it was estimated that 20,000 people were present. Before the meeting began, a number of men marched to the location in military array to the shouts of 'right wheel' and 'left wheel', from various Chartist commanders.[1038] At the venue was 'a more than ordinary' display of flags and banners, along with several bands. The staffs of some of the small tricolours were tipped with spikes and spears, one of which bore the ominous representation of a dagger pointed to a heart.[1039]

When the meeting got under way, the crowd set free a number of carrier pigeons, intending that they would reach Chartist cells in Halifax. This was done to inform their comrades that the meeting had gone ahead despite attempts made by the authorities to prevent it. Whilst the crowds listened to a number of speakers, including Dr Peter McDouall, stones were thrown at the platform, and a pistol was fired as David Lightowler was speaking. Many fled but what particularly alarmed the authorities was the size of the crowd and its menacing aspect. When the meeting ended, a huge procession marched through the centre of Bradford and many people took to the streets to welcome it.[1040]

Grey became very concerned about the chain of events. After receiving a report of the speech made by McDouall, the Home Secretary told the town's magistrates not to take any proceedings against the Chartist, even though the language that he had used was clearly 'illegal and seditious'.[1041] He also warned the Mayor and Justices of the Peace that 'the marching of great numbers of persons in military array through a town in such a way to strike terror' was illegal.[1042] Grey told them to enforce the Unlawful Drilling Act 'without delay'.[1043]

Following the episode, the authorities in and around Bradford tried to regain control of the situation as the town had virtually become ungovernable. The magistrates decided to pursue 'the Chartist leaders and orators, armourers and drill-sergeants'.[1044] The strategy led to disagreements, especially amongst the Justices of the Peace and the Military, over the deployment of the Metropolitan Police. The army wanted to use the force to gather intelligence about the activities of the Chartists who were at the forefront of the arming and drilling. Whilst the generals petitioned the Home Secretary for Metropolitan Police assistance, local magistrates such as John Tempest objected to its use on the familiar grounds of cost. He argued that the magistracy had insufficient funds available to pay for their expenses and upkeep.[1045] Tempest and his colleagues, were overruled by the Home Office and two constables from the Detective Force were later sent to Bradford and Halifax to assist with the repression of arming and drilling.[1046] Grey told the personnel in charge of both the civil and military powers in Bradford that the force was deployed because of a 'peculiar case' and that it could only be used 'for a very short time'.[1047] The magistrates were also warned by the Home Secretary to increase the efficiency of their local police by adopting the 1839 and 1840 County Police Acts.[1048]

The deployment of the Metropolitan Police coincided with the gradual build-up of a military presence within Bradford. On 25 May, the infantry entered the town and they were met by a large body of Chartists on the Leeds Road who goaded the soldiers and defiantly marched in military order within full view of them.[1049] The arrival of the infantry was followed by the cavalry in the shape of ninety men of the West Yorkshire Yeomanry Regiment. They arrived on the 28 May, at the same time that a huge Chartist meeting was being held at Pudding Hill in the neighbourhood of Wilsden. By the following day, when 800 soldiers had descended on the town, it was effectively now in a state of 'military occupation'.[1050] Sir George Grey had earlier told the Mayor to remind the magistrates that the military force with which they had been provided was not to be used as a substitute for the police but to aid them.[1051]

In the early hours of 29 May 1848, the town magistrates, various military-generals, the Lord Lieutenant and the Mayor gathered at Bradford Court House. The special constables were later summoned to attend a 'council of war' to discuss and decide on a 'plan of operations'.[1052] At nine o'clock in the morning, the superintendent constable William Brigg and one-hundred special constables set off from the Court House. The intention was to arrest the Chartist leaders who resided at Manchester Road. This included the colourful Isaac Jefferson, better known as 'Wat Tyler', a Chartist blacksmith and pike-maker. When Brigg and the specials reached the top of Adelaide Street, they were met by a large number of men, boys and women who jeered them. The superintendent constable, along with a group of detectives, entered Jefferson's blacksmiths shop and home, but he was nowhere to be seen.[1053]

When Brigg and his force were about to depart from the location they were assaulted by a crowd. Stones and brickbats 'flew about like hail' and several constables were hit by the missiles, causing injuries.[1054] Many special constables were unarmed and without staves to defend themselves. Some of the cudgels that belonged to them had been seized by the Chartists. They were used with great effect to inflict injuries to the heads and backs of the constables. Following the melée, as the police and the specials hastily retreated along the Manchester Road in the direction of the Court House, a large mob followed in pursuit, whilst women among them who were said to have been 'violent in tone and gesture', threw stones from the windows of their houses.[1055]

At mid-morning, a huge crowd gathered in front of the Court House which was heavily garrisoned by troops of the 5th Dragoon Guards, a detachment of the 81st Infantry and army pensioners. The shops in the town centre were closed and as special constables ventured to and from the Court House, many were kicked by women and boys at the scene. For the rest of the entire morning, the magistrates and military plotted their next course of action. At noon, three companies of the 52nd Infantry from Colne and Manchester entered the town. The magistrates issued the following notice:

Borough of Bradford, in the West Riding of Yorkshire – Caution – Whereas processions of large numbers of people, accompanied with circumstances tending to excite terror and alarm in the minds of her Majesty's subjects, and training and drilling, or practising military movements or exercise, are highly criminal and illegal; and whereas not only those persons who take an active part at any such processions and drillings, but all who by their presence wilfully countenance them, are acting contrary to the law: all persons are hereby cautioned and strictly

enjoined not to attend or take part in or be present at any processions
or drillings: and all well-disposed persons are hereby called upon and
required to aid in enforcing the provisions of the law, and effectually
to protect the public peace, and to suppress any attempt to disturb the
same.[1056]

At half-past three in the afternoon, a large number of special constables
began to enter the yard of the Court House. These were made up of men
of property – merchants, manufacturers and tradesmen. Thirty minutes
later, they were addressed by Colonel Tempest who relayed instructions
given to him by the magistrates. They were told to return to the Manchester
Road. The news was greeted by loud cheers. The Colonel, who was assisted
by a few magistrates, said that the police would lead the procession with
the specials following eight or ten abreast. Positioned to the rear of them
were infantry and cavalry troops. The special constables were told to seize
any Chartist leaders that came their way and if anyone used violence or
obstructed them, they were to be secured and placed in the custody of the
soldiers. In total, 500 special constables, fifty policemen, 160 of the 81st, 32nd
and 39th Regiments, along with fifty of the 5th Dragoons assembled in front
of the Court House. They were led by the mayor and a posse of magistrates
on horseback who gave orders and advice whenever needed.[1057]

The formidable procession set off from the Court House and when it
arrived at the top of Adelaide Street, it came to a brief halt and was greeted
by a large crowd. Magistrates gave the police a command to march into the
street and revisit Wat Tyler's home. In so doing, the ranks of the special
constables were broken up by 'an immense volley of stones and brickbats'
thrown by the crowd which was situated on the other side of the street.[1058] A
pistol was fired and several specials who were struck by the stones sustained
serious cuts and bruises. At this stage, the cavalry intervened and charged
at the crowd. This distraction enabled the constables to conduct thorough
searches of the buildings along Adelaide Street and Earl Street. As the cavalry
roared up the road, the crowd hastily retreated and a number of people
were arrested. These included the men who had thrown the stones and fired
the pistol. Some protesters, such as Mary Mortimer who was captured in
the doorway of a house, were also taken into custody for offering resistance.
In order to restrain her, the sword of a dragoon was used to pin her to a
wall! She was one of many women who had thrown stones 'with the greatest
intrepidity and fierceness' and 'swore like a trooper', when seized.[1059] She
was one of seventeen people arrested at the scene and escorted back to the
Court House by police and soldiers who later put down a bold attempt

to rescue some of the prisoners. After visiting the Manchester Road, the procession conducted a full search of the neighbourhood as they continued on to Bower Street, Portland Street, Queen's Cut and Broomfield. They searched 'dirty and wretched abodes', along with deserted workshops, for widespread and intense pike-making and a number of weapons which were seized.[1060]

The violence attached to the suppression of this incident revealed much about the lack of adequate protection afforded to the special constables and the dangers that they faced. George Brown, a worsted spinner, received a cut on the head after being hit by a stone; Thomas Dewhurst, a share-broker, 'had his face and shoulder dreadfully cut'; Daniel Illingworth, a worsted spinner and later founder of an industrial dynasty, was hit below the knee-cap by a stone.[1061] Several 'other gentlemen' also received 'several cuts and bruises' but hardly any of those were of a 'serious nature'.[1062] However, none of the military were injured. Despite the lengths to which the civil and military forces went, only nineteen people were arrested. One of those was sent to York Castle for drilling, along with nine others who were later charged with rioting. The remainder of those captured were discharged on the basis that there was 'not sufficient evidence to justify their committal'.[1063]

The blame for the chaotic response of the civil forces in the battle for Bradford was firmly placed at the hands of the police, in particular Superintendent Constable Brigg who was drunk and had failed to properly organise the special constables.[1064] His misconduct and negligence led to instant dismissal. The officer-in-charge later claimed that he had gone down with an 'an attack of fever'.[1065] Sir George Grey expressed huge regret that 'the ends of justice' had been 'frustrated by the inefficiency' and 'misconduct of a person'.[1066] In response to this lapse, the Home Secretary ordered an inspector from the Metropolitan Police to be sent to Bradford. The local magistrates also issued a proclamation which banned marches through the town.[1067]

After this major incident, the borough detectives monitored the people who were responsible for the frequent arming and drilling that had taken place. At Busy Brigg they observed men who were formed into divisions two deep, step in-time with their feet as they marched up and down the field. The detectives watched them march towards White Abbey, a notoriously deprived part of Bradford, but because they did not have a warrant, no arrests could be made. When the magistrates gave them a warrant, the Bradford detectives John Shuttleworth and Joseph Field, along with a number of police officers, apprehended the ringleader, Benjamin Plant, at his home in Mill Street. It was there that they found a pike and a 'green velvet cap of liberty'.[1068] Similar raids were carried out on the homes of Daniel Holroyd, William Gill and Henry Woodhead, all of whom were later charged with drilling.[1069] However, the person that the authorities especially wanted was the Chartist leader Isaac Jefferson (Wat Tyler). When he later resurfaced, the authorities had him in their grasp only for the police to lose him again after a group came to his rescue. On 21 July 1848, the Bradford magistrate Robert Milligan wrote to Sir George Grey:

> One of our day Police happening to see Wat Tyler in the street (who had returned after having been out of the way for some weeks) watched him into a house' and 'without consulting any one took two other police men' and 'apprehended there' and 'were on their way to the lockup when the mob who have colluded in the mean time offended a rescue...'We regret the circumstance' and 'believe that if our Chief Constable had been informed he would have sent a force sufficient to have prevented the rescue.[1070]

A few weeks later, the pike-maker along with many others involved in arming and drilling were rounded up and arrested.[1071] What was interesting about this incident was that despite the innovation of the electric telegraph, the authorities in Bradford still relied heavily on the postmaster, who was in frequent contact with George Cornewall Lewis at the Home Office. This evidence would suggest that despite the availability of this technology, it was not being fully utilised by the authorities to aid repression.[1072]

With the Chartist movement in Bradford effectively defeated, the attention of the Home Office swiftly turned towards the suppression of its close allies the Irish Confederates. This revealed much about the strength of the surveillance mechanisms that were deployed within the region. On the day that the authorities in Bradford tried to arrest David Lightowler and Isaac Jefferson for their part in causing civil unrest, the Home Office received information about a bigger plot. The Irish Confederate leader Joe Grady, who led a cell in Bradford, spoke openly about the need for an insurrection in Ireland. He suggested that it was 'the duty of every Irishman' within Chartist ranks to 'double their exertions' and step up the agitation in order to prevent the British government from sending any more troops to Ireland.[1073]

Much of Grady's anger was centred upon the outcome of the trial of John Mitchel. The Irish Confederate leader argued that if he was found guilty, 'a revolution' would 'immediately commence'.[1074] However, Grady also suggested that if Mitchel was not found guilty a revolt would still go ahead but not 'until the first of August next'.[1075] The plot was given further impetus when Sir Thomas Arbuthnot received information from spies and informants that the Irish wanted to cause a widespread uprising in the North of England. This scheme centred upon Bradford, Manchester and Liverpool.[1076]

In analysing how this plot unfolded and was suppressed, on 24 July 1848 the Bradford magistrate John Tempest told Sir George Grey that Chartist and Irish Confederate Clubs had held meetings in their private houses. The ringleaders expected that, in the event of any outbreak of violence within Ireland, troops would be moved from Bradford. Their departure was to act as a signal for an uprising on the mainland in order to distract the authorities from putting down an even larger one in Ireland. The plot was given added impetus when local magistrates told the Home Secretary that Irish Confederate leaders from Dublin had visited Lancashire and Yorkshire.[1077] From this visit, the Home Office unearthed a scheme to destroy gas and water works, along with factories and mills in the three designated places. The intention was to create a chain of simultaneous uprisings in order to make the region ungovernable.[1078]

The Irish Confederates' and Chartists' attempt to carry the plot into effect was a failure. As the ringleaders in Bradford waited for further instructions from cells in Manchester about the plot, they were captured by the authorities. Also arrested were leaders of the Chartist Confederate Council, its secretary and various other sections which had also been behind much of the community arming and drilling that had previously taken place.[1079] Whilst only ten men were arrested in the raids, this was enough to prevent the beleaguered Irish Confederates from carrying their designs into action. In effect, the suppression of this plot killed off any further violent protest in the West Riding and with it the threat of 'physical force' Chartism.[1080]

Despite the later efforts of Ernest Jones to keep the movement afloat, Chartism never really recovered from the devastating blow which it received during the autumn of 1848. In the long-term, the movement fell into steady decline. During the early-1850s, which was quite a prosperous time for the West Riding, many veteran Chartists became active in local council politics, engaging in issues such as public health and urban improvement.[1081] This was especially the case in places such as Bradford which, after the huge political crisis that shook the town in 1848, was later changed by liberalism and transformed into what Theodore Koditschek described as being a 'more orderly urban community of the mid-Victorian age'.[1082] In neighbouring Halifax, Chartism failed to regain the same momentum that it had ten years previously. As Kate Tiller has pointed out, despite contesting elections, the movement withered away and became the preserve of 'a handful of disillusioned enthusiasts with little to concentrate on but past glories'.[1083] Throughout 1848 there was a clear attempt by the Home Office to suppress any dissent expressed by the Chartists and the Irish Confederate movement, in order to prevent the state and its institutions from succumbing to revolutionary turmoil. The move included a major clampdown on the Chartists use of written language, speech and freedom of assembly. The measures introduced by the Home Office were largely anti-democratic and supports James Vernon's view that there was a closure of the political space in which the Chartists conducted their protestations. This coercive response subsequently led to their demise as a mass movement for social change.

The Home Office tactics employed in London during 1848 were mimicked throughout the country, especially in places such as the West Riding, but on a much lesser scale. However, there were significant differences over the way in which Chartist unrest was suppressed in London compared to the West Riding. First of all, with Chartist protest being conducted nearer to the seat of government, the Home Office never left anything to chance. In London, the response to Chartist agitation was better coordinated and much more cohesive than anywhere else in the country. This was largely because the Home Secretary, Metropolitan Police Commissioners and various Military Generals worked quite closely together on the spot in planning and coordinating police and military responses to disorder. In tandem were crucial factors such as the use of propaganda and control of public space which ensured that civil unrest did not gain a foothold.

The use of press propaganda had a major impact on Chartist protest as the movement could not muster enough support to trouble the authorities on a mass scale, especially in London. The turn-out for the presentation of the Chartist National Petition and the demonstrations that followed were transformed by the authorities into a major police and military operation. The threat of revolution, and the danger which the Chartists and the Irish Confederate movement posed to the security of the nation was reported extensively in mainstream newspapers. It clearly had a major effect on the way in which the middle classes formed their opinions towards the protesters. In doing so, the fear of revolution encouraged many of them to come forward in large numbers and volunteer their services as special constables to overwhelm the Chartists.

In the closure of public space within London, the Home Office had greater resources at its disposal and the Chartists found many avenues and thoroughfares closed when they tried to engage in any form of political protest which challenged the authority of the state. The systematic closure of public spaces entailed the protection from assault by the Chartists of strategic buildings such as military barracks and railway stations, along with economic concerns such as factories and mills. Further, there was also a major clampdown, initiated by the Home Office, on the right of the Chartists to assemble in parks and open spaces, which severely weakened their protest. The closure of public space was extended to the use of language, both spoken and written, through legislation such as the Crown Government and Security Act which did much to silence and criminalise Chartist protests.

If the measures used to control public space in London proved highly effective in the suppression of Chartism during 1848, within the West Riding the situation was not as clear cut. This was despite the fact that the Home Office could exert greater control than ever before over the machinery of public order that existed within the provinces. The response to Chartist agitation in the West Riding was not as well organised or cohesive as it was in the capital, despite the fact that many lessons had been learned from the handling of the 1842 Plug Plot disturbances from which better apparatus for dealing with civil unrest had emerged.

There were serious difficulties policing provincial Chartist agitation. Whilst London had a centrally controlled and uniform police force which operated within a 15-mile radius of Charing Cross, in the West Riding the police forces were divided along borough and parish lines. The forces had different customs and practices, and there was a lack of cooperation amongst them which allowed Chartist unrest to gain a foothold. A further difference between the police forces in the West Riding and London was the lack of numbers, a deficiency clearly demonstrated by incidents in Bingley and Bradford in which the military had to act as a guiding hand in suppressing violent disorder.

The use of the military as a back-up force in the suppression of Chartist unrest was also problematic for a number of reasons. Unlike previous Home Secretaries, Sir George Grey did not show the same willingness to part with troops, Instead, holding them in reserve and allowing the police to take up a position as the front line of defence. Secondly, in relation to the deployment of the military during 1848, there were still the same difficulties that existed almost ten years earlier, particularly over the lack of troop accommodation. However, despite these problems, Chartist agitation in the West Riding was suppressed because ultimately the Home Office could draw on a range of greater resources. In the end, by 1848 this proved too much for the Chartists to deal with as the movement was backed into a corner from which there was no escape.

7. CONCLUSION

It is clear that the Home Office policy of state coercion was certainly an important factor in the decline of Chartism. Improvements to the machinery of public order, changes to the spatial dynamics of the state and new forms of communications (railways, press and the electric telegraph) go some way in supporting James Vernon's assertion that throughout the period, there was a gradual closure and disciplining of the political system. However, this was serpentine in its development and evidently not as clear cut as it might seem, largely because the Home Office had to overcome a number of barriers in relation to the development of the state and its apparatus.

At the beginning of the Chartist period, the Home Office's control over the machinery of public order in the West Riding, as elsewhere, was fairly weak due to poor internal communications, geographical obstacles, embryonic policing and barrack provision. As a consequence, the Lord Lieutenant, along with the magistracy and military forces in the localities, enjoyed much independence and strength due to their detachment from central government influence. By 1848, the situation had changed considerably, as the second wave of railway construction and the electric telegraph reduced geographical isolation and a frontier mentality. This did much to eliminate the gulf that existed between the centre and localities, particularly in mining areas, and so enabled the British state to become a far more cohesive and integrated entity. As the pace of communications quickened, so the Home Office suppression of Chartist agitation became much easier.

The changes over time to the spatial dynamics of the state between the core and the periphery fed directly into the development of the machinery of public order. Beginning with the Home Office, the powers of the state became more centralised and its effectiveness as an agency of control grew significantly as it gained additional powers through legislation in the areas of police and communications. However, the suppression of Chartist agitation was hindered by the personalised and uneven approaches of the Home Secretaries who served the Home Office during the ten years of unrest. As a consequence, there was a lack of uniformity and, at times, consistency over its policy. Whilst Lord John Russell and Sir George Grey were moderate in their approaches, the Marquis of Normanby and Sir James Graham resorted to violent suppression and autocratic governance to exert control over the Chartists.

The preservation of the state and its institutions would not have been possible without utilising better lines of communication which enabled the Home Office to exert greater authority over the machinery of public order. This occurred in the West Riding where there were major changes to the way in which the apparatus functioned. Whereas in the mass agitations of 1838-40 and 1842, the first line of defence was the magistracy followed by the military and special constables, during 1848 the situation was reversed, and the police were positioned on the front line with the magistracy and the military in the background. This new alignment was the shape of things to come as future responses to disorder were conducted along similar lines with the Home Office orchestrating matters from Whitehall. However, this was not as straightforward as it seems insofar as protracted infighting amongst elites, personality clashes, financial considerations and community-based Chartist solidarity all provided important obstacles to state control prevailing over unrest. Such stresses and strains surely point towards a need for a more nuanced view of how we approach the concept of a united ruling class.

The Home Office suppression of Chartist unrest also brought about changes in the composition of the machinery of public order. During the period, the influence of traditional forms of control such as the Lord Lieutenant, yeomanry and militia waned, even though these forces were used in the suppression of Chartist disturbances in January 1840. The decline in the use of these mechanisms of control coincided with the steady growth of policing which was far better suited to the protection of urban, industrial towns within the West Riding. Furthermore, the three major stages of intense Chartist unrest – 1838-40, 1842 and 1848 – each brought about a response from the Home Office which gave rise to provincial policing improvements. At the beginning of the period, in the late 1830s, the policing provisions in the West Riding were extremely weak and minimal. Whilst towns such as Leeds and Sheffield had relatively well organised police forces, the policing of many places, such as Bradford, was almost non-existent. By the time Chartist unrest was suppressed in September 1848, all the main urban, industrial centres within the region had professional paid police forces in operation, along with fairly adequate lock-up facilities. Necessity had been the *modus operandi* as the transition from traditional forms of control such as the yeomanry and militia to policing were problematic.

Whilst Justices of the Peace wanted a police presence in towns across the West Riding following the January 1840 Chartist disturbances they were, like elsewhere, unwilling to pay for its cost. This was particularly apparent in the parishes where there was an overwhelming rejection of the 1839 and 1840 Rural Constabulary Acts. The biggest turning point was the 1842 Plug Plot disturbances, which were badly handled by the magistracy and military. The agencies fell out amongst themselves and in doing so highlighted that the ruling class was not as united as we have been led to believe. It was from this moment onwards that the Home Office put pressure on magistrates within the West Riding to adopt police measures. Whilst the 1842 Parish Constables Act proved to be a much cheaper alternative to the 1839 Rural Police legislation, this measure catered for the creation of police forces in growing industrial towns. However, they were not as well resourced or integrated as the Metropolitan Police in London. The continued division of police forces within the region, along parish and borough lines, meant that throughout 1848 the response to mass Chartist disorder by watching men and women alike was uneven. Furthermore, the failure of the police to deal with mass demonstrations and the arming and drilling of Chartists in places such as Bradford meant a continued reliance upon the military for support.

Chartism was a powerful community force which staged protests across the West Riding and attracted much support, especially from the dispossessed, the disenfranchised and the influx of Irish immigrants. However, the movement was ultimately doomed to failure, regardless of the impact of the reforms that the Peel government introduced, as it came up against a range of forces that were too powerful. In simple terms, the Chartist movement was outfought and outmanoeuvred by the Home Office and its machinery of public order, which led to the collapse of mass political protest and helped bring about an age of stability.

NOTES

Introduction: The Home Office and Chartist Historiography

1   *Northern Star*, 11 August 1838, 'The London Democratic Association'; HO 45/2410/608-15 (609), 'The People: Their Rights and Liberties, their duties and their interests', 27 May 1848.
2   See John K. Walton, *Chartism*, London: Routledge, 1999; Neville Kirk, 'In Defence of Class' in *International Review of Social History*, 32, 1987, 2-47; Miles Taylor, 'Rethinking The Chartists: Searching for Synthesis in the Historiography of Chartism' in *The Historical Journal*, 39, 1996, 479-495.
3   Gareth Stedman Jones, 'Rethinking Chartism' in *Languages of Class*, Cambridge: Cambridge University Press, 1983, pp. 90-178.
4   Arvel B. Erickson, *The Public Career of Sir James Graham*, Oxford: Basil Blackwell, 1952; J.T. Ward, *Sir James Graham*, London: Macmillan, 1967; John Prest, *Lord John Russell*, London: Macmillan, 1970; Paul Scherer, *Lord John Russell: A Biography*, London: Associated University Press, 1999.
5   See D.F. Smith, 'Sir George Grey at the Mid-Victorian Home Office', unpublished doctoral thesis, University of Toronto, 1972; A.P. Donajgrodzki, 'The Home Office 1822-48', unpublished doctoral thesis, University of Oxford, 1974; Jill Pellew, *The Home Office, 1848-1914: from Clerks to Bureaucrats*, London: Heinemann, 1982.
6   Sir Edward Troup, *The Home Office*, London: G.P. Putnam's Sons, 1926.
7   Ibid., pp. 1-6; 7-25.
8   Sir Frank Newsam, *The Home Office*, London: George Allen and Unwin, 1954.
9   Ibid., p. 13.
10 Henry Parris, 'The Nineteenth-Century Revolution in Government: A Reappraisal Reappraised' in *Historical Journal*, 3, 1960, 17-37; Oliver MacDonagh, 'The Nineteenth-Century Revolution in Government: A Reappraisal' in *Historical Journal*, 1, 1958, 52-67.
11 Ibid.
12 A. V. Dicey, *Lectures on the relation between Law and Public Opinion in England during the nineteenth century*, London: Macmillan, 1905, p. 135.
13 Ibid., p. 32; 133.
14 Peter Jupp, *The Governing of Britain, 1688-1848: The Executive, Parliament, and the People*, London: Routledge, 2006, p. 109; 159.
15 A. V. Dicey, (1905), p. 187.
16 D. F. Smith, 'Sir George Grey at the Mid-Victorian Home Office', unpublished doctoral thesis, University of Toronto, 1972; A. P. Donajgrodzki, 'The Home Office 1822-48', unpublished doctoral thesis, University of Oxford, 1974.
17 D. F. Smith, (1972).
18 Ibid., pp. 4-7; 46-7.
19 Ibid., p. 40.
20 Ibid., p. 25.
21 Ibid., pp. 167-213; 292-358; 363-6.
22 Ibid., pp. 373-5.

23   A. P. Donajgrodzki, (1974).

24   Ibid., pp. 366-413; 414-39; 440-86.

25   Ibid., p. 23.

26   Ibid., p. 147.

27   Ibid., pp. 52-150; 151-87.

28   Ibid., p. 255.

29   Ibid., p. 9

30   Jill Pellew, (1982).

31   Ibid., pp. 12-15; A. P. Donajgrodzki, 'New roles for old: The Northcote Report and the Clerks of the Home Office 1822-48' in Gillian Sutherland (ed.), *Studies in the Growth of Nineteenth-Century Government*, London: Routledge and Kegan Paul, 1972, pp. 82-109.

32   Jill Pellew, (1982), pp. 33-120; 121-182.

33   Malcolm Chase, *Chartism: A New History*, Manchester: Manchester University Press, 2007; Janette Martin, 'Popular political oratory and itinerant lecturing in Yorkshire and the North East in the age of Chartism, 1837-60', unpublished doctoral thesis, University of York, 2010.

34   James Vernon, *Politics and the People: A Study in English Political Culture, c.1815-1867*, Cambridge: Cambridge University Press, 1993, pp. 46-63.

35   Robert G. Gammage, *History of the Chartist Movement, 1837-1854*, 2nd ed, London: Frank Cass, 1969; Mark Hovell, *The Chartist Movement*, 3rd ed., Manchester: Manchester University Press, 1966.

36   See Asa Briggs (ed.), *Chartist Studies*, London: Macmillan, 1959; F.C. Mather, *Chartism*, London: Historical Association Pamphlet 1965.

37   Asa Briggs (ed.), (1959), p. 2.

38   Ibid., p. 14.

39   See Gareth Stedman Jones, 'Languages of Class' in James Epstein and Dorothy Thompson (eds.), *The Chartist Experience: Studies in Working-class Radicalism and Culture, 1830-1860*, London: Macmillan 1982, p. 5; F. C. Mather, *Public Order in the Age of the Chartists*, Manchester: Manchester University Press, 1959, pp. 4-5.

40   Asa Briggs (ed.), (1959), pp. 2-3.

41   See PRO 30/22/5F, Lord John Russell papers, November to December 1846; PRO 30/22/6F, September to October 1847.

42   F. C. Mather, (1965), p. 6.

43   G. D. H Cole, *Chartist Portraits*, London: Macmillan, 1940, pp. 80-105.

44   For further reading see Cecil Driver, *Tory Radical: The Life of Richard Oastler*, New York: Oxford University Press, 1946.

45   A. V. Dicey, (1905), pp. 225-31.

46   E. P. Thompson, *The Making of the English Working Class*, 2nd ed., Harmondsworth: Penguin, 1980.

47   Ibid., p. 909.

48   Dorothy Thompson (ed.), *The Early Chartists*, London: Macmillan, 1971, p. 12.

49   Ibid., p. 14.

50   Ibid.

51   Ibid., p. 11.
52   Ibid.
53   Ibid.
54   Ibid.
55   Dorothy Thompson in *The Early Chartists* touched on a number of themes but at the same time left a number of opportunities for a broader analysis of the government and state suppression of Chartism. For instance, only three pages are devoted to the 1839 Bull Ring disturbances, whilst there is very little mention of the attempted uprisings at Dewsbury, Sheffield and Bradford during 1840.
56   Peter Jupp, (2006), pp. 109-110; Adam Smith, *An inquiry into the nature and causes of the Wealth of Nations*, Oxford: Clarendon Press, 1869; Thomas Paine, *Rights of Man*, Dublin: 1792; Jeremy Bentham, *An Introduction to the Principles of Morals and Legislation*, Oxford: Clarendon Press, 1879.
57   Ibid., p. 181.
58   J. T. Ward, *Chartism*, London: B.T. Batsford, 1973, p. 11.
59   Ibid., p. 11.
60   Ibid., p. 12.
61   David Jones, *Chartism and the Chartists*, London: Allen Lane, 1975, p. 26.
62   Ibid., p. 61.
63   James Epstein, *The Lion of Freedom: Feargus O'Connor and the Chartist Movement*, London: Croom Helm, 1982, p. 2.
64   Malcolm Chase, 'What next for Chartist Studies?', Chartism Annual International Conference paper, University of Paris IV - Sorbonne, 2 July 2010; But see W. Hamish Fraser, *Chartism in Scotland*, London: Merlin Press, 2010.
65   Roger Swift, 'Policing Chartism, 1839-1848: The Role of the 'Specials' Reconsidered' in *English Historical Review*, 122, 2007, 669-699 (p. 669).
66   Gareth Stedman Jones, (1983), p. 19.
67   Neville Kirk, (1987), pp. 2-47 (p. 5).
68   Ibid., p. 27.
69   Ibid., p. 44; See Gareth Stedman Jones, (1983), pp. 163-178.
70   Ibid., p. 44.
71   Patrick Joyce, *Visions of the People: Industrial England and the Question of Class, 1848-1914*, Cambridge: Cambridge University Press, 1991, p. 113.
72   Ibid., p. 342.
73   Ibid., p. 61; 329.
74   See James Vernon, (1993); James Vernon, *Re-reading the Constitution: New Narratives in the Political History of England's Long Nineteenth Century*, Cambridge: Cambridge University Press, 1996.
75   James Vernon, (1993), pp. 1-2
76   James Vernon, (1996), p. 4.
77   James Vernon, (1993), pp. 8-9.
78   Ibid., pp. 46-63
79   Ibid., p. 250.
80   Ibid., pp. 336-7.

81 Jon Lawrence, 'The Decline of English Popular Politics' in *Parliamentary History*, 13, 1994, 333-337.

82 Lisa Keller, *The Triumph of Order: Democracy and Public Space in New York and London*, New York: Columbia University Press, 2009; Antony Taylor, 'Commons-Stealers, Land-Grabbers and Jerry-Builders: Space, Popular Radicalism and the Politics of Public Access in London, 1848-1880' in *International Review of Social History*, 40, 1995, 383-407.

83 Katrina Navickas, 'Moors, Fields and Popular Protest in South Lancashire and the West Riding, 1800-1848' in *Northern History*, 46, March 2009, 93-111 (p. 19).

84 Miles Taylor, (1996), p. 482.

85 Ibid., p. 480-1.

86 Andrew Messner, 'Land, Leadership, Culture and Emigration: Some Problems in the Chartist Historiography' in *Historical Journal*, 42, 1999, 1093-1109 (p. 1094).

87 Ibid., pp. 1095-1100.

88 Ibid., pp. 1100-1108; See Paul A. Pickering, '"Mercenary Scribblers" and "Polluted Quills": The Chartist Press in Australia and New Zealand' in Joan Allen and Owen R. Ashton (eds.), *Papers for the People: A study of the Chartist press*, London: Merlin Press, 2005, pp. 190-215.

89 Peter Jupp, (2006), p. 151.

90 Mike Sanders, *The Poetry of Chartism: Aesthetics, Politics, History*, Cambridge: Cambridge University Press, 2009; Ian Haywood, *The Revolution in Popular Literature: Print, Politics and the People, 1790-1860*, Cambridge: Cambridge University Press, 2009.

91 See Malcolm Chase, (2007).

92 See F. C. Mather, (1959).

93 F. C. Mather, 'The Machinery of Public Order in England during the Chartist period, 1837-48', unpublished master's thesis, University of Manchester, 1948.

94 F. C. Mather, 'The Railways, the Electric Telegraph and Public Order during the Chartist period' in *History*, 38, 1953, 40-53.

95 F. C. Mather, (1959), pp. 75-95; 96-140; 141-181; 182-225.

96 John Saville, *1848: The British State and the Chartist Movement*, Cambridge: Cambridge University Press, 1987.

97 Ibid., p. 1.

98 Stanley H. Palmer, *Police and Protest in England and Ireland, 1750-1850*, Cambridge: Cambridge University Press, 1988.

99 Ibid., p. 427.

100 Ibid., p. 417.

101 John K. Walton, (1999), p. 65.

102 Miles Taylor, (1996), p. 491.

103 Ibid.,p. 491

104 Ibid., p. 493.

105 Ibid.

106 Ibid., p. 492.

107 Malcolm Chase, 'Rethinking Welsh Chartism'; Joe England, '"Engaged in a

Righteous Cause": Chartism in Merthyr Tydfil'; Owen Ashton, 'Chartism in Llanidloes: The "Riot" of 1839 Revisited' in *Llafur: The Journal of Welsh People's History*, 3, (2010), 39-57; 58-75; 76-85.

108 J. T. Ward, (1973), p. 89.

109 Ibid.

110 Edward Royle, '"Radical Riding?", Myth and Reality in the Long Nineteenth-Century', unpublished seminar paper taken from *Radical Riding! Radical Cultures in the West Riding of Yorkshire, c.1760 to 1960*, University of Bradford Conference, 14 April 2007.

111 W. G. Rimmer, 'The Industrial Profile of Leeds, 1740-1840' in *Publications of the Thoresby Society*, 113, 1967, p. 132.

112 *1851 Census of Great Britain* (London, Longman, 1854), p. 192.

113 Ibid., p. 101.

114 J. F. C. Harrison, 'Chartism in Leeds' in Asa Briggs (ed.), (1959), pp. 65-98 (p. 65).

115 Ibid.

116 Ibid.

117 Ibid. p. 82.

118 See David G. Wright, 'Politics and Opinion in Nineteenth-Century Bradford, 1832-1880', unpublished doctoral thesis, University of Leeds, 1966.

119 F. C. Mather, (1965), p. 22

120 Ibid.

121 David G. Wright, (1966), pp. 35-50.

122 *Northern Star*, 17 February 1838.

123 *Northern Star*, 7 April 1838.

124 Theodore Koditschek, *Class Formation and Urban-Industrial Society: Bradford, 1750-1850*, Cambridge: Cambridge University, 1990.

125 Ibid., pp. 18-19.

126 Ibid., p. 165.

127 Ibid., p. 581.

128 Ibid., p. 488; 494.

129 Ibid., p. 581.

130 Alfred Peacock, *Bradford Chartism, 1838-40*, York: St Anthony's Press, 1969, p. 2.

131 Ibid., p. 11.

132 Ibid., p. 39.

133 Ibid., p. 27.

134 Ibid.

135 Ibid.

136 See H. M. Docton, 'Chartism in Dewsbury', unpublished dissertation, University of Leeds, 1972.

137 Frederick J. Kaijage, 'Labouring Barnsley, 1816-1856: A Social and Economic History', unpublished doctoral thesis, University of Warwick, 1975.

138 Ibid., p. 463.

139 Ibid., p. 510.

140 Ibid., p. 511

141 Ibid., pp. 522-3.

142 John L. Baxter, 'The origins of the social war in South Yorkshire: A study of capitalist evolution and labour class realization in one industrial region, c.1750-1855', unpublished doctoral thesis, University of Sheffield, 1976.

143 Ibid., p. 443, 505.

144 Kate Tiller, 'Late Chartism: Halifax 1847-58' in Epstein and Thompson (eds.), (1982), pp. 311-344; John A. Hargreaves, *Benjamin Rushton: 1785-1853, Handloom Weaver and Chartist*, Halifax: Friends of Lister Lane Cemetery, 2006; Suzanne Grason, 'The Sheffield Chartist Uprising' in *Yorkshire History*, 1, 1996, 5-7.

145 James Vernon, (1993), p. 250.

The Home Office and the Network of Repression

146 See David Philips, 'A "Weak" State?' The English State, the Magistracy and the Reform of Policing in the 1830s' in *English Historical Review*, 119, 2004, 873-91; Andrew Vincent, *Theories of the State*, Oxford: Basil Blackwell, 1987, p. 2.

147 John Brewer, *The Sinews of Power: War, Money and the English State, 1688-1783*, London: Unwin Hyman, 1989, pp. 199-217.

148 Richard Vogler, *Reading The Riot Act: The Magistracy, the Police and the Army in Civil Disorder*, Milton Keynes: Open University, 1991; David Eastwood, *Governing Rural England: Tradition and Transformation in Local Government, 1780-1840*, Oxford: Oxford University Press, 1994.

149 David Eastwood, (1994), p. 2

150 David Philips, (2004), pp. 873-891.

151 See Joe Painter and Alex Jeffrey (eds.), *Political Geography: An Introduction to Space and Power*, London: Sage, 2009; Carolyn Gallaher, *Key Concepts in Political Geography*, London, Sage, 2009; Martin Jones, An *Introduction to Political Geography: Space, Place and Politics*, London: Routledge, 2004.

152 David Storey, *Territory: The Claiming of Space*, Harlow: Prentice Hall, 2001, pp. 1-3.

153 Michael Mann, 'The Autonomous Power of the State: Its Origins, Mechanisms and Results' in Neil Brenner, Bob Jessop, Martin Jones, and Gordon MacLeod (eds.), *State/Space: A Reader*, Oxford: Blackwell, 2003, pp. 53-64 (p. 54).

154 Ibid.

155 See Max Weber, *Essays from Max Weber*, London: Routledge and Kegan Paul, 1946, p. 78; Neil Brenner, Bob Jessop, Martin Jones and Gordon MacLeod (eds.), (2003), pp. 1-26 (1-2); Michael Mann, (2003), p. 53.

156 David Storey, *Territory: The Claiming of Space*, Harlow: Prentice Hall, 2001, pp. 1-3.

157 Sir Edward Troup, (1926) and Sir Frank Newsam, (1954) contend that the Home Secretary had absolute power over the Home Office, whilst D. F. Smith (1972) and A. P. Donajgrodzki, (1974) suggest that public order responsibilities were more evenly spread out amongst the staff at the department.

158 A. P. Donajgrodzki, (1974), p. 18.

159 Ibid., pp. 16-18; p. 67.

160 A. P. Donajgrodzki, (1974), pp. 18-19; Sir Edward Troup, (1926), pp. 2-3; 70-1.

161 Ibid., p. 75.

162 Ibid., p. 70.

163 Ibid., pp. 102-6.

164 Jill Pellew, (1982), p. 3.

165 Henry Parris, *Government and the Railways in Nineteenth-Century Britain*, London: Routledge and Kegan Paul, 1965, p. 202.

166 Jeremy Bentham, *A Fragment on Government and an Introduction to the Principle of the Morals and Legislation*, Oxford: Basil Blackwell, 1967, pp. 125-131.

167 David G. Wright, *Democracy and Reform, 1815-1885*, Harlow: Longman, 1970, p. 24.

168 Peter Jupp, (2006), p. 159.

169 Ibid., pp. 180-1.

170 HO 41/13/11-12, Samuel March Phillipps to R.H. Batty, Huddersfield, 17 June 1837.

171 HO 41/13/14-16, Samuel March Phillipps to Joseph Armitage, Huddersfield, 21 June 1837.

172 HO 41/13/102-4, Samuel March Phillipps to J.G. Paley and Matthew Thompson, Bradford, 24 November 1837.

173 HO 41/15/411-2, Samuel March Phillipps to Mayor and Magistrates of Leeds, 6 March 1840

174 Sir Edward Troup, (1926), pp. 76-7.

175 TS 11/814/2678, The Queen versus The Editor of the *Northern Star*, 6 May 1839; TS 11/813/2677, Case respecting persons apprehended at Sheffield, January 1840.

176 TS 11/496-505, Regina v John Frost and others for chartist disturbances at Newport, Monmouth: Monmouth special commission, 1839-40; TS 36/24, The Queen v John Frost and others, 1839; TS 36/24, The Queen v John Frost: Court of Exchequer Chamber, 1840.

177 Sir Edward Troup, (1926), p. 73.

178 Ibid., p. 2; 55.

179 HO 41/13/173-4, Samuel March Phillipps to the Magistrates acting at Dewsbury, 22 August 1838.

180 Ibid.

181 Hew Strachan, *Wellington's Legacy: The Reform of the British Army, 1830-54*, Manchester: Manchester University Press, 1984, pp. 229-30; See HO 41/13-9, Disturbance Entry Books from 1837-52 that contain numerous examples of the Home Office enlisting the use of Regular Soldiers to support Civil Power, when Chartist riots and disturbances took place.

182 John Brewer, (1989), p. 46.

183 Return of the Number of Troops, Officers and Men, employed in Great Britain on the 25th day of January in the Years 1829, 1835, 1840 and 1847, p. 5.

184 F.C. Mather, *Public Order in the Age of the Chartists*, Manchester: Manchester University Press, 1959, p. 153.

185 Ibid.

186 HO 41/13/6-7, Lord John Russell to Earl of Harewood, 13 June 1837.

187 HO 41/13/108-9, Samuel March Phillipps to J. G. Paley, Matthew Thompson, Bradford, 25 November 1837.

188 HO 41/13/106-8, Samuel March Phillipps to Major-General Sir Richard Jackson K.C.B., 25 November 1837

189 HO 41/13/60-1, Lord John Russell to Earl of Harewood, 7 July 1837.

190 Edward Troup, (1926), pp. 46-7.

191 Richard Vogler, (1991); W.S. Hamer, *The British Army, Civil Military Relations 1885-1905*, Oxford: Clarendon, 1970, p. 5.

192 Ibid.,p. 84.

193 1839 (169), First Report of the Commissioners appointed to inquire as to the best means of establishing an efficient constabulary in the counties of England and Wales, p. 83.

194 Ibid.

195 Ibid.

196 Ibid.

197 Ibid., p. 84.

198 Ibid.

199 *Northern Star,* 17 February 1838.

200 Ibid.

201 Ibid.

202 Ibid.

203 Ibid.

204 *Northern Star,* 24 February 1838

205 See David Philips and Robert Storch, *Policing Provincial England, 1829-1856: The Politics of Reform*, London: Leicester University Press, 1999, pp. 63-70; 70-75; Clive Emsley, *The English Police: A Political and Social History, 2nd ed.,* London: Longman, 1996, pp. 1-4.

206 Robert D. Storch, 'The Plague of the Blue Locusts: Police Reform and Popular Resistance in Northern England, 1840-57' in *International Review of Social History*, 20, 1975, 61-90.

207 Stanley H. Palmer, *Police and Protest in England and Ireland, 1750-1850*, Cambridge: Cambridge University Press, 1988, p. 297; See Appendix I, for the total number of officers employed by the Metropolitan Police during 1837-1848.

208 HO 97/27, Enquiry into the transaction of business at the Home Office, 29 August 1848.

209 1833 (718) Select Committee Report on Cold Bath Fields Meeting, 23 August 1833, p. 15; Troup, *The Home Office*, p. 97.

210 Ibid., p. 5

211 HO 41/13/1-3, Samuel March Phillipps to Joseph Armitage, Huddersfield, 9 June 1837; HO 41/13/172, Samuel March Phillipps to B. Wheatley, J. Ingham, Mirfield, 17 August 1838; 1837-38 (602) Constables on Public Works. A Bill for the Payment of Constables for Keeping the Peace near Public Works, 18 July 1838.

212 1837 (118) Bradford (Poor Law Amendment Act), Return of the Metropolitan Police sent to Bradford, with correspondence on the subject (118), 11 December 1837, p. 3.

213 Ibid., p. 2; HO 41/13/98-9, Samuel March Phillipps to E. C. Lister, 16 November 1837.

214 Richard Vogler, (1991), p. 97.

215 David A. Campion, 'Policing the Peelers: Parliament, the Public and the Metropolitan Police, 1829-33' in Matthew Cragoe and Antony Taylor (eds.), *London Politics, 1760-1914*, Basingstoke: Palgrave Macmillan, 2005, pp. 38-56; Robert D. Storch, (1975), 61-90.

216 Richard Vogler, (1991), p. 97.

217 1833 (718) Select Committee Report on Cold Bath Fields Meeting, 23 August 1833, p. 4.

218 Ibid., p. 10; 25; pp. 43-4.

219 Ibid, pp. 48-9.

220 Ibid., p. 21.

221 Ibid., p. 25; 44.

222 Ibid., pp. 23-46; See David Taylor, *The New Police in Nineteenth-Century England: Crime, Conflict and Control*, Manchester: Manchester University Press, 1997, pp. 97-9; Clive Emsley, (1996), p. 29,40.

223 D. F. Smith, (1972), p. 64.

224 A. P. Donajgrodzki, (1974), p. 172.

225 Ibid., p. 151; Edward Troup, (1926), p. 254.

226 A. P. Donajgrodzki, (1974), p. 152; pp. 161-4.

227 Ibid., pp. 164-6; Edward Troup, (1926), p. 76.

228 See HO 41/17, Home Office Disturbance Entry Book, August 1842 to July 1843 for a number of examples.

229 HO 97/27, Enquiry into the transaction of business at the Home Office: the evidence of Thomas Henry Plasket, p. 15.

230 HO 45/264/62, Letter from Mayor Rawson of Leeds to Lieutenant Colonel Beckett regarding troops for Leeds, 15 August 1842.

231 HO 51/166/43, War Office Letter Book, 1838-51.

232 HO 51/166/13; 26-7, War Office Letter Book, 1838-51.

233 Hansard, House of Commons debate, 3 May 1838, vol.42., cc.819-20.

234 HO 51/166/13; HO 51/166/26-27, War Office Letter Book, 1838-51.

235 Donald Read, *Peterloo: The 'Massacre' and its Background*, Manchester: Manchester University Press, 1973; Robert Poole, '"By the Law or the Sword": Peterloo Revisited' in *History*, 91, 2006, 254-276.

236 John Brewer, (1989), p. 33.

237 See HO 51/121, Militia and Volunteers, 1829-56.

238 Stanley H. Palmer, (1988), pp. 267-9.

239 HO 51/121/56-60, Home Office circular from Lord John Russell to Lord Lieutenants of England and Wales, 3 March 1838.

240 HO 97/27, Enquiry into the transaction of business at the Home Office: the evidence of Thomas Henry Plasket, p. 68.

241 WO 30/111, 'Warrant regulating the grant of pension, allowance and relief to

soldiers on their discharge from the army', 7 February 1833.

242 HO 97/27, Enquiry into the transaction of business at the Home Office: the evidence of Thomas Henry Plasket, p. 70.

243 Ibid.

244 HO 387/31, Folios 1-6, Secret Service accounts; Correspondence with Audit Office, Affidavits and Miscellaneous Papers, James Graham (ff 1-6).

245 HO 387/30, Folios 1-5, Secret Service accounts; Correspondence with Audit Office, Affidavits and Miscellaneous Papers, Lord Normanby (ff 1-5).

246 See Clive Emsley, 'The Home Office and Its Sources of Information and Investigation 1791-1801' in *The English Historical Review*, 94, 1979, 532-561.

247 1833 (48) 3 Will. IV.- Session. 1833. A Bill to Regulate the Labour of Children and Young Persons in the Mills and Factories of the United Kingdom.

248 *Northern Star*, 25 July 1840.

249 HO 33/4/24, General Post Office to Samuel March Phillipps, 14 July 1838.

250 Edward Troup, (1926), p. 108.

251 HO 33/4/8, Samuel March Phillips to General Post Office, 11 March 1838.

252 HO 45/264/84-85, William Moore, the Huddersfield Postmaster, to Sir James Graham, 15 August 1842.

253 HO 33/4, General Post Office to Lord John Russell, 17 March 1838.

254 HO 33/4/16-18, Colonel Maberly to Samuel March Phillipps, 3 May 1838.

255 HO 33/4/67, Sir John Campbell to General Post Office, 17 June 1840.

256 HO 33/4/41, Extract from Penny Postage Act 1.Vict.C.35.Sec.17, 2 December 1839.

257 HO 33/4/35, General Post Office to Fox Maule, 28 March 1839.

258 HO 97/27, Enquiry into the transaction of business at the Home Office: the evidence of Francis Walpole, p. 75.

259 Ibid., pp. 69-70.

260 Ibid., pp. 72-73.

261 HO 97/27, Enquiry into the transaction of business at the Home Office: The evidence of Richard Noble, p. 14.

262 Ibid., p. 15.

263 Ibid., p. 14.

264 HO 97/27, Enquiry into the transaction of business at the Home Office: The evidence of Samuel Redgrave, p. 94-5.

265 Ibid., pp. 108-111.

266 Ibid., pp. 119-120.

267 Ibid., p. 120.

268 Ibid., p. 121.

269 HO 97/27, Enquiry into the transaction of business at the Home Office: The evidence of George Everest, p. 11.

270 Ibid., pp. 11-2.

271 Ibid., pp. 12-3.

272 HO 41/13/63-4, Lord John Russell to Duke of Wellington, 19 August 1837.

273 Sir Norman Chester, *The English Administrative System*, 1780-1870, Oxford: Clarendon Press, 1981, p. 53.

274 David Eastwood, (1994), p. 14; 51.

275 1835 (574) Municipal Corporations. A Bill, (with the amendments made by the Lords) entitled an Act to provide for the Regulation of Municipal Corporations in England and Wales, 6.Will. IV, 28 August 1835.

276 John Saville, (1987), p. 20.

277 Stanley H. Palmer, (1988), p. 432.

278 F. C. Mather, (1959), p. 49; Sir Edward Troup, (1926), p. 74.

279 HO 41/13/6-7, Lord John Russell to Earl of Harewood, 13 June 1837.

280 John Saville, (1987), p. 20; F. C. Mather, (1959), pp. 49-52.

281 HO 52/35/17/40-45, A report from the magistrates acting at Huddersfield to the Earl of Harewood, 22 June 1837.

282 HO 41/13/23-32, Lord John Russell to Earl of Harewood, 5 July 1837.

283 John Saville, *The Consolidation of the Capitalist State, 1800-1850*, London: Pluto Press, 1994, p. 59.

284 HO 41/13/1-3, Samuel March Phillipps to Joseph Armitage, Huddersfield, 10 June 1837.

285 HO 41/13/6-7, Lord John Russell to Earl of Harewood, 13 June 1837.

286 HO 41/13/23-32, Lord John Russell to Earl of Harewood, 5 July 1837.

287 HO 97/27/67-8, Enquiry into the transaction of business at the Home Office: The evidence of Richard Noble, p. 16.

288 1852-3 (715) (715-I), Second Report from the Select Committee on Police; Together with the proceedings of the Committee, Minutes of Evidence and Appendix, 5 July 1853, pp. 25-6.

289 *Leeds Mercury*, 17 April 1841.

290 1833 (150) 3 Will. IV. Sess.1833, A Bill to alter and extend the provisions of an act of the eleventh year of King George the Fourth, for Lighting and Watching of parishes in England and Wales, 2 April 1833.

291 Robert Pearce, *Government and Reform*, 1815-1918, London: Hodder and Stoughton, 1994, p. 83; R. Quinault, 'The Warwickshire County Magistracy and Public Order, c.1830-1870', in John Stevenson and Roland Quinault (eds.), *Popular Protest and Public Order: Six Studies in British History, 1790-1920*, London: George Allen and Unwin Ltd, 1974, pp. 181-214 (181-2).

292 HO 41/13/1-3, Samuel March Phillipps to J. Armitage, 10 June 1837.

293 HO 41/13/14-6, Samuel March Phillipps to Joseph Armitage, Huddersfield, 21 June 1837.

294 HO 41/13/19, Samuel March Phillipps to J.C. Laycock, Clerk to the Magistrates, Huddersfield, 26 June 1837.

295 1833 (718), Select Committee Report on Cold Bath Fields Meeting, 23 August 1833, p. 15.

296 Ibid., p. 16.

297 HO 41/13/23-32, Lord John Russell to Earl of Harewood, 5 July 1837.

298 Ibid.

299 See Felix Driver, *Power and Pauperism: The Workhouse System, 1834-1884*, Cambridge University Press: Cambridge, 1993, pp. 120-130; Cecil Driver, *Tory Radical: The Life of Richard Oastler*, New York: Oxford University Press, 1946, pp. 353-5.

300 HO 41/13/23-32, Lord John Russell to Earl of Harewood, 5 July 1837.

301 Ibid.

302 Ibid.

303 Ibid.

304 HO 41/13/6-7, Samuel March Phillipps to R. Battye, Huddersfield, 15 June 1837.

305 HO 41/13/16, Samuel March Phillipps to R. Battye, Huddersfield, 21 June 1837.

306 1852-3 (715) (715-I), Second Report from the Select Committee on Police, p. 91.

307 HO 41/13/23-32, Lord John Russell to Earl of Harewood, 5 July 1837.

308 1839 (169), First Report of the Commissioners appointed to inquire as to the best means of establishing an efficient constabulary in the counties of England and Wales, pp. 86-7.

309 HO 41/13/171-2, Samuel March Phillipps to Major-General Sir Richard Jackson, K.C.B., 14 August 1838.

310 HO 41/13/104-6, Samuel March Phillipps to the Magistrates acting at Bradford, 24 November 1837;

311 HO 41/13/97-8, Samuel March Phillipps to Major-General Sir Richard Jackson, K.C.B., 11 November 1837.

312 HO 41/13/106-8, Samuel March Phillipps to Major-General, Sir Richard Jackson, K.C.B., 25 November 1837; HO 41/13/108-9, Samuel March Phillipps to J.G. Paley and Matthew Thompson, Bradford, 25 November 1837.

313 HO 41/13/97-8, Samuel March Phillipps to Major-General, Sir Richard Jackson, K.C.B., 11 November 1837.

314 HO 41/13/110, Samuel March Phillipps to Matthew Thompson, Bradford, 6 December 1837.

315 HO 41/13/117-8, Samuel March Phillipps to Colonel Wemyss, Manchester, 21 December 1837.

316 HO 41/13/186, Fox Maule to Major-General, Sir Richard Jackson K.C.B., 20 September 1838.

317 See David Philips and Robert D. Storch (eds.), (1999); David Taylor, *The New Police: Crime, Conflict and Control in Nineteenth Century England*, Manchester: Manchester University Press, 1997; Clive Emsley, *The English Police: A Political and Social History*, Harvester Wheatsheaf: Hemel Hempstead, 1991; David J. V. Jones, 'The New Police, Crime and the People in England and Wales, 1829-1888' in *Transactions of the Royal Historical Society*, 33, 1983, pp. 151-68.

318 *Northern Star*, 22 December 1838.

319 *Northern Star,* 2 February 1839; 25 May 1839.

320 See Clive Emsley, (1991) for various examples about the problematic nature of early policing.

321 *Northern Star*, 22 December 1838; 7 December 1839; 19 September 1840.

322 Ibid., 16 October 1847.

323 Ibid., 11 March 1848; 15 April 1848; 24 June 1848.

324 *Leeds Intelligencer*, 26 September 1840.

325 Ibid., 12 December 1840.

326 Philip Rawlings, *Policing: A Short History*, Cullompton: Willan Publishing,

2002, p. 116; 129.

327 *Leeds Intelligencer*, 12 December 1840.

328 1839 (169), First Report of the Commissioners appointed to inquire as to the best means of establishing an efficient constabulary in the counties of England and Wales, pp. 102-3.

329 Ibid., p. 102.

330 HO 52/35/17/40-45, A report from Joseph Walker, Joseph Armitage, R. Batty and William Battye, Huddersfield magistrates to the Earl of Harewood, 22 June 1837.

331 Figures taken from Palmer, *Police and Protest in England and Ireland*, p. 397; 1852-3 (715) (715-I), Second Report from the Select Committee on Police, p. 91; HO 45/310, Memorandums reflecting the Town and Neighbourhood of Leeds, p. 1.

332 *Leeds Intelligencer*, 26 September 1840.

333 Ibid.

334 *Leeds Intelligencer*, 12 December 1840.

335 Ibid.

336 Apart from Jennifer Hart, 'Reform of the Borough Police, 1835-56' in *English Historical Review*, 70, 1955, 411-27, in recent times there have only been isolated studies of the Borough Police such as Richard Godfrey, *Newbury Borough Police, 1836-1875*, Newbury: Richard Godfrey, 2008; Chris A. Williams, 'Expediency, Authority and Duplicity: Reforming Sheffield's Police' in Robert J. Morris and Richard H. Trainor (eds.), *Urban Governance: Britain and Beyond Since 1750*, Aldershot: Ashgate, 2000, pp. 115-27; James Fairhurst, *Policing Wigan: The Wigan Borough Police Force, 1836-1969*, Blackpool: Landy, 1996.

337 *Leeds Intelligencer*, 12 December 1840.

338 HO 45/310, Memorandums reflecting the Town and Neighbourhood of Leeds, p. 1.

339 1839 (169), First Report of the Commissioners appointed to inquire as to the best means of establishing an efficient constabulary in the counties of England and Wales, pp. 164-6.

340 F. C. Mather, (1959), p. 117.

341 1839 (169), First Report of the Commissioners appointed to inquire as to the best means of establishing an efficient constabulary in the counties of England and Wales, pp. 143-4.

3 Lord John Russell: Containment and Moderation, 1838-39

342 Paul Scherer, *Lord John Russell: A Biography*, London: Associated University Press, 1999, p. 12.

343 Ibid.

344 For further reading see Spencer Walpole, *The Life of Lord John Russell*, 2 vols., London: Longmans, 1889; W. F. Reddaway, 'Lord John Russell' in F. J. C. Hearnshaw, *Political Principles of some notable Prime Ministers of the Nineteenth Century*, London: Ernest Benn Ltd, 1926, pp. 129-76; John Prest, *Lord John*

Russell, London: Macmillan, 1972; A. J. P. Taylor, 'Lord John Russell: The Last Great Whig' in A. J. P. Taylor (ed.), *From Napoleon to the Second International: Essays on Nineteenth-Century Europe*, London: Hamilton, 1993, pp. 145-51.

345 John Prest, (1972), p. 140.

346 Ibid.

347 Hansard, House of Commons debate, 20 November 1837, vol.39 cc.31-91.

348 Ibid.

349 Ibid.

350 See HO 52/35, Home Office Counties Correspondence relating to Yorkshire, 1837.

351 Edward Vallance, *A Radical History of Britain: Visionaries, Rebels and Revolutionaries – The men and women who fought for our freedoms*, London: Little, Brown, 2009, p. 370.

352 Charles Tilly, *Popular Contention in Great Britain, 1758-1834*, London: Harvard University Press, 1995, p. 372.

353 J. T. Ward, *Chartism*, London: B.T. Batsford, 1973, p. 105; *Northern Star*, 16 October 1838; *Leeds Times*, 20 October 1838.

354 *Halifax Guardian*, 2 November 1838.

355 *Halifax Guardian*, 20 October 1838.

356 Ibid.

357 *Halifax Guardian*, 2 November 1839.

358 Ibid.

359 Ibid.

360 F. C. Mather, *Public Order in the Age of the Chartists*, Manchester: Manchester University Press, 1959, p. 75.

361 *Northern Star*, 18 August 1838.

362 Ibid.

363 Ibid.

364 Ibid.

365 Ibid.

366 *Northern Star*, 8 September 1838.

367 HO 41/13/13/261-3, Samuel March Phillipps to Magistrates acting in the West Riding, 16 December 1838.

368 Ibid.

369 Ibid.

370 HO 41/13/413-4, Samuel March Phillipps to Magistrates acting in the West Riding, 25 April 1839.

371 HO 41/13/269-70, Lord John Russell to Duke of Newcastle, 21 December 1838.

372 HO 41/13/265-8, Samuel March Phillipps to the Mayor and Magistrates at Stockport, 18 December, 1838.

373 *Bradford Observer*, 31 January, 1839.

374 Ibid.

375 See Cecil Driver, *Tory Radical: The Life of Richard Oastler*, New York: Oxford University Press, 1946.

376 *Bradford Observer*, 31 January 1839.

377 HO 41/13/320, Samuel March Phillipps to Major-General Sir Richard Jackson, K. C. B., 23 February 1839.

378 HO 41/13/340, Samuel March Phillipps to J. C. Laycock, Clerk to the Magistrates Acting at Huddersfield, 5 March 1839.

379 HO 41/13/385, Samuel March Phillipps to Mayor of Leeds, 8 April 1839.

380 *Northern Star*, 13 April 1839.

381 David Jones, *Chartism and the Chartists*, London: Allen Lane, 1975, pp. 149-50.

382 Ibid.

383 Paul Ward, *Red Flag and Union Jack: Englishness, Patriotism and the British Left, 1881-1924*, Woodbridge: Royal Historical Society/Boydell Press, 1998, p. 116.

384 David Jones, (1975), p. 154.

385 *Northern Star*, 23 February 1839.

386 *Bradford Observer*, 7 March 1839.

387 Ibid.

388 Ibid.

389 Ibid.

390 Ibid.

391 Ibid.

392 Ibid.

393 HO 41/13/256, Samuel March Phillipps to Lieutenant-General, Sir Richard Jackson K.C.B., 14 December 1838.

394 *Bradford Observer*, 28 March 1839.

395 Ibid.

396 Stanley H. Palmer, 'Major-General Sir Charles James Napier: Irishman, Chartist and Commander of the Northern District in England, 1839-41' in *Irish Sword*, 15, 1982, 89-100.

397 Ibid., 89-100 (p. 93).

398 Sir William Francis Patrick Napier, *Life and Opinions of General Sir Charles James Napier*, London: Murray, 1857, p. 6.

399 Ibid., p. 15.

400 HO 41/14/14-15, Samuel March Phillipps to Lieutenant-General, Lord Fitzroy Somerset, 10 May 1839.

401 Sir William Francis Patrick Napier (1857), p. 17.

402 HO 41/14/23-4, Samuel March Phillipps to Major-General Sir Charles Napier, 11 May 1839.

403 HO 41/14/127, Samuel March Phillipps to H.B. Cooke, Barnsley, 11 June 1839; Lord John Russell to Earl of Harewood, 12 June 1839.

404 HO 41/14/106-7, Samuel March Phillipps to Major-General Sir Charles Napier, 30 May 1839.

405 HO 41/14/433, Samuel March Phillipps to Major-General Sir Charles Napier, 10 August 1839.

406 *Northern Star*, 11 May 1839.

407 HO 41/14/14, Lord John Russell to Earl of Harewood, 10 May 1839.

408 WYL 1352/D3/7/17/1-2, J. G. Horsfall to Earl of Harewood, 19 March 1839.

409 WYL 1352/D3/7/17/1-2, Lord Wharncliffe to Home Office, 23 April 1839.

410 WYL 1352/D3/7/17/1-2, Matthew Thompson to Earl of Harewood, 7 May 1839.

411 Ibid.

412 *Northern Star*, 6 April 1839.

413 Ibid.

414 Ibid.

415 Ibid.

416 Ibid.

417 Hansard, House of Commons Debate, 15 May 1839, vol.47, cc.1025-8.

418 Ibid.

419 Ibid.

420 Ibid.

421 Ibid.

422 Ibid.

423 Ibid.

424 Ibid.

425 Ibid.

426 Ibid.

427 1839 (169), First Report of the Commissioners appointed to inquire as to the best means of establishing an efficient constabulary in the counties of England and Wales, p. 82.

428 Ibid.

429 Copy of a letter written by Lord John Russell to the Lord Lieutenants' of certain Counties suggesting the formation of Associations for the Protection of Life and Property, Parliamentary Accounts and Papers 1839, Vol.9, p. 3.

430 HO 41/14/328-30, Lord John Russell to Earl of Harewood, 30 July 1839.

431 WYL 1352/D3/7/17/1-2, Abraham Horsfall to Earl of Harewood, 25 May 1839.

432 Ibid.

433 1839 (169), First Report of the Commissioners appointed to inquire as to the best means of establishing an efficient constabulary in the counties of England and Wales, p. 82.

434 *Leeds Mercury*, 15 June 1839.

435 *Halifax Guardian*, 25 May 1839.

436 Ibid.

437 Ibid.

438 Ibid.

439 Ibid.

440 Ibid.

441 Malcolm Chase, *Chartism: A New History*, Manchester: Manchester University Press, 2007, pp. 76-80.

442 Ibid., p. 81; *The Times*, 6 July 1839; *Aris's Birmingham Gazette*, 8 July 1839.

443 Antony Taylor, 'Commons-Stealers, Land-Grabbers and Jerry-Builders: Space, Popular Radicalism and the Politics of Public Access in London, 1848-1880' in *International Review of Social History*, 40, 1995, 383-407 (p. 387).

444 *The Times*, 6 July 1839; *Aris's Birmingham Gazette*, 8 July 1839.

445 Ibid.

446 Ibid.

447 Ibid.

448 Malcolm Chase, (2007), pp. 81-2.

449 TS 11/813/2677, 'Yorkshire Lent Assizes, Bradford Riots: The Queen against Robert Peddie', 5 March 1840.

450 MEPO 2/61, The Statement of Superintendent John May respecting the riot on Monday evening, 15 July 1839.

451 Ibid.

452 Ibid.

453 Ibid.

454 Ibid.

455 Ibid.

456 Ibid.

457 Ibid.

458 Ibid.

459 Ibid.

460 Ibid; See account given in Aris' *Birmingham Gazette*, 22 July 1839.

461 Ibid.

462 Ibid.

463 MEPO 2/61, Metropolitan Police: Observations made by the Office of the Commissioner concerning the Birmingham Riots of 15 July 1839.

464 Ibid.

465 Ibid.

466 Ibid.

467 Ibid.

468 Ibid.

469 *The Times*, 17 July 1839.

470 Michael Weaver, 'The Bayonet, the Cutlass and the Truncheon: Maintaining Public Order in Chartist Birmingham' in *Consortium on Revolutionary Europe, 1750-1850*, 24, 1994, 224-36; Michael Weaver, 'The New Science of Policing: Crime and the Birmingham Police Force, 1839-1842' in *Albion*, 26, 1994, 289-308.

471 *The Times*, 11 July 1839.

472 Ibid.

473 Ibid.

474 Ibid.

475 1839 (484) Birmingham Police. (No.2.), A Bill for improving the police in Birmingham, 2 August 1839; 1839 (499) Manchester Police: A bill for improving the police in Manchester; 7 August 1839; 1839 (500) Bolton Police: A Bill for improving the police in Bolton, 7 August 1839.

476 1839 (445) Birmingham Police: A Bill to authorise an advance out of the Consolidated Fund for the purposes of the Police of the Borough of Birmingham, 23 July 1839.

477 *Leeds Mercury*, 18 April 1840.

478 *Leeds Intelligencer,* 11 April 1840.
479 See David Philips and Robert D. Storch, *Policing Provincial England, 1829-1856: The Politics of Reform,* London: Leicester University Press, 1999, pp. 202-6.
480 *Leeds Mercury,* 20 July 1839.
481 Ibid.
482 WYL 1352/D3/7/17/1-2, Lord John Russell to the Huddersfield Magistrates. 9 August 1839.
483 See HO 41/14 for various examples of Arming and Drilling across the West Riding that occurred during May to August 1839.
484 Peter Gurney, 'Exclusive Dealing in the Chartist Movement' in *Labour History Review,* 74, 2009, 90-110; Peter Gurney, '"Rejoicing in Potatoes": The Politics of Consumption in England during the "Hungry Forties"' in *Past and Present,* 203, 2009, 99-136.
485 *Leeds Mercury,* 27 July 1839.
486 *Halifax Guardian,* 27 July 1839.
487 HO 41/14/323-5, Lord John Russell to Mayor or Magistrates acting in towns across the West Riding, 31 July 1839
488 Ibid.
489 Ibid.
490 *Bradford Observer,* 1 August 1839.
491 Ibid.
492 Ibid.
493 Ibid.
494 Ibid.
495 HO 41/14/301, Samuel March Phillipps to Mayor of Leeds, 26, July 1839.
496 HO 41/14/334, Samuel March Phillipps to Mayor of Leeds, 31 July 1839.
497 *Northern Star,* 22 June 1839; 6 July 1839; 20 July 1839; 29 May 1841; 11 September 1841.
498 Ibid., 22 January 1842; 21 March 1846; *Bradford Observer,* 4 January 1844.
499 *Northern Star,* 24 July 1847; 15 April 1848.
500 *Bradford Observer,* 1 August 1839.
501 WYL 1352/D3/7/17/1-2, Earl of Harewood to E. C. Lister and J. W. Hird, 6 August 1839.
502 Ibid.
503 Ibid.
504 HO 41/14/378-9, Lord John Russell to Earl of Harewood, 5 August 1839.
505 HO 41/14/385-6, Samuel March Phillipps to Earl of Harewood, 6 August 1839; Samuel March Phillips to Office Commanding the Troops at the Barracks, Leeds, 6 August 1839.
506 HO 41/14/384, Samuel March Phillipps to H. Watkins, Silkstone, Barnsley, 4 August 1839.
507 WYL 1352/D3/7/17/1-2, Earl of Harewood to E. C. Lister and J.W. Hird, 6 August 1839.
508 HO 41/14/399-405, Samuel March Phillipps to Sir Charles Napier, 9 August 1839.

509 Ibid.

510 Ibid.

511 Ibid.

512 Ibid.

513 Ibid.

514 *Bradford Observer*, 8 August 1839.

515 Ibid.

516 Ibid.

517 *Leeds Mercury*, 17 August 1839.

518 *Halifax Guardian*, 10 August 1839.

519 *Leeds Mercury*, 10 August 1839.

520 Ibid.

521 *Leeds Mercury*, 17 August 1839.

522 WYL 1352/D3/7/17/1-2, Earl of Harewood to Lord John Russell, 11 August 1839.

523 WYL 1352/D3/7/17/1-2, 'The Writer' to Earl of Harewood, 26 July 1839.

524 Ibid.

525 *Northern Star*, 10 August 1839.

526 WYL 1352/D3/7/17/1-2, Bradford Magistrates to Earl of Harewood, 10 August 1839.

527 HO 41/14/424-5, Samuel March Phillipps to the Magistrates Acting at Bradford, 9 August 1839.

528 *Bradford Observer*, 17 October 1839; *The Times*, 14 October; 23 October 1839.

529 HO 41/15/42, Samuel March Phillipps to Colonel Angelo, 29 August 1839.

530 *Leeds Mercury*, 17 August 1839.

531 *Halifax Guardian*, 17 August 1839.

532 *Leeds Mercury*, 17 August 1839.

533 *Leeds Mercury*, 17 August 1839.

534 Ibid.

535 WYL 1352/D3/7/17/1-2, Bradford Magistrates (Lister, Thompson, Busfield and Hind) to Earl of Harewood, 16 August 1839.

536 Ibid.

537 Ibid.

538 Ibid.

539 WYL 1352/D3/7/17/1-2, Lord John Russell to the Earl of Harewood, copy letter sent to Bradford magistrates, 23 August 1839.

4 The Marquis of Normanby: Disturbance, Division and Stagnation, 1839-41

540 *Leeds Intelligencer*, 9 May 1840.

541 Keith Laybourn, *British Political Leaders: A Biographical Dictionary*, Oxford: ABC-Clio, 2001, pp. 237-8.

542 *Bradford Observer*, 26 September 1839.

543 Ibid.

544 Ibid.

545 Ibid.

546 Ibid.

547 Ibid.

548 *The Times*, 30 September 1839.

549 *Halifax Guardian*, 28 September 1839.

550 Ibid.

551 F. C. Mather, (1959), pp. 56-7.

552 HO 52/40/250-251, Earl of Harewood to Lord John Russell, 10 October 1839.

553 WYL 1352/D3/7/17/1-2, Lord Normanby to the Earl of Harewood, 16 October 1839.

554 Ibid.

555 WYL 1352/D3/7/17/1-2, Earl of Harewood to Matthew Thompson, 8 November 1839.

556 See David Jones, *The Last Rising: The Newport Insurrection of 1839*, Oxford: Clarendon Press, 1985; Ivor Wilks, *South Wales and the Rising of 1839: Class Struggle as Armed Struggle*, London: Croom Helm, 1984.

557 *The Times*, 7 November 1839.

558 Edward Vallance, (2009), pp. 383-4; Ivor Wilks, (1984), pp. 183-207.

559 John K. Walton, (1999), p. 18.

560 Ibid.

561 TS 11/813/2677, 'Yorkshire Lent Assizes, Bradford Riots: The Queen against Robert Peddie', 5 March 1840.

562 Ibid.

563 David Jones, (1985), p. 196

564 Ibid., p. 196; 213.

565 Ibid., pp. 206-7.

566 Ibid., p. 207.

567 WYL 1352/D3/7/17/1-2, Earl of Harewood to Lord Normanby, 19 December 1839.

568 Ibid.

569 *Bradford Observer*, 26 December 1839.

570 Ibid.

571 Ibid.

572 *The Times*, 17 December 1839.

573 Ibid.

574 Sir William Francis Patrick Napier (1857), p. 22.

575 *Wakefield Journal and West Riding Herald*, 17 January 1840.

576 Ibid.

577 Ibid.

578 *The Times*, 11 January 1840.

579 Ibid.

580 HO 40/57/141-144, Ledgard (Clerk to the Dewsbury Magistrates) to the Secretary of State for the Home Department, 1 January 1840.

581 Ibid.

582 Ibid.

583 Ibid.

584 Ibid.

585 Ibid.

586 HO 40/57/149, The depositions of Thomas Oldroyd and Henry Cullingworth, 2 January 1840.

587 Ibid.

588 HO 41/15/262-3, Fox Maule to Sir Charles Napier, 2 January 1840.

589 HO 40/57/209-11, The deposition of John Hirst, Deputy Constable of Dewsbury, 12 January 1840.

590 Ibid.

591 HO 40/57/181-2, Earl of Harewood to the Marquis of Normanby, 13 January 1840.

592 Ibid.

593 Ibid.

594 TS 11/813/2677, Sheffield Treason 1840: The evidence of Samuel Foxhall, p. 17.

595 TS 11/813/2677, Sheffield Treason 1840: The evidence of Samuel Powell Thompson, p. 11.

596 See Baxter, (1976), pp. 461-5; Bill Moore, *Samuel Holberry, 1814-1842, Sheffield's Revolutionary Democrat*, Sheffield: Holberry Society Publications, 1978; John Baxter, *Armed Resistance and Insurrection: The early Chartist experience*, London: Communist Party History Group, 1984; Catherine Lewis, 'Samuel Holberry: Chartist Conspirator or Victim of a State Conspiracy?' in *Crimes and Misdemeanours: Deviance and the Law in Historical Perspective*, 3, 2009, 109-24.

597 TS 11/813/2677, Sheffield Treason 1840: The evidence of Samuel Powell Thompson, p. 11.

598 TS 11/813/2677, Sheffield Treason 1840: The evidence of Samuel Foxhall, p. 17; Thomas Raynor, p. 7.

599 TS 11/813/2677, Sheffield Treason 1840: The evidence of Thomas Raynor, pp. 7-8.

600 HO 41/15/276-7, Samuel March Phillipps to the Magistrates at Sheffield, 13 January 1840.

601 TS 11/813/2677, Sheffield Treason 1840: The evidence of Samuel Howe, Police Watchman, p. 2.

602 TS 11/813/2677, Sheffield Treason 1840: The evidence of Thomas Hague, Police Watchman, pp. 2-3.

603 HO 41/15/277-8, Fox Maule to Hugh Parker, Sheffield, 14 January 1840.

604 HO 40/57/181-182, Earl of Harewood to the Marquis of Normanby, 13 January 1840.

605 *The Times*, 16 January 1840.

606 Ibid.

607 HO 40/57/205, Dewsbury – Bingham, Wheatley and Hague to Marquis of Normanby, 15 January 1840.

608 Ibid.

609 HO 41/15/284-5, Samuel March Phillipps to the Magistrates acting at Dewsbury, 17 January 1840.

610 HO 41/15/364-5, Samuel March Phillipps to H. Parker, Sheffield, 13 February

1840.

611 W. Hamish Fraser, *Dr John Taylor, Chartist, Ayrshire Revolutionary*, Ayr: Ayrshire Archaeological and Natural History Society, 2006, pp. 57-8; 66-8; 77.

612 TS 11/813/2677, Bradford Riots: The case against Robert Peddie, p. 3; The evidence of John Smith, Horton, p. 28.

613 TS 11/813/2677, Bradford Riots: The case against Robert Peddie, p. 4.

614 HO 41/15/377, Samuel March Phillipps to the Magistrates acting at Bradford, 17 February 1840.

615 TS 11/813/2677, Bradford Riots: The case against Robert Peddie, pp. 11-12. See Frederick J. Kaijage, (1976), section titled 'The Barnsley Chartists'.

616 Ibid.

617 Ibid.

618 Ibid.

619 HO 40/57/295, Bradford Magistrates to the Marquis of Normanby, 29 January 1840.

620 Ibid.

621 Ibid.

622 TS 11/813/2677, Bradford Riots 1840: Proofs, Charles Ingham, Deputy Constable, p. 1.

623 HO 40/57/349-50, Bradford Magistrates to the Marquis of Normanby, 19 February 1840.

624 *Bradford Observer*, 6 February 1840.

625 Ibid.

626 *Leeds Mercury*, 18 April 1840; Clive Emsley, (1996), p. 43.

627 *Leeds Intelligencer*, 11 April 1840.

628 Ibid.

629 Ibid.

630 Ibid.

631 Ibid.

632 Ibid.

633 *Leeds Intelligencer*, 18 April 1840.

634 Ibid.

635 Ibid.

636 Ibid.

637 Ibid.

638 *Leeds Intelligencer*, 19 September 1840.

639 Ibid.

640 Ibid.

641 Ibid.

642 *Leeds Intelligencer*, 26 September 1840.

643 Ibid.

644 1840 (119) County Constabulary. A Bill to amend the Act for the Establishment of County and District Constables, 3.Vict., 17 March 1840.

645 *Leeds Intelligencer*, 26 September 1840.

646 Ibid.

647 Ibid.

648 Ibid.
649 Ibid.
650 *Leeds Intelligencer*, 5 December 1840; *Leeds Mercury*, 13 February 1841.
651 *Leeds Mercury*, 13 February 1841.
652 Ibid.
653 Ibid.
654 Ibid.
655 Ibid.
656 Ibid.
657 Clive Emsley, (1996), pp. 43-5; 54-9.
658 *Leeds Mercury*, 17 April 1841.
659 *Leeds Intelligencer*, 17 April 1841.
660 Ibid.
661 Ibid.
662 *Leeds Mercury*, 17 April 1841.
663 Ibid.
664 Ibid.
665 Ibid.
666 Ibid.
667 HO 50/451, Sir Charles James Napier's Report into the state of the Northern District Barracks, 23 May 1840; Hew Strachan, (1984), pp. 60-1.
668 HO 50/451, Sir Charles James Napier's Report into the state of the Northern District Barracks, 23 May 1840, p. 3.
669 Ibid., p. 16.
670 Ibid., p. 13.
671 Ibid.
672 Ibid.
673 Ibid.
674 Ibid., pp. 17-22.

Sir James Graham: Barracks, Plug Plots and Reform, 1841-46

675 Norman Gash, *Peel*, London: Longman, 1976, pp. 93-9; Robert Blake, *The Conservative Party from Peel to Thatcher*, London: Methuen, 1985, pp. 39-41.
676 Paul Adelman, *Peel and the Conservative Party*, London: Longman, 1989, pp. 11-12; 89-90.
677 *The Times*, 18 December 1834.
678 Ibid.
679 David Philips and Robert D. Storch (eds.), (1999), pp. 62-3.
680 Ibid., p. 64.
681 John Prest, 'Peel, Sir Robert, second baronet (1788–1850)', *Oxford Dictionary of National Biography*, Oxford: Oxford University Press, 2004, online ed., May 2009, http://www.oxforddnb.com/view/article/21764.
682 *The Times*, 8 September 1841; Arvel B. Eriksson, *The Public Career of Sir James Graham*, Oxford: Basil Blackwell, 1952, p. 157.
683 F. C. Mather, (1959), p. 36.

684 Malcolm Chase, (2007), p. 225. According to Chase, 'history failed to turn for the Chartists in 1842'.

685 *The Times*, 14 September 1841.

686 J. T. Ward, *Sir James Graham*, London: Macmillan, 1967, pp. 185-6.

687 *The Times*, 17 September 1841.

688 Ibid.

689 *The Times*, 14 September 1841.

690 Ibid.

691 Boyd Hilton, *A Mad, Bad, and Dangerous People? England 1783-1846*, Oxford: Clarendon Press, 2008, p. 600.

692 Hew Strachan, (1984), p. 61; F. C. Mather, (1959), p. 171.

693 HO 45/649/8, Report into the 'Bradford Barracks', 31 January 1844.

694 Ibid.

695 Ibid.

696 HO 41/16/230, Henry Manners Sutton to Magistrates Acting at Bradford, 2 November 1841; HO 45/649/9, Report into the 'Bradford Barracks', 31 January 1844.

697 HO 45/649/9-10; HO 45/264/32, John Hignett Solicitor to R.Byham at Board of Ordnance, 4 July 1842.

698 See John Burke, *A Genealogical and Heraldic History of the Commoners of Great Britain and Ireland, Vol. I*, London: Henry Colburn, 1883, pp. 288-292 (p. 288).

699 *Bradford Observer*, 17 March 1842.

700 Ibid.

701 Ibid.

702 HO 45/264/45-47, Letter from R Byham to Office of Ordnance regarding wasteland attached to the site for the Bradford Barracks, 7 July 1842.

703 Ibid.

704 Theodore Koditschek, (1990), p. 92; 98; 261.

705 HO 45/264/37, John Hignett Solicitor to R.Byham at Board of Ordnance, 4 July 1842.

706 HO 45/649/10, Report into the 'Bradford Barracks', 31 January 1844.

707 HO 45/649/36-7, Bradford Magistrates to Sir James Graham, 28 September 1844; HO 45/649/40, Charles Trevelyan to Samuel March Phillipps, 12 November 1844.

708 Malcolm Chase, (2007), p. 193.

709 Ibid., p. 209.

710 Ibid., p. 229.

711 *Bradford Observer*, 2 June 1842.

712 Ibid, 16 June 1842; Paul A. Pickering and Alex Tyrrell (eds.)., *The People's Bread: A History of the Anti-Corn Law League*, London: Leicester University Press, 2000, p. 147-8.

713 Ibid.

714 HO 41/16/410, Henry Manners Sutton to Colonel Wemyss, 10 August 1842; HO 41/16/415, Henry Manners Sutton to Major-General Sir William Warre, 11 August 1842.

715 HO 41/16/428-9, Henry Manners Sutton to Magistrates acting at Oldham, 12 August 1842.

716 HO 45/264/49-52, Letter from Mr Moreton to Colonel Maberly regarding Turn-Outs in Huddersfield, 14 August 1842.

717 Ibid.

718 Ibid.

719 Simon Garfield, *The Last Journey of William Huskisson: How a Day of Triumph became a Day of Despair at the Turn of a Wheel*, London: Faber and Faber, 2002, p. 209; 217.

720 HO 41/16/442, Henry Manners Sutton to Major-General Sir William Warre, 13 August 1842.

721 *Leeds Mercury*, 20 August 1842.

722 Ibid.

723 Ibid.

724 Ibid.

725 HO 45/264/55-56, Letter from the Huddersfield Magistrates to the Home Secretary about the state of Huddersfield.

726 HO 45/264/127, Huddersfield Magistrates to Sir James Graham, 16 August 1842.

727 HO 41/16/450-1, Henry Manners Sutton to Lieutenant-General Lord Fitzroy-Somerset, 15 August 1842.

728 HO 41/16/470-2, Sir James Graham to Earl of Harewood, 15 August 1842.

729 Ibid.

730 Ibid.

731 Ibid.

732 HO 45/264/80-82, Bradford Magistrates to Sir James Graham reporting intelligence, 15 August 1842.

733 Ibid.

734 Ibid.

735 HO 45/264/112-114, Conflict between the Military and the Turn Outs at Salter Hebble, 15 August 1842.

736 Ibid.

737 Ibid.

738 HO 45/264/84-85, William Moore, Huddersfield Postmaster to Sir James Graham, 15 August 1842.

739 HO 45/264/136-137, Letter from the Huddersfield Magistrates to Sir James Graham, 16 August 1842.

740 HO 45/264/84-85, William Moore, Huddersfield Postmaster to Sir James Graham, 15 August 1842.

741 HO 45/264/136-137, Letter from the Holmfirth Magistrates to Sir James Graham, dated 16 August 1842.

742 Ibid.

743 HO 45/264/139-40, Letter from the Clerk to the Magistrates of Holmfirth to Sir James Graham regarding mill stoppages, 16 August 1842.

744 Ibid.

745 HO 45/264/142-145, John Rawson to Sir James Graham regarding the Holbeck

Riots, 17 August 1842.
746 Ibid.
747 Ibid.
748 Ibid.
749 Ibid.
750 Ibid.
751 Ibid.
752 Ibid.
753 C. S. Parker, *Sir Robert Peel: From His Private Papers, Vol.2*, London: 1899, p. 541.
754 J. T. Ward, (1967), pp. 209-210; Boyd Hilton, (2008), p. 607.
755 HO 41/17/16, Sir James Graham to Duke of Wellington, 17 August 1842.
756 F. C. Mather, (1959), p. 155; A. J. Arbuthnot, 'Sir Thomas Arbuthnot (1776–1849)', rev. S. Kinross, in *Oxford Dictionary of National Biography*, ed. H. C. G. Matthew and Brian Harrison, Oxford: Oxford University Press, 2004, online ed., http://www.oxforddnb.com/view/article/613.
757 *Leeds Intelligencer*, 20 August 1842.
758 HO 41/17/27, Henry Manners Sutton to Magistrates acting at Huddersfield, 17 August 1842.
759 *Leeds Mercury*, 20 August 1842.
760 Ibid.
761 Ibid.
762 Ibid.
763 *Leeds Mercury*, 20 August 1842.
764 Ibid.
765 HO 41/17/37-8, Henry Manners-Sutton to Magistrates acting at Huddersfield, 18 August 1842.
766 HO 41/17/46-7, Henry Manners-Sutton to George Portland, Halifax, 18 August 1842.
767 HO 41/17/58-9, Henry Manners-Sutton to Magistrates acting at Huddersfield, 19 August 1842.
768 J. T. Ward, (1967), pp. 191-2; Arvel B. Erickson, (1952), p. 164.
769 A. P. Donajgrodzki, (1974), pp. 126-7; Norman Gash, *Sir Robert Peel: The Life of Sir Robert Peel after 1830*, London: Longman, 1972, p. 352.
770 F. C. Mather, (1959), p. 155.
771 Figures taken from *Ibid.*, p. 159; Stanley H. Palmer, (1988), p. 463.
772 Hew Strachan, (1984), pp. 181-2; 198-202.
773 *Leeds Intelligencer*, 27 August 1842.
774 Ibid.
775 Gareth Stedman Jones, (1983), pp. 177-8.
776 Dorothy Thompson, (1984); Neville Kirk, (1987), pp. 2-47.
777 Dorothy Thompson, (1984), p. 295.
778 Boyd Hilton, (2008), p. 607.
779 J. T. Ward, (1967), pp. 191-2.
780 *Leeds Intelligencer*, 28 January 1843
781 Ibid.

782 Ibid., 11 February 1843.

783 Ibid., 28 January 1843.

784 HO 41/17/294, Sir James Graham to Lord Wharncliffe, 30 September 1842.

785 Ibid.

786 Ibid.

787 Ibid.

788 HO 41/17/298, Sir James Graham to Lord Wharncliffe, 4 October 1842.

789 Ibid.

790 Ibid.

791 Ibid.

792 Ibid.

793 HO 41/17/300-303, Samuel March Phillipps to the Magistrates acting at Huddersfield, 4 October 1842.

794 Ibid.

795 HO 41/17/320-1, Samuel March Phillipps to Francis Ledgard, Dewsbury, 31 October 1842.

796 Philip Rawlings, (2002), pp. 137-8; Robert D. Storch and David Philips (eds.), (1999), pp. 213-5; Clive Emsley, (1996), p. 48.

797 QC/4, West Riding Quarter Sessions Lock-Up Committee minutes, 1843-59, p. 1.

798 1842 (432), Parish Constables Bill, 11 July 1842, pp. 1-2.

799 Ibid., TS 25/62, Parish Constables Act 1842: The Appointment of Paid Constables.

800 Clive Emsley, (1996), p. 48.

801 *Leeds Intelligencer*, 24 September 1842.

802 *Leeds Intelligencer*, 17 September 1842.

803 Ibid.

804 Ibid., 10 December 1842.

805 Ibid., 12 November 1842.

806 Philip Rawlings, (2002), pp. 137-8.

807 Clive Emsley, (1996), pp. 48-9.

808 QC/4, West Riding Quarter Sessions Lock-Up Committee minutes, 1843-59, p. 1.

809 Ibid., p. 5.

810 Ibid., pp. 3-4.

811 Ibid., p. 6.

812 Ibid., p. 13; 18.

813 Ibid., p. 8.

814 Ibid.

815 Ibid., p. 11.

816 Ibid., p. 8.

817 Ibid., p. 31.

818 Ibid., p. 33.

819 Ibid., p. 33.

820 Ibid., p. 35.

821 Ibid.

822 Ibid., pp. 35-6.

823 David Eastwood, (1994), p. 241; See Appendix II, for the total number of Police employed in England, Wales, Ireland and Scotland during 1837-1848.

824 See HO 45/292, Police: Origins of Detective Force, 1842.

825 *Northern Star*, 18 July 1840.

826 HO 45/724, Metropolitan Police Office to H. Manners Sutton MP, 23 August 1842.

827 HO 45/724, Richard Mayne to Samuel March Phillipps, 17 October 1844.

828 Ibid.

829 Ibid.

830 HO 45/292, Sir Richard Mayne to Samuel March Phillipps, 'Memorandum relative to Detective Powers of Police', 14 June 1842

831 Ibid.

832 Ibid.

833 Ibid.

834 Ibid.

835 Ibid.

836 HO 45/724, Richard Mayne to Samuel March Phillipps, 2 November 1844.

837 Ibid.

838 HO 45/724, Memorandum concerning pay-scales of the Detective Force.

839 HO 41/19/192, Henry Waddington to J. P. Tempest, Bradford, 29 May 1848.

840 Harold Perkin, *The Age of the Railway*, Newton Abbot: David and Charles, 1971, p. 169.

841 David Joy, *A Regional History of the use of Railway, Volume 8: South and West Yorkshire*, London: David and Charles, 1975, p. 12.

842 Ibid., p. 15.

843 HO 45/729, Samuel March Phillipps to Metropolitan Police Office, 12 December 1844.

844 HO 45/729, Sir James Graham to the Metropolitan Police Office, 26 February 1845.

845 HO 45/729, List of Railway Companies with which agreements have been made for the conveyance of Police under the 7 and 8 Vic. C.85 sec.12.

846 HO 45/1560, A Bill for forming and regulating "The Electric Telegraph Company", 9.Vict.Sess.1846, p. 1.

847 Edward Troup, (1926), pp. 109-110.

848 David Vincent, *The Culture of Secrecy: Britain, 1832-1998*, Oxford: Oxford University Press, 1998, p. 1.

849 Ibid., pp. 1-2.

850 Ibid., p. 2; 30.

851 HO 45/1560, A Bill for forming and regulating "The Electric Telegraph Company", 9.Vict., Sess., 1846.

852 Ibid.

853 F. C. Mather, (1953), pp. 40-53 (48).

854 See HO 45/2410, Part 1, London: Electric Telegraph papers, arrangements and messages from various places, March to July 1848.

855 *Northern Star*, 'Treatment of Feargus O'Connor', 18 July 1840; 'The Case and

Treatment of Robert Peddie', 5 September 1840.

856 *Leeds Intelligencer*, 25 June 1842; See Bill Moore, *Samuel Holberry and the Chartist Movement in Sheffield*, 1837-1851, Sheffield: Holberry Society Publications, 1987.
857 Ibid.
858 Ibid.
859 Ibid.
860 Ibid.
861 Ibid.
862 Michel Foucault, *Discipline and Punish: The Birth of the Prison*, 2nd ed., New York: Vintage Books, 1995, pp. 47-8; p. 78; 179.
863 A. P. Donajgrodzki, (1974), p. 477.
864 HO 45/1585, Major Sir Joshua Jebb to Sir James Graham, 'Report on Tread Wheel Labour and the absence of an authorised scheme of Hard Labour for short-terms of Imprisonment', 11 April 1846.
865 Ibid.
866 HO 45/1585, Whitworth Russell and William Crawford to Samuel March Phillipps, 30 April 1846.
867 Ibid.
868 Ibid.
869 Ibid.
870 Ibid.
871 Ibid.
872 HO 45/772, John G. Perry, Inspector of Prisons to Samuel March Phillipps, 23 November 1844.
873 Ibid.
874 HO 45/1585, Whitworth Russell to Samuel March Phillipps, 30 April 1846.
875 Ibid.
876 Ibid.
877 HO 45/1585, Major Sir Joshua Jebb to Sir James Graham, 'Report on Tread Wheel Labour and the absence of an authorised scheme of Hard Labour for short-terms of Imprisonment', 11 April 1846; Whitworth Russell to Samuel March Phillipps, 30 April 1846.
878 Ibid.
879 HO 45/1585, Diagram and Description of Major Jebb's Crank Machinery.
880 HO 45/1585, Whitworth Russell to Samuel March Phillipps, 30 April 1846.
881 Ibid.
882 HO 45/1585, Major Sir Joshua Jebb to Sir James Graham, 'Report on Tread Wheel Labour and the absence of an authorised scheme of Hard Labour for short-terms of Imprisonment', 11 April 1846.
883 Ibid.
884 Ibid.
885 Ibid.
886 Ibid.
887 Ibid.
888 D. F. Smith, (1972), p. 171.

889 A. P. Donajgrodzki, (1974), p. 478.

890 Malcolm Chase, (2007), p. 225; Miles Taylor, *The Decline of British Radicalism, 1847-1860*, Oxford: Clarendon, 1995, p. 103.

6 Sir George Grey: The Challenge of Chartism, 1846-48

891 D. F. Smith, (1972); D. F. Smith, 'Sir George Grey at the Mid-Victorian Home Office' in *Canadian Journal of History*, 19, 1984, 361-86.

892 *Manchester Guardian*, 4 July 1846.

893 Ibid.

894 D. F. Smith (1972), pp. 46-9.

895 James Vernon, (1993), p. 250.

896 Ibid., p. 296.

897 John Belchem, '1848: Feargus O'Connor and the Collapse of the Mass Platform' in James Epstein and Dorothy Thompson (eds.), *The Chartist Experience: Studies in Working-Class Radicalism and Culture, 1830-60*, London: Macmillan, 1982, pp. 269-310.

898 David Storey, *Territory: The Claiming of Space*, Harlow: Prentice Hall, 2001, p. 72.

899 *The Times*, 1 March 1844.

900 *The Times*, 24 May 1844; *The Times*, 30 May 1844; *The Times*, 3 September 1844.

901 Roger Magraw, *France 1815-1914: The Bourgeois Century*, 3rd ed, London: Fontana, 1992, pp. 70-2.

902 PRO 30/22/5F, Viscount Palmerston: Memorandum on comparative state of defences of Britain and France, December 1846.

903 Edward Royle, *Revolutionary Britannia? Reflections on the threat of revolution in Britain, 1789-1848*, Manchester: Manchester University Press, 2000, pp. 127-128.

904 PRO 30/22/5F; WO 55/1563/6, Sir John Burgoyne's observations on the probable results of a war with France, 7 November 1846.

905 Kay Boardman and Christine Kinealy (eds.), *1848: The Year the World Turned?* Newcastle Upon Tyne: Cambridge Scholars, 2007, p. 17.

906 H. Parris, *Government and the Railways in Nineteenth-Century Britain*, London: Routledge and Kegan Paul, 1965, p. 120; T. R. Gourvish, *Railways and the British Economy, 1830-1914*, London: Macmillan, 1980, pp. 12-19.

907 WO 30/112, Sir George Grey to Duke of Wellington, 14 December 1846.

908 *Leeds Intelligencer*, 27 March 1847.

909 Ibid.

910 WO 30/112, Duke of Wellington to Sir George Grey, 15 December 1846.

911 WO 30/112, Memorandum relative to difficulties anticipated in carrying into effect the proposed Warrant for extending the privilege of free discharges in the Army, 22 January 1847.

912 Ibid.

913 WO 30/112, Duke of Wellington to Sir George Grey, 22 January 1847.

914 *Morning Chronicle*, 4 January 1848; Hew Strachan, (1984), p. 198.

915 PRO 30/22/5F; WO 55/1563/6, Sir John Burgoyne's observations on the probable results of a war with France, 7 November 1846.

916 Ibid.

917 PRO 30/22, Lord John Russell: Papers; See John Saville, (1987), p. 60; Hew Strachan, (1984), pp. 198-9.

918 Dorothy Thompson, (1984), p. 295; Stephen Roberts, *The Chartist Prisoners: The Radical Lives of Thomas Cooper (1805-1892) and Arthur O'Neill (1819-1896)*, Oxford: Peter Lang, 2008, pp. 17-82.

919 Antony Taylor, (1995), pp. 383-407 (388).

920 *Northern Star*, 11 February 1843; 26 July 1843.

921 *Northern Star*, 11 February 1843; 27 April 1844.

922 *Northern Star*, 30 August 1845.

923 *Northern Star*, 7 June 1845; 14 June 1845; 19 July 1845; 9 August 1845.

924 *Northern Star*, 17 October 1846; 12 December 1846; 13 March 1847; 28 August 1847; 27 November 1847

925 *Northern Star*, 14 March 1846; 22 August 1846.

926 *Northern Star*, 9 January 1847; 12 June 1847; 4 September 1847; 29 January, 1848.

927 *Northern Star*, 8 January 1848; 25 March 1848; 1 April 1848; 6 May 1848.

928 *The Times*, 9 November 1847; 31 May 1848; See Malcolm Chase, (2007), pp. 274-5; 292; 324-6; See also Edward Royle, *Chartism*, 3rd ed., London: Longman, 1996, pp. 39-41; 116-118.

929 HO 45/2410/544-6, Thomas Paterson, Bingley to Sir George Grey, 28 April 1848; *Northern Star*, 13 May 1838; Paul A. Pickering, *Feargus O' Connor: A Political Life*, Monmouth: Merlin Press, 2008.

930 F. C. Mather, (1965), p. 24; See HO 45/2410 papers.

931 Fabrice Bensimon, 'Britain During the 1848 Revolutions and the Changing of "Britishness"' in Kay Boardman and Christine Kinealy (eds.), *1848: The Year the World Turned?*, Newcastle Upon Tyne: Cambridge Scholars, 2007, pp. 83-107 (86); Dorothy Thompson, *Outsiders: Class, Gender and Nation*, London: Verso, 1993, Ch.4, 'Ireland and the Irish in English Radicalism before 1850', pp. 103-133.

932 Kay Boardman and Christine Kinealy (eds.), (2007), p. 2.

933 James Vernon, (1993), p. 105.

934 David Ayerst, *Guardian: Biography of a Newspaper*, London: Collins, 1971, p. 94.

935 *The Times*, 6 June 1846.

936 Ibid.

937 David Ayerst, (1971), p. 93.

938 Ibid. p. 94.

939 Wilfred Hindle, *The Morning Post, 1772-1937: Portrait of a Newspaper*, London: Routledge, 1937, p. 176.

940 Hannah Barker, *Newspapers, Politics and English Society, 1695-1855*, Harlow: Longman, 2000, p. 223.

941 William Newarch, 'Mechanics' Institutes' in *Westminster Review*, 41, 1844, in Andrew King and John Plunkett (eds.), *Popular Print Media, 1820-1900*,

London: Routledge, 2004, pp. 416-445; Aled Jones, *Powers of the Press: Newspapers, Power and the Public in Nineteenth-Century England*, Aldershot: Scolar Press, 1996, pp. 183-6.

942 David Ayerst, (1971), p. 98.

943 Figures taken from Newspaper stamps: Return of the number of newspaper stamps at one penny, issued to newspapers in England, Ireland, Scotland and Wales, 1837 to 1850; 1852 (42) XXVIII.497, House Of Commons Papers: Accounts and Papers, 10 February 1852.

944 *Northern Star*, 19 October 1844.

945 Ibid.

946 Ibid.

947 Malcolm Chase, (2007), pp. 252-3.

948 See Appendix III, for a return of the number of Newspaper Stamps during 1837-1848.

949 Henry Richard Fox Bourne, *English Newspapers: Chapters in the History of Journalism, Vol.II*, London: 1887, p. 185.

950 Ibid., p. 187.

951 HO 41/19/25-6, Samuel March Phillipps to Lt-Gen. Sir Thomas Arbuthnot K.C.B., 9 March 1848.

952 HO 41/19/24-5, Samuel March Phillipps to Mayor of Manchester, 9 March 1848.

953 HO 41/19/100, Denis Le Marchant to the Mayors and Commanding Officers, 9 April 1848.

954 Ibid.

955 HO 41/19/108-110, Sir George Grey to John Lewis Ricardo MP, 10 April 1848.

956 John Saville, (1987), pp. 126-8; pp. 137-8.

957 Antony Taylor, (1995), 383-407 (p. 388).

958 WO 30/111, Chartist riots, 1848, Wellington letters concerning the disposition of Troops assembled in the Metropolis, 6-8 April 1848.

959 Ibid.

960 Antony Taylor, (1995), 383-407 (p. 387).

961 Ibid.

962 HO 41/19/86, Denis Le Marchant to Mayor and Magistrates of England and Wales, 6/7 April 1848.

963 *The Times*, 15 April 1848

964 Ibid.

965 Ibid; HO 45/2410/975-6, J. P. Tempest to Sir George Grey, 3 May 1848.

966 *The Times*, 19 April 1848.

967 Edward Vallance, (2009), p. 419.

968 Hansard, House of Commons Debate on the Removal of Aliens Bill, 1 May 1848, vol.98, cc.560-84; 1847-8 (281) Removal of Aliens, A Bill intituled an act to authorise during a limited time, the Removal of Aliens from the Realm, 18 April 1848.

969 Hansard, House of Lords Debate on the Removal of Aliens Bill, 16 May 1848, vol.98, cc.1060.

970 HO 45/2410/452-8; 459-62, The report of Sir Richard Mayne and his meeting

with Feargus O'Connor, 10 April 1848.

971 HO 45/2410/557, Thomas Clutton Salt, 'The Real Chartist: Designed to show the only way in which true liberty, genuine equality and elevated fraternity are to be sought, acquired and established', 1848.

972 WO 30/111, Chartist riots, 1848; HO 41/19/120-1, Sir George Grey to Duke of Wellington, 12 April 1848.

973 HO 45/2410/459-60, Chartist demonstration: Metropolitan Police Office, 10 April 1848; *The Times*, 11 April 1848.

974 See David Goodway, *London Chartism, 1838-1848*, Cambridge: Cambridge University Press, 1982, p,74; pp. 130-2.

975 Ibid.

976 HO 45/2410/490-3, Memorandum upon the further and more permanent organisation of the Special Constables, 1848.

977 John Belchem, *Popular Radicalism in Nineteenth-Century Britain*, Basingstoke: Macmillan, 1996, p. 91.

978 Roger Swift, (2007), 669-699 (p. 680).

979 HO 45/2410/762-763, Leeds: Letter from William Dawson to Sir George Grey, 15 April 1848.

980 HO 45/2410/490-3, Memorandum upon the further and more permanent organisation of the Special Constables, 1848; HO/2410/495-500, Proposed association to be named the 'Loyal Association Police', 5 April 1848.

981 Ibid.

982 Ibid.

983 HO 45/2410/486-9, Note concerning the payment of Special Constables.

984 HO 45/2410/501-3, Metropolitan Police Office to Sir George Grey, 5 April 1848.

985 Theodore Koditschek, (1990), p. 492.

986 HO 45/2410/1181-2, Thomas Marshall, Clerk to the Barnsley Magistrates to Sir George Grey, 16 April 1848.

987 HO 45/2410/1031-4, Bradford Chartists, S.L. Binns to Sir George Grey, 25 May 1848.

988 Ibid.

989 See Asa Briggs, (ed.), (1959), pp. 1-28.

990 HO 45/2410/1031-4, Bradford, S.L. Binns to Sir George Grey, 25 May 1848

991 *Bradford Observer*, 16 March 1848; Stephen Roberts, *Radical Politicians and Poets in Early Victorian Britain: The Voices of Six Chartist Leaders*, Lampeter: Edwin Mellen Press, 1993, George White, pp. 11-38, particularly 22-34.

992 Ibid., 6 April 1848.

993 Ibid.

994 Ibid.

995 Ibid.

996 Ibid.

997 Ibid.

998 *Leeds Intelligencer*, 1 May 1847.

999 John Saville, (1987), p. 127.

1000 HO 45/2410/961-962, Bradford Magistrates to Sir George Grey, 10 April 1848.

1001 Ibid.

1002 HO 45/19/115, Denis Le Marchant to Mayor and Magistrates of Bradford, 11 April 1848.

1003 HO 45/2410/715, Statement written by George Hall of Leeds, Police Officer.

1004 HO 45/2410/772-774 – Leeds: Letter from J Corbett, the Mayor of Leeds to Sir George Grey, 17 April 1848.

1005 HO 41/19/17, Denis Le Marchant to Mayor of Leeds, 29 February 1848.

1006 HO 45/2410/433, John Waterhouse to Major-General Thorn, 27 May 1848.

1007 HO 45/2410/1013, Mayor and Magistrates of Bradford to Sir George Grey, 22 May 1848.

1008 HO 45/2410/1075-6, Bradford magistrates to Sir George Grey, 9 June 1848; HO 45/2410/1086-7, Mayor and Magistrates of Bradford to Sir George Grey, 13 June 1848.

1009 *Leeds Intelligencer*, 3 June 1848.

1010 HO 41/19/137-8, Sir George Grey to Earl of Harewood, 17 April 1848.

1011 Ibid.

1012 HO 45/2410/1169-70, Letter to Sir George Grey, 7 April 1848.

1013 HO 45/2410/1175-6, Thomas Marshall, Clerk to the Barnsley Magistrates to Sir George Grey, 14 April 1848; HO 45/2410/1184-5, Thomas Marshall, Clerk to the Barnsley Magistrates to Sir George Grey, 19 April 1848.

1014 HO 45/2410/1179-80, Denis Le Marchant to Barnsley Magistrates, 18 April 1848; HO 45/2410/1188-9, Note written by Sir George Grey, 7 June 1848.

1015 HO 41/19/150, Denis Le Marchant to Lieutenant-General. Sir Thomas Arbuthnot K.C.B, 22 April 1848.

1016 Ibid.

1017 HO 45/2410/1186-7, Thomas Marshall, Clerk to the Barnsley Magistrates to Sir George Grey, 7 June 1848.

1018 HO 45/2410/1111, John Houghton to Sir George Grey, 21 May 1848.

1019 HO 45/2410/1197-9, Bingley Magistrates to Sir George Grey, 29 March 1848.

1020 HO 45/2410/1203-4, William Busfield Ferrand to Sir George Grey, 24 May 1848.

1021 HO 41/19/182, Henry Waddington to William Ellis, Bingley, 25 May 1848.

1022 HO 45/2410/1214-8, William Busfield Ferrand to Sir George Grey, 27 May 1848.

1023 HO 45/2410/435-441, Letter and enclosures, Sir Thomas Arbuthnot to Henry Waddington, 28 May 1848.

1024 HO 41/19/191, Henry Waddington to William Busfield Ferrand, Bingley, 29 May 1848.

1025 HO 45/2410/1031-1034, S. L. Binns to Sir George Grey, 25 May 1848.

1026 See QC/4, West Riding Quarter Sessions Lock-Up Committee minutes, 1843-59.

1027 QC/4, West Riding Quarter Sessions Lock-Up Committee minutes, 1843-59, p. 71.

1028 HO 45/2410/975-6, J. P. Tempest, Bradford magistrate to Sir George Grey, 3 May 1848.

1029 Ibid.

1030 *Bradford Observer*, 13 April 1848.

1031 Ibid.

1032 HO 41/19/167-8, Denis Le Marchant to J. P. Tempest, 4 May 1848.

1033 *Bradford Observer*, 18 May 1848.

1034 Ibid.

1035 Ibid.

1036 Ibid.

1037 Ibid.

1038 *Bradford Observer*, 25 May 1848.

1039 Ibid.

1040 Ibid.

1041 HO 41/19/183-4, Henry Waddington to Mayor and Magistrates of Bradford, 25 May 1848.

1042 Ibid.

1043 Ibid.

1044 *Bradford Observer*, 1 June 1848.

1045 HO 45/2410/1045-6. J. P. Tempest to Sir George Grey, 28 May 1848

1046 HO 41/19/192, Henry Waddington to J. P. Tempest, 29 May 1848; HO 45/2410/456-457, Colonel Thorn to Colonel Yorke, 29 May 1848.

1047 HO 45/2410/1049, Permanent Under-Secretary of State to Bradford Magistrates, 29 May 1848.

1048 Ibid.

1049 *Bradford Observer*, 1 June 1848.

1050 Ibid.

1051 HO 41/19/185, Henry Waddington to Mayor of Bradford, 26 May 1848.

1052 *Bradford Observer*, 1 June 1848.

1053 Ibid.

1054 Ibid.

1055 Ibid.

1056 Ibid.

1057 Ibid.

1058 Ibid.

1059 Ibid.

1060 Ibid.

1061 *Leeds Intelligencer*, 3 June 1848.

1062 Ibid.

1063 HO 45/2410/1060-1, Mayor and Magistracy to Sir George Grey, 30 May 1848.

1064 HO 45/2410/1063-4, Mayor and Magistrates of Bradford to Sir George Grey, 31 May 1848.

1065 HO 45/2410/1053, Mayor and Magistrates of Bradford to Sir George Grey, 29 May 1848.

1066 HO 45/2410/477, Colonel Thorn to Colonel Barnard, 30 May 1848.

1067 Ibid.

1068 *Bradford Observer*, 1 June 1848.

1069 Ibid.

1070 HO 45/2410/1119-1120. Robert Milligan, Bradford Magistrate to Sir George

Grey, 19 July 1848.

1071 HO 45/2410/1145, Bradford magistrates to Sir George Grey, 14 September 1848.

1072 HO 45/2410/802, General Post Office to George Cornewall Lewis, 30 May 1848.

1073 HO 45/2410/1038-1039, Mayor and magistrates of Bradford to Sir George Grey, concerning the Irish Confederate, Joe Grady, 26 May 1848.

1074 Ibid.

1075 Ibid.

1076 HO 45/2410/436-441, Thomas Arbuthnot to Henry Waddington (Under Secretary of State at the Home Office), 28 May 1848.

1077 HO 45/2410/1122, J. P. Tempest to Sir George Grey, 24 July 1848.

1078 Ibid.

1079 HO 45/2410/1132-1133, Letter from J.P. Tempest, Robert Milligan, John Rand to Sir George Grey, 18 August 1848.

1080 HO 45/2410/1135-1136, Letter from Tempest, Pollard, Milligan to Sir George Grey, 24 August 1848.

1081 Theodore Koditschek, (1990), p. 537-8.

1082 Ibid., p. 581

1083 Kate Tiller, 'Late Chartism: Halifax 1847-58' in James Epstein and Dorothy Thompson (eds.), (1982), pp. 311-344 (p. 318).

APPENDICES

APPENDIX I

The total number of officers employed by the Metropolitan Police,
1837-1848

Year	Superintendents*	Inspectors	Sergeants	Constables	Total
1837	17	74	340	3,071	3,502
1838	17	76	339	3,043	3,475
1839	17	79	345	3,058	3,499
1840	19	101	349	3,218	3,687
1841	19	105	446	3,768	4,338
1842	19	109	459	3,807	4,394
1843	19	110	465	3,799	4,393
1844	19	111	478	4,065	4,673[1]
1845	19	112	479	4,027	4,637[2]
1846	19	114	485	4,131	4,749[3]
1847	19	114	493	4,166	4,792[4]
1848	19	125	588	4,781	5,513[5]

* Figures include 1 Inspecting Superintendent

1   Figures taken from Police: A return of the number of the Irish Police Force, and of the Metropolitan Police, in each year since they were established, and the amount of public money voted for the same in each year, 1844 (189) XXXIX.689, House of Commons Papers: Accounts and Papers, 16 February 1844.

2   Metropolitan Police: Accounts showing the sums received and expended for the purposes of the Metropolitan Police, Police Superannuation Fund, and police courts, in the year ended the 31st December 1844 (114) XXXVII.711, House of Commons Papers: Accounts and Papers, 11 March 1845.

3   Metropolitan Police: Accounts showing the sums received and expended for the purposes of the Metropolitan Police, Police Superannuation Fund, and Police Courts, in the year ended the 31st December 1845 (20) XXXIV.795, House of Commons Papers: Accounts and Papers, 3 February 1846.

4   Metropolitan Police: Accounts showing the sums received and expended for the purposes of the Metropolitan Police, Police Superannuation Fund, and police courts, in the year ended the 31st December 1846 (28) XLVII.643, House of Commons Papers: Accounts and Papers, 29 January 1847.

5   Figures taken from Metropolitan Police: Abstract return of the number of divisions into which the Metropolitan Police district is now divided; and the letter and name of each division; the parishes and places comprised in each division, and population thereof, with number of police in each division; and the salaries and allowances of each class, (24) XLIV.479, House of Commons Papers: Accounts and Papers, 13 February 1849.

APPENDIX II

The total number of Police in England, Wales, Ireland and Scotland, 1837-1848 [1]

Year	England and Wales	Scotland	Ireland	Total
1837	5,884	629	8,423	14,936
1838	6,014	665	8,532	15,211
1839	6,101	684	9,217	16,002
1840	7,174	750	9,428	17,352
1841	9,613	679	9,783	20,075
1842	10,454	1,086	9,799	21,339
1843	10,567	1,091	10,399	22,057
1844	10,664	1,100	10,177	21,941
1845	11,240	1,086	10,290	22,616
1846	11,373	1,095	10,550	23,018
1847	11,722	1,122	11,269	24,113
1848	11,876	1,146	12,188	25,210

1   Statistics taken from Abstract of return for each year of the number of Police in England and Wales, Ireland and Scotland, 1835-6 to 1851-2; 1852 (260) XXX.1, House Of Commons Papers: Accounts and Papers, 25 March 1852.

APPENDIX III

A return of the number of Newspaper Stamps during 1837-1848 [2]

Title	1837	1838	1839	1840	1841	1842	1843	1844	1845	1846	1847	1848
Morning Post	797,000	875,500	1,006,000	1,125,000	1,165,210	1,195,025	1,090,000	1,002,000	1,002,500	1,045,500	990,100	964,500
Morning Chronicle	2,200,000	2,075,000	2,028,000	2,075,500	2,079,000	1,918,500	1,784,000	1,628,000	1,554,000	1,356,000	1,233,000	1,151,304
Morning Herald	2,078,000	1,925,000	1,820,000	1,956,000	1,630,000	1,559,500	1,516,000	1,609,070	2,018,025	1,752,500	1,510,000	1,335,000
Sun	896,000	1,344,000	1,231,000	1,281,000	1,225,000	1,173,000	1,098,000	868,000	1,098,500	1,105,000	909,000	893,312
Times	3,355,000	3,650,000	4,300,000	5,060,000	5,650,000	6,305,000	6,250,000	6,900,000	8,100,000	8,950,000	9,025,230	11,021,500
Manchester Guardian	526,750	545,000	602,000	609,000	637,451	710,700	761,800	859,000	967,000	1,002,000	1,009,000	968,000
Bradford Observer	23,000	32,500	34,000	27,879	30,500	36,000	55,500	48,000	54,000	54,000	54,000	55,598
Halifax Guardian	23,000	16,650	38,000	33,000	41,000	56,000	59,000	74,000	69,000	82,000	117,450	109,000
Leeds Intelligencer	165,000	173,000	173,000	212,500	187,000	188,500	190,000	200,000	210,000	208,480	201,480	220,174
Leeds Mercury	408,975	459,728	527,000	493,500	517,000	513,000	459,006	464,190	489,250	500,000	500,000	521,000
Leeds Times	171,000	132,000	118,000	169,500	182,000	163,000	176,000	204,000	241,000	234,650	254,000	281,500
Northern Star	52,000	572,640	1,851,000	976,500	706,000	651,000	454,500	384,000	337,500	322,000	455,000	626,000
Sheffield Independent	66,500	66,000	108,500	118,000	121,000	123,500	134,600	131,999	156,000	174,000	168,500	170,000
Sheffield Iris	44,000	40,500	44,000	39,500	16,500	17,000	27,125	28,000	35,500	34,500	26,500	21,000
Sheffield Mercury	95,975	92,500	90,750	90,000	67,500	71,500	76,250	64,000	70,000	67,000	54,000	37,000
West Riding Herald	29,000	31,000	35,000	33,000	23,000	23,000	24,000	32,180	31,000	43,800	36,000	36,000

2   Figures taken from Newspaper stamps: Return of the number of newspaper stamps at one penny, issued to newspapers in England, Ireland, Scotland and Wales, 1837 to 1850; 1852 (42) XXVIII.497, House Of Commons Papers: Accounts and Papers, 10 February 1852.

BIBLIOGRAPHY

PRIMARY SOURCES

Archives

National Archives
HO 33/4, Correspondence from the General Post Office concerning administrative matters, intelligence reports, the notification of political meetings and disturbances, 1838-50.

HO 40/57, Yorkshire disturbance papers, 1840.

HO 41/13, Home Office: Disturbances Entry Book, June 1837 to May 1839.

HO 41/14, Home Office: Disturbances Entry Book, May 1839 to August 1839.

HO 41/15, Home Office: Disturbances Entry Book, August 1839 to July 1840.

HO 41/16, Home Office: Disturbances Entry Book, July 1840 to August 1842.

HO 41/17, Home Office: Disturbances Entry Book, August 1842 to July 1843.

HO 41/18, Home Office: Disturbances Entry Book, July 1843 to January 1848.

HO 41/19, Home Office: Disturbances Entry Book, January 1848 to April 1852.

HO 41/20, Home Office: Disturbances Entry Book, June 1852 to October 1867.

HO 45/264, Chartist Disturbance Papers, 1842.

HO 45/310, Memorandums reflecting the Town and Neighbourhood of Leeds, 1838.

HO 45/649, Yorkshire Disturbance Papers: The provision of barracks at Bradford, 1844.

HO 45/292, Police: Origins of Detective Force, 1842.

HO 45/724, Detective Force: Pay and Rewards, 1843-8

HO 45/729, Police: Conveyance by Railway, 1844-5.

HO 45/772, Prisons and Prisoners: Enforcement of Authorized Dietary Regime, 1844.

HO 45/1560, Telegraph: A Bill for regulating Electric Telegraphs, 1846.

HO 45/1585, Prisons and Prisoners, Treadmill Labour: Report by Major Joshua Jebb, 1846-1847.

HO 45/2410, Disturbances: Threat of revolution 1848: London. Chartists, and Irish Confederates. Reports indicating plan for sabotage and revolution. Arms traffic, plans for demonstrations, enrolment of special constables and pensioners and provision for military assistance if required. Reports on meetings, posters, arrests. Use of the Electric Telegraph Company by the government. Reports from the provinces. Alleged police brutality. Claims for compensation following riots and looting. Protection of key government offices. Connections with French revolutionaries, 1848.

HO 50/451, War Office and Chelsea Hospital: Contains reports by Sir Charles Napier on Barracks in Northern District, 1840.

HO 51/121, Circulars: Militia and Volunteers, 1829-56.

HO 51/166, War Office Letter Book, 1838-1851.

HO 52/35, Home Office: Counties Correspondence relating to Yorkshire, 1837.

HO 52/40, Home Office: Counties Correspondence relating to Yorkshire, 1839.

HO 97/27, Enquiry into the Transaction of Business at the Home Office: Transcripts of Oral Evidence, 1848.

HO 387/31, Folios 1-6, Secret Service accounts; Correspondence with Audit Office, Affidavits and Miscellaneous Papers, James Graham (ff 1-6).

HO 387/30, Folios 1-5, Secret Service accounts; Correspondence with Audit Office, Affidavits and Miscellaneous Papers, Lord Normanby (ff 1-5).

MEPO 2/61, Chartist riots at Birmingham, 1839.

PRO 30/22/5F, Lord John Russell: Papers, 1846.

PRO 30/22/6F, Lord John Russell: Papers, 1847.

TS 11/496-505, Regina v John Frost and others for Chartist disturbances at Newport, Monmouth: Monmouth Special Commission, 1839-40.

TS 11/813/2677, 'Yorkshire Lent Assizes, Bradford Riots: The Queen against

Robert Peddie', 1840.

TS 25/62, Parish Constables Act 1842: The Appointment of Paid Constables, 1843.

TS 36/24, The Queen v John Frost and others, 1839.

TS 36/24, The Queen v John Frost: Court of Exchequer Chamber, 1840.

WO 30/111, Chartist riots, 1848.

WO 30/112, Army Reforms: Between Duke of Wellington, The Lord Fitzroy Somerset, The Earl Grey, The Lord John Russell and Major General Sir H.D. Ross, K.C.B., regarding proposed Bill to limit the time of service in the Army, to extend the principle of free discharges with deferred pensions to all soldiers of 10 years service, and to render effective the services of the Chelsea and Greenwich Out-Pensioners as a Reserve Militia.

WO 55/1563/6, Sir John Burgoyne's observations on the probable results of a war with France, with the Duke of Wellington's reply.

West Yorkshire Archives

WYL1352/D3/7/17/1-2, Letters from Lord Harewood, Lord Lieutenant of the West Riding, to magistrates about riots in the West Riding and the formation of Armed Associations to protect life and property, 1838.

QC/4, West Riding Quarter Sessions Committees: Minutes and Reports, Lock-Up Committee Minutes, 1843-59.

Parliamentary Papers

Debates

Hansard, House of Commons debate, 3 May 1838, vol. 42., cc.819-20

Hansard, House of Commons debate, 20 November 1837, vol. 39 cc.31-91.

Hansard, House of Commons debate, 15 May 1839, vol. 47, cc.1025-8.

Hansard, House of Commons debate on the Removal of Aliens Bill, 1 May 1848, vol.98, cc.560-84

Hansard, House of Lords debate on the Removal of Aliens Bill, 16 May 1848, vol.98, cc.1060.

Parliamentary Reports and Commissions

1833 (48) 3 Will. IV.--Sess. 1833. A Bill to Regulate the Labour of Children and Young Persons in the Mills and Factories of the United Kingdom.

1833 (150) 3 Will.IV. – Sess.1833, A Bill to alter and extend the provisions of an act of the eleventh year of King George the Fourth, for lighting and watching of parishes in England and Wales, 2 April 1833.

1833 (718) Select Committee Report on Cold Bath Fields Meeting, 23 August 1833

1835 (574) Municipal Corporations. A Bill, (with the amendments made by the Lords) entitled an Act to provide for the Regulation of Municipal Corporations in England and Wales, 6.Will. IV, 28 August 1835.

1837 (118) Bradford (Poor Law Amendment Act), Return of the Metropolitan Police sent to Bradford, with correspondence on the subject (118), 11 December 1837.

1839 (169) First Report of the Commissioners appointed to inquire as to the best means of establishing an efficient constabulary in the counties of England and Wales.

1839 (499) Manchester Police: A bill for improving the police in Manchester.

1840 (119) County constabulary. A Bill to amend the Act for the Establishment of County and District Constables, 3.Vict., 17 March 1840.

Copy of a letter written by Lord John Russell to the Lord Lieutenants' of certain Counties suggesting the formation of Associations for the Protection of Life and Property, Parliamentary Accounts and Papers 1839, Vol.9, p.3.

1842 (456) A copy of all communications that have passed between the Secretary of State for the Home Department and the authorities of York Castle, from the beginning of September 1841 to the present time, relative to the state of health and death of Samuel Holberry, House Of Commons Papers ; Accounts and Papers, Vol.XXXII.569

Return of the Number of Troops, Officers and Men, employed in Great Britain on the 25th day of January in the Years 1829, 1835, 1840 and 1847.

1842 (432) Parish Constables Bill, 11 July 1842.

1844 (189) Police: A return of the number of the Irish Police Force, and of the Metropolitan Police, in each year since they were established, and the amount of public money voted for the same in each year, 16 February 1844.

1845 (114) Metropolitan Police: 1844. Accounts showing the sums received and expended for the purposes of the Metropolitan Police, Police Superannuation Fund, and police courts, in the year ended the 31st December 1844, 11 March 1845.

1846 (20) Metropolitan Police: 1845. Accounts showing the sums received and expended for the purposes of the Metropolitan Police, Police Superannuation Fund, and Police Courts, in the year ended the 31st December 1845, 3 February 1846.

1847 (28) Metropolitan Police: 1846. Accounts showing the sums received and expended for the purposes of the Metropolitan Police, Police Superannuation Fund, and police courts, in the year ended the 31st December 1846, 29 January 1847.

1847-8 (281) Removal of Aliens, A Bill intituled an act to authorise during a limited time, the Removal of Aliens from the Realm, 18 April 1848.

1849 (24) Metropolitan Police: Abstract return of the number of divisions into which the Metropolitan Police district is now divided; and the letter and name of each division; the parishes and places comprised in each division, and population thereof, with number of police in each division; and the salaries and allowances of each class, 13 February 1849.

1852 (260) Abstract of return for each year, 1835-6 to 1851-2 of the number of Police in England and Wales, Ireland and Scotland, 29 June 1852.

1852-3 (715) (715-I), Second Report from the Select Committee on Police; Together with the proceedings of the Committee, Minutes of Evidence and Appendix, 5 July 1853.

1852 (42) Newspaper stamps: Return of the number of newspaper stamps at one penny, issued to newspapers in England, Ireland, Scotland and Wales, from the year 1837 to the year 1850, 10 February 1852.

1854 (127) Police: A Bill to render more effectual the police in Counties and Boroughs in England and Wales, 2 June 1854.

1856 (215), Police (Counties and Boroughs): A Bill (as amended by the Lords) intituled an act to render more effectual the police in Counties and Boroughs in England and Wales, 1 July 1856.

Printed Primary Sources

1851 Census of Great Britain, London: Longman, 1854.

Bentham, J., *An Introduction to the Principles of Morals and Legislation*, Oxford: Clarendon Press, 1879.

Napier, W. F. P. N., *Life and Opinions of General Sir Charles James Napier*, London: Murray, 1857.

Paine, T., *Rights of Man*, Dublin: 1792.

Smith, A., *An inquiry into the nature and causes of the Wealth of Nations*, Oxford: Clarendon Press, 1869.

Newspapers

Aris's Birmingham Gazette

Bradford Observer

Halifax Guardian

Leeds Intelligencer

Leeds Mercury

Manchester Guardian

Northern Star

The Times

Wakefield Journal and West Riding Herald

SECONDARY SOURCES

Books and Pamphlets

Adelman, P., *Peel and the Conservative Party*, London: Longmans, 1989.

Ashton, O. R. and Allen J. (eds.), *Papers for the People: A Study of the Chartist Press*, London: Merlin Press, 2005.

Ayerst, D., *Guardian: Biography of a Newspaper*, London: Collins, 1971.

Barker, H., *Newspapers, Politics and English Society, 1695-1855*, Harlow: Longman, 2000.

Baxter, J., *Armed Resistance and Insurrection: The early Chartist experience*, London: Communist Party History Group, 1984.

Belchem, J., '1848: Feargus O'Connor and the Collapse of the Mass Platform' in J. Epstein and D. Thompson (eds.), *The Chartist Experience: Studies in Working-Class Radicalism and Culture, 1830-60*, London: Macmillan, 1982, pp.269-310.

Belchem, J., *Popular Radicalism in Nineteenth-Century Britain*, Basingstoke: Macmillan, 1996.

Belchem, J., (ed.), *Popular Politics, Riot and Labour: Essays in Liverpool History, 1790-1940*, Liverpool: Liverpool University Press, 1992.

Bensimon, F., 'Britain During the 1848 Revolutions and the Changing of "Britishness"' in K. Boardman and C. Kinealy (eds.), *1848: The Year the World Turned?*, Newcastle Upon Tyne: Cambridge Scholars, 2007, pp.83-107.

Bentham, J., *A Fragment on Government and an Introduction to the Principle of the Morals and Legislation*, Oxford: Basil Blackwell, 1967.

Blake, R., *The Conservative Party from Peel to Thatcher*, London: Methuen, 1985.

Boardman, K. and Kinealy, C. (eds.), *1848: The Year the World Turned?*, Newcastle Upon Tyne: Cambridge Scholars, 2007.

Bourne, H. R. F., *English Newspapers: Chapters in the History of Journalism, Vol.II*, London: 1887.

Brenner, N., Jessop, B., Jones, M., MacLeod, G. (eds.), *State/Space: A Reader*, Oxford: Blackwell, 2003.

Brewer, J., *The Sinews of Power: War, Money and the English State, 1688-1783*, London: Unwin Hyman, 1989.

Briggs, A. (ed), *Chartist Studies*, London: Macmillan, 1959.

Burke, B., *A Genealogical and Heraldic History of the Commoners of Great Britain and Ireland, Vol. I*, London: Henry Colburn, 1883.

Campion, D. A., 'Policing the Peelers: Parliament, the Public and the Metropolitan Police, 1829-33' in M. Cragoe and A. Taylor (eds.), *London Politics, 1760-1914*, Basingstoke: Palgrave Macmillan, 2005, pp.38-56.

Chase, M., *Chartism: A New History*, Manchester: Manchester University Press, 2007.

Chester, N., *The English Administrative System*, 1780-1870, Oxford: Clarendon Press, 1981.

Cole, G. D. H., *Chartist Portraits*, London: Macmillan, 1940.

Dicey, A. V., *Lectures on the relation between Law and Public Opinion in England during the nineteenth century*, London: Macmillan, 1905,

Donajgrodzki, A. P., 'New roles for old: The Northcote Report and the Clerks of the Home Office 1822-48' in G. Sutherland (ed.), *Studies in the Growth of Nineteenth-Century Government*, London: Routledge and Kegan Paul, 1972, 82-109.

Driver, C., *Tory Radical: The Life of Richard Oastler*, New York: Oxford University Press, 1946.

Driver, F., *Power and Pauperism: The Workhouse System, 1834-1884*, Cambridge: Cambridge University Press, 1993.

Eastwood, D., *Governing Rural England: Tradition and Transformation in Local Government, 1780-1840*, Oxford: Oxford University Press, 1994.

Emsley, C., *The English Police: A Political and Social History*, 2nd ed., London: Longman, 1996.

Epstein, J., *The Lion of Freedom: Feargus O'Connor and the Chartist Movement*, London: Croom Helm, 1982.

Epstein, J. and Thompson, D. (eds.), *The Chartist Experience: Studies in Working Class Radicalism and Culture, 1830-1860*, London: Macmillan 1982.

Erickson, A. B., *The Public Career of Sir James Graham*, Oxford: Basil Blackwell, 1952.

Fairhurst, J., *Policing Wigan: The Wigan Borough Police Force, 1836-1969*, Blackpool, Landy, 1996).

Foster, J., *Class Struggle and the Industrial Revolution: Early Industrial Capitalism in Three English Towns*, London: Weidenfeld and Nicolson, 1974.

Foucault, M., *Discipline and Punish: The Birth of the Prison*, 2nd ed., New York: Vintage Books, 1995.

Fraser, W. H., *Dr John Taylor, Chartist, Ayrshire Revolutionary*, Ayr: Ayrshire Archaeological and Natural History Society, 2006.

Gallaher, C., *Key Concepts in Political Geography*, London: Sage, 2009.

Gammage, R. G., *History of the Chartist Movement, 1837-1854*, 2nd ed., London: Frank Cass, 1969.

Garfield, S., *The Last Journey of William Huskisson: How a Day of Triumph became a Day of Despair at the Turn of a Wheel*, London: Faber and Faber, 2002.

Gash, N., *Sir Robert Peel: The Life of Sir Robert Peel after 1830*, London: Longman, 1972.

Gash, N., *Peel*, London: Longmans, 1976.

Godfrey, R., *Newbury Borough Police, 1836-1875*, Newbury: Richard Godfrey, 2008.

Goodway, D., *London Chartism, 1838-1848*, Cambridge: Cambridge University Press, 1982.

Gourvish, T. R., *Railways and the British Economy, 1830-1914*, London: Macmillan, 1980.

Hovell, M., *The Chartist Movement*, 3rd ed., Manchester: Manchester University Press, 1966.

Hall, R. G., *Voices of the People: Democracy and Chartist Political Identity 1830–1870*, Monmouth: Merlin Press, 2007.

Hamer, W. S., *The British Army, Civil Military Relations 1885-1905*, Oxford: Clarendon, 1970.

Hargreaves, J. A., *Benjamin Rushton: 1785-1853, Handloom Weaver and Chartist*, Halifax: Friends of Lister Lane Cemetery, 2006.

Haywood, I., *The Revolution in Popular Literature: Print, Politics and the People, 1790-1860*, Cambridge: Cambridge University Press, 2009.

Hilton, B., *A Mad, Bad, and Dangerous People? England 1783-1846*, Oxford: Clarendon Press, 2008.

Hindle, W., *The Morning Post, 1772-1937: Portrait of a Newspaper*, London: Routledge, 1937.

Jones, A., *Powers of the Press: Newspapers, Power and the Public in Nineteenth-Century England*, Aldershot: Scolar Press, 1996.

Jones, D., *Chartism and the Chartists*, London: Allen Lane, 1975.

Jones, G. S., *Languages of Class: Studies in English Working Class History, 1832-1982*, Cambridge: Cambridge University Press, 1983.

Jones, M., An *Introduction to Political Geography: Space, Place and Politics*, London: Routledge, 2004.

Joy, D., *A Regional History of the use of Railway, Volume 8: South and West Yorkshire*, London: David and Charles, 1975.

Joyce, P., *Work, Society and Politics: The Culture of the Factory in Later Victorian-England*, Brighton: Harvester Press, 1980.

Joyce, P., *Visions of the People: Industrial England and the Question of Class, 1848-1914*, Cambridge: Cambridge University Press, 1991.

Jupp, P, *The Governing of Britain, 1688-1848: The Executive, Parliament, and the People*, London: Routledge, 2006,

Keller, L., *The Triumph of Order: Democracy and Public Space in New York and London*, New York: Columbia University Press, 2009.

Koditschek, T., *Class Formation and Urban-Industrial Society: Bradford, 1750-1850*, Cambridge: Cambridge University, 1990.

Laybourn, K., *British Political Leaders: A Biographical Dictionary*, Oxford: ABC-Clio, 2001.

Magraw, R., *France 1815-1914: The Bourgeois Century, 3rd ed*, London: Fontana, 1992.

Mather, F. C., *Public Order in the Age of the Chartists*, Manchester: Manchester University Press, 1959.

Mather, F. C., *Chartism*, London: Historical Association Pamphlet 1965.

Miliband, R., *Parliamentary Socialism: A Study in the Politics of Labour*, London: Allen and Unwin, 1961.

Mitchell J., and Oakley A., (eds.), *The Rights and Wrongs of Women*, New York: Harmondsworth, 1976.

Moore, B., *Samuel Holberry, 1814-1842, Sheffield's Revolutionary Democrat*, Sheffield: Holberry Society Publications, 1978.

Moore, B., *Samuel Holberry and the Chartist Movement in Sheffield, 1837-1851*, Sheffield: Holberry Society Publications, 1987.

Newarch, W., 'Mechanics' Institutes', *Westminster Review*, 41, 1844, in King, A. and Plunkett J., (eds.), *Popular Print Media, 1820-1900*, London: Routledge, 2004, pp.416-445.

Newsam, F., *The Home Office*, London: George Allen and Unwin, 1954.

Painter, J. and Jeffrey, A. (eds.), *Political Geography: An Introduction to Space and Power*, London: Sage, 2009.

Palmer, S. H., *Police and Protest in England and Ireland, 1750-1850*, Cambridge: Cambridge University Press, 1988.

Parker, C. S., *Sir Robert Peel: From His Private Papers, Vol.2*, London: 1899.

Parris, H., *Government and the Railways in Nineteenth-Century Britain*, London: Routledge and Kegan Paul, 1965.

Peacock, A., *Bradford Chartism, 1838-40*, York: St Anthony's Press, 1969.

Pearce, R., *Government and Reform*, 1815-1918, London: Hodder and Stoughton, 1994.

Pellew, J., *The Home Office, 1848-1914: from Clerks to Bureaucrats*, London: Heinemann, 1982.

Philips, D. and Storch, R. D., *Policing Provincial England, 1829-1856: The Politics of Reform*, London: Leicester University Press, 1999.

Pickering, P. A. and Tyrrell, A. (eds.)., *The People's Bread: A History of the Anti-Corn Law League*, London: Leicester University Press, 2000.

Pickering, P. A., '"Mercenary Scribblers" and "Polluted Quills": The Chartist Press in Australia and New Zealand', in J. Allen and O. R. Ashton (eds.), *Papers for the People: A study of the Chartist press*, London: Merlin Press, 2005, pp.190-215.

Pickering, P. A., *Feargus O'Connor: A Political Life*, London: Merlin Press, 2008.

Prest, J., *Lord John Russell*, London: Macmillan, 1970.

Quinault, R., 'The Warwickshire County Magistracy and Public Order, c.1830-1870', in J. Stevenson and R. Quinault (eds.), *Popular Protest and Public Order: Six Studies in British History, 1790-1920*, London: George Allen and Unwin Ltd, 1974, pp.181-214.

Rawlings, P., *Policing: A Short History*, Cullompton: Willan Publishing, 2002.

Read, D., *Peterloo: The 'Massacre' and its Background*, Manchester: Manchester University Press, 1973.

Reddaway, W. F., 'Lord John Russell' in F. J. C. Hearnshaw, *Political Principles of some notable Prime Ministers of the Nineteenth Century*, London: Ernest Benn Ltd, 1926, pp.129-76.

Roberts, S., *Radical Politicians and Poets in Early Victorian Britain: The Voices of Six Chartist Leaders*, Lampeter: Edwin Mellen Press, 1993.

Roberts, S., *The Chartist Prisoners: The Radical Lives of Thomas Cooper (1805-1892) and Arthur O'Neill (1819-1896)*, Oxford: Peter Lang, 2008.

Royle, E, *Chartism*, 3rd ed., London: Longman, 1996.

Royle, E., *Revolutionary Britannia? Reflections on the threat of revolution in Britain, 1789-1848*, Manchester: Manchester University Press, 2000.

Sanders, M., *The Poetry of Chartism: Aesthetics, Politics, History*, Cambridge: Cambridge University Press, 2009.

Savage, M. and Miles A. (eds.), *The Remaking of the British Working Class, 1840-1940*, London: Routledge, 1994.

Saville, J., *1848: The British State and the Chartist Movement*, Cambridge: Cambridge University Press, 1987.

Saville, J., *The Consolidation of the Capitalist State, 1800-1850*, London: Pluto Press, 1994.

Scherer, P., *Lord John Russell: A Biography*, London: Associated University Press, 1999.

Schwarzkopf, J., *Women in the Chartist Movement*, London: Macmillan, 1991.

Stevenson, J. and Quinault, R. (eds.), *Popular Protest and Public Order: Six Studies in British History, 1790-1920*, London: George Allen and Unwin Ltd, 1974.

Storey, D., *Territory: The Claiming of Space*, Harlow: Prentice Hall, 2001.

Strachan, H., *Wellington's Legacy: The Reform of the British Army, 1830-54*, Manchester: Manchester University Press, 1984.

Taylor, A. J. P., 'Lord John Russell: The Last Great Whig' in A. J. P. Taylor (ed.), *From Napoleon to the Second International: Essays on Nineteenth-Century Europe*, London: Hamilton, 1993, pp.145-51.

Taylor, D., *The New Police: Crime, Conflict and Control in Nineteenth Century England*, Manchester: Manchester University Press, 1997.

Taylor, M. *The Decline of British Radicalism, 1847-1860*, Oxford: Clarendon, 1995.

Taylor, M., *Ernest Jones, Chartism and the Romance of Politics, 1819-1869*, Oxford: Oxford University Press, 2004.

Thompson, D., (ed.), *The Early Chartists*, London: Macmillan, 1971.

Thompson, D., *The Chartists: Popular Politics in the Industrial Revolution*, London: Wildwood House, 1984.

Thompson, E. P., *The Making of the English Working Class*, 2nd ed., Harmondsworth, Penguin, 1980.

Tilly, C., *Popular Contention in Great Britain, 1758-1834*, London: Harvard University Press, 1995.

Troup, E., *The Home Office*, London: G.P. Putnam's Sons, 1926.

Vallance, E., *A Radical History of Britain: Visionaries, Rebels and Revolutionaries – The men and women who fought for our freedoms*, London: Little, Brown, 2009.

Vernon, J., *Politics and the People: A Study in English Political Culture, c.1815-1867*, Cambridge: Cambridge University Press, 1993.

Vernon, J., *Re-reading the Constitution: New Narratives in the Political History of England's Long Nineteenth Century*, Cambridge: Cambridge University Press, 1996.

Vincent, A., *Theories of the State*, Oxford: Basil Blackwell, 1987.

Vincent, D., *The Culture of Secrecy: Britain, 1832-1998*, Oxford: Oxford University Press, 1998.

Vogler, R., *Reading The Riot Act: The Magistracy, the Police and the Army in Civil Disorder*, Milton Keynes: Open University, 1991.

Walpole, S., *The Life of Lord John Russell*, 2 vols., London: Longmans, 1889.

Walton, J. K, *Chartism*, London: Routledge, 1999.

Ward, J. T., *Sir James Graham*, London: Macmillan, 1967.

Ward, J. T., *Chartism*, London: B.T. Batsford, 1973.

Ward, P., *Red Flag and Union Jack: Englishness, Patriotism and the British Left, 1881-1924*, Woodbridge: Royal Historical Society/Boydell Press, 1998.

Weber, M., *Essays from Max Weber*, London: Routledge and Kegan Paul, 1946.

Wilks, I., *South Wales and the Rising of 1839: Class Struggle as Armed Struggle*, London: Croom Helm, 1984.

Williams, C. A., 'Expediency, Authority and Duplicity: Reforming Sheffield's Police', in R. J. Morris and R. H. Trainor (eds.), *Urban Governance: Britain and Beyond Since 1750*, Aldershot: Ashgate, 2000, pp.115-27.

Wright, D. G., *Democracy and Reform, 1815-1885*, Harlow: Longman, 1970.

Wright, D. G., *The Chartist Risings in Bradford*, Bradford: Bradford Libraries and Information, 1987.

Articles

Ashton, O., 'Chartism in Llanidloes: The "Riot" of 1839 Revisited' in *Llafur: The Journal of Welsh People's History*, 3, 2010, 76-85.

Belchem, J., 'Liverpool in 1848: Image, Identity and Issues' in *Transactions of the Historic Society of Lancashire and Cheshire*, 147, 1998, 1-26.

Chase, M., 'Rethinking Welsh Chartism' in *Llafur: The Journal of Welsh People's History*, 3, 2010, 39-57.

Cronin, J. E., 'The British State and the Structure of Political Opportunity' in *The Journal of British Studies*, 27, 1988, pp.199-231.

Emsley, C., 'The Home Office and Its Sources of Information and Investigation 1791-1801' in *The English Historical Review*, 94, 1979, 532-561.

England, J., '"Engaged in a Righteous Cause": Chartism in Merthyr Tydfil', *Llafur: The Journal of Welsh People's History*, 3, 2010, 58-75.

Grason, S., 'The Sheffield Chartist Uprising' in *Yorkshire History*, 1, 1996, 5-7.

Gurney, P., 'Exclusive Dealing in the Chartist Movement' in *Labour History Review*, 74, 2009, 90-110.

Gurney, P., '"Rejoicing in Potatoes": The Politics of Consumption in England during the "Hungry Forties"' in *Past and Present*, 203, 2009, 99-136.

Hart, J., 'Reform of the Borough Police, 1835-56' in *English Historical Review*, 70, 1955, 411-27.

Hobsbawm, E., 'The Forward March of Labour Halted?' in *Marxism Today*, 1978, 279-86.

Jones, D. J. V., 'The New Police, Crime and the People in England and Wales, 1829-1888' in *Transactions of the Royal Historical Society*, 33, 1983, 151-68.

Kirk, N., 'In Defence of Class' in *International Review of Social History*, 32, 1987, 2-47.

Lawrence, J., 'The Decline of English Popular Politics' in *Parliamentary History*, 13, 1994, 333-337.

Lewis, C., 'Samuel Holberry: Chartist Conspirator or Victim of a State Conspiracy?' in *Crimes and Misdemeanours: Deviance and the Law in Historical Perspective*, 3, 2009 109-24.

Mather, F. C., 'The Railways, the Electric Telegraph and Public Order during the Chartist period' in *History*, 38, 1953, 40-53.

Messner, A., 'Land, Leadership, Culture and Emigration: Some Problems in the Chartist Historiography' in *Historical Journal*, 42, 1999, 1093-1109.

Navickas, K., 'Moors, Fields and Popular Protest in South Lancashire and the West Riding, 1800-1848' in *Northern History*, 46, 2009, 93-111.

Parris, H., 'The Nineteenth-Century Revolution in Government: A Reappraisal Reappraised' in *Historical Journal*, 3, 1960, 17-37.

MacDonagh, O., 'The Nineteenth-Century Revolution in Government: A Reappraisal' in *Historical Journal*, 1, 1958, 52-67.

Palmer, S. H., 'Major-General Sir Charles James Napier: Irishman, Chartist and Commander of the Northern District in England, 1839-41' in *Irish Sword*, 15, 1982, 89-100.

Philips, D., 'A 'Weak' State? The English State, the Magistracy and the Reform of Policing in the 1830s' in *English Historical Review*, 119, 2004, 873-91.

Poole, R., '"By the Law or the Sword": Peterloo Revisited' in *History*, 91, 2006, 254-276.

Rimmer, W. G., 'The Industrial Profile of Leeds, 1740-1840' in *Publications of the Thoresby Society*, 113, 1967.

D. F. Smith, 'Sir George Grey at the Mid-Victorian Home Office' in *Canadian Journal of History*, 19, 1984, 361-86.

Storch, Robert D., 'The Plague of the Blue Locusts: Police Reform and Popular Resistance in Northern England, 1840-57' in *International Review of Social History*, 20, 1975, 61-90.

Swift, R., 'Policing Chartism, 1839-1848: The Role of the Specials Reconsidered' in *English Historical Review*, 122, 2007, 669-699.

Taylor, A., 'Commons-Stealers, Land-Grabbers and Jerry-Builders: Space, Popular Radicalism and the Politics of Public Access in London, 1848-1880' in *International Review of Social History*, 40, 1995, 383-407.

Taylor, M., 'Rethinking The Chartists: Searching for Synthesis in the Historiography of Chartism' in *The Historical Journal*, 39, 1996, 479-495.

Weaver, M., 'The Bayonet, the Cutlass and the Truncheon: Maintaining Public Order in Chartist Birmingham' in *Consortium on Revolutionary Europe, 1750-1850*, 24, 1994, 224-36.

Weaver, M., 'The New Science of Policing: Crime and the Birmingham Police Force, 1839-1842' in *Albion*, 26, 1994, 289-308.

Conference Papers

Chase, M., 'What next for Chartist Studies?', Chartism Annual International Conference paper, University of Paris IV - Sorbonne, 2 July 2010.

Royle, E., '"Radical Riding?", Myth and Reality in the Long Nineteenth Century', from *Radical Riding! Radical Cultures in the West Riding of Yorkshire, c.1760 to 1960*, University of Bradford Conference, 14 April 2007.

Online Sources

Arbuthnot, A. J., 'Sir Thomas Arbuthnot (1776–1849)', rev. S. Kinross, in *Oxford Dictionary of National Biography*, (eds.), H. C. G. Matthew and Brian Harrison, Oxford: Oxford University Press, 2004, online ed.,

http://www.oxforddnb.com/view/article/613.

Chartist Ancestors, http://www.chartists.net/

Prest, J., 'Peel, Sir Robert, second baronet (1788–1850)', *Oxford Dictionary of National Biography*, Oxford: Oxford University Press, 2004, online ed., May 2009, http://www.oxforddnb.com/view/article/21764.
Spartacus Educational, http://www.spartacus.schoolnet.co.uk/

Unpublished Theses

Baxter, J. L., 'The origins of the social war in South Yorkshire: A study of capitalist evolution and labour class realization in one industrial region, c.1750-1855', unpublished doctoral thesis, University of Sheffield, 1976.

Docton, H. M., 'Chartism in Dewsbury', unpublished thesis, University of Leeds, 1972.

Donajgrodzki, A. P., 'The Home Office 1822-48', unpublished doctoral thesis, University of Oxford, 1974.

Kaijage, F. J., 'Labouring Barnsley, 1816-1856: A Social and Economic History', unpublished doctoral thesis, University of Warwick, 1975.

Mather, F. C., 'The Machinery of Public Order in England during the Chartist period, 1837-48', unpublished masters thesis, University of Manchester, April, 1948.

Martin, J., 'Popular political oratory and itinerant lecturing in Yorkshire and the North East in the age of Chartism, 1837-60', unpublished doctoral thesis, University of York, 2010.

Smith, D. F., 'Sir George Grey at the Mid-Victorian Home Office', unpublished doctoral thesis, University of Toronto, 1972.

Wright, D. G., 'Politics and Opinion in Nineteenth Century Bradford, 1832-1880', unpublished doctoral thesis, University of Leeds, 1966.

INDEX

Chartist Studies from Merlin Press

CHARTISM IN SCOTLAND
W. Hamish Fraser

This new study recognises the importance of setting events and attitudes within the wider context of social, political and religious movements between 1830 and the end of the 1860s.

The process of industrialisation was creating huge changes for working people, not only in the big cities but also in towns and villages across Scotland. The decades of the eighteen thirties, forties and fifties were a time of intense intellectual debate about relations with the rest of Britain, about the place of religion in the state, about the relationship between social classes and about the nature of politics. The movement in Scotland, while conscious of being part of a wider working-class political movement, has to be seen in the context of these debates.

Making extensive use of both the Chartist press and local newspapers this comprehensive re-examination sheds much new light on the activities of Char ists in localities from Orkney and Wick in the north of Scotland to Dumfries in the south. It challenges the long-held view that Chartism in Scotland was markedly moderate in its demands and approaches compared with the movement in England.

'It is hard to see how it might be bettered in the years to come. This is a book that deserves to be read – and argued over – widely.' *Scottish Labour History*

Chartist Studies Series No. 10
264 pages ISBN. **978 0 85036 666 2 paperback £18.95**

VOICES OF THE PEOPLE
Democracy and Chartist Political Identity, 1830-1870
Robert G. Hall

"A study of one of the most active Chartist districts which interrogates and expands the insights that the last half century has brought into the study of popular social and political history. Hall's exploration of the experience of a community at the heart of the cotton industry during the period of mechanisation throws light on the period which goes well beyond its purely local interest."– Dorothy Thompson.

This book explores the development and decline of Chartism as a coherent political identity between 1830 and 1860 and illustrates the creation of Chartist identity from the perspective of plebeian intellectuals and activists in Ashton-under-Lyne and other militant localities of Greater Manchester and Lancashire. It questions myths, memories, and identities and will appeal to students of history, sociology and culture, and challenges the approach of Gareth Stedman-Jones, Patrick Joyce and James Vernon.

Chartists Studies series No. 8
228 pages
hardback 978 0 85036 564 1 £45.00;   paperback 978 0 85036 557 3 £15.95

FEARGUS O'CONNOR
Paul A. Pickering

A survey of Feargus O'Connor's career (1795-1855) for a general and academic audience. This full length biography provides an overview of a turbulent and active political career: journalism, the House of Commons, mass demonstrations for the People's Charter, working for the Chartist Land company. At the height of his popularity as a leader of the Chartists' campaign for democratic reform, O'Connor enjoyed the support of millions. More than any other popular leader of his generation, he sought to bring the 'working Saxon and Celt' together in a common struggle, an aspiration that had its roots deep in the Irish past. Uniquely, this book restores the Irish dimension of O'Connor's career to its proper place by offering, for the first time, an evaluation of his heritage, his ideas, and his public life on both sides of the Irish Sea.

Chartist Studies Series No. 9
176 pages
hardback 978 0 85036 562 7 £ 40.00   paperback   978 0 85036 561 0 £14.95

CHARTISM AFTER 1848
The Working Class and the Politics of Radical Education
Keith Flett

This work looks at independent working-class radical education and politics in England from the year of revolutions, 1848, to the passage of the 1870 Education Act. It takes as its starting point Richard Johnson's analysis of really useful knowledge but argues that radical ideas and radical working-class education and schools, far from disappearing after 1848, in fact flourished. The main source used is the late Chartist and radical working-class press focusing on radical meetings and events, and the ideas that informed them. The introductory chapter situates the research in its theoretical, historical and particularly chronological context. This book considers the events of 1848 and how these influenced working-class ideas and education. It surveys the period after 1848, the later 1850s and the little discussed educational strategy for political change put forward by G.J. Holyoake and opposed by W.E Adams. Two final chapters consider the development of radical education in the post-Chartist period of the 1860s and, finally, suggest conclusions from the work in respect of the politics of the 1870 Education Act and beyond.

Chartist Studies Series No. 6
221 pages
Hardback 978 0 85036 544 3 £45.00   Paperback 978 0 85036 539 9 £15.95

PAPERS FOR THE PEOPLE
A Study of the Chartist Press
Edited by Joan Allen & Owen Ashton

An original study of the role of the Chartist press in the campaign for democracy in Victorian Britain, and overseas, it includes a study of the press from 1838 to the late 1850s, it considers the press in England, Scotland, Wales, Ireland, Australia and New Zealand. Almost all of the contributors are well known specialists in the history of Chartism, they write from both innovative and revisionist perspectives. The editors provide set contributions in context and discuss how these essays expand our knowledge of Chartism;

Chartist Studies Series No. 7
225 pages
Hardback 978 0 85036 545 0 £45.00   Paperback 978 0 85036 540 5 £15.95

THE PEOPLE'S CHARTER
Democratic Agitation in Early Victorian Britain
Edited by Stephen Roberts

Hostile MPs, police spies, mass arrests, picked juries, jails - just some of the difficulties faced by working people who campaigned for the vote and some measure of equality before the law in the early Victorian period. Essays from: Eileen Yeo on Christianity and Chartism; Brian Harrison on Teetotal Chartism; Paul Pickering on selling Chartist goods and merchandise; Robert Hall on remembering Chartism; Malcolm Chase on Chartism in Middlesbrough and Stockton; Stephen Roberts on Chartism in Leicestershire; Philip Howell on Chartist lecturers; Chris Yelland on Speech and Writing in the *Northern Star*.

Chartist Studies Series No. 4
217 pages
Paperback 978 0 85036 514 6 £ 14.95